Southern Colorado State College
Pueblo, Colorado

The Modern Nations in
Historical Perspective

ROBIN W. WINKS, *General Editor*

The volumes in this series deal with individual nations or groups of closely related nations throughout the world, summarizing the chief historical trends and influences that have contributed to each nation's present-day character, problems, and behavior. Recent data are incorporated with established historical background to achieve a fresh synthesis and original interpretation.

ROBERT E. QUIRK, author of this book, is Professor of History, Indiana University. He is the author of *The Mexican Revolution, 1914–1915,* and *An Affair of Honor: Woodrow Wilson and the Occupation of Veracruz.* He was the managing editor of *Hispanic American Historical Review* from 1965 to 1970.

MEXICO

0   100   200   300   400
Miles

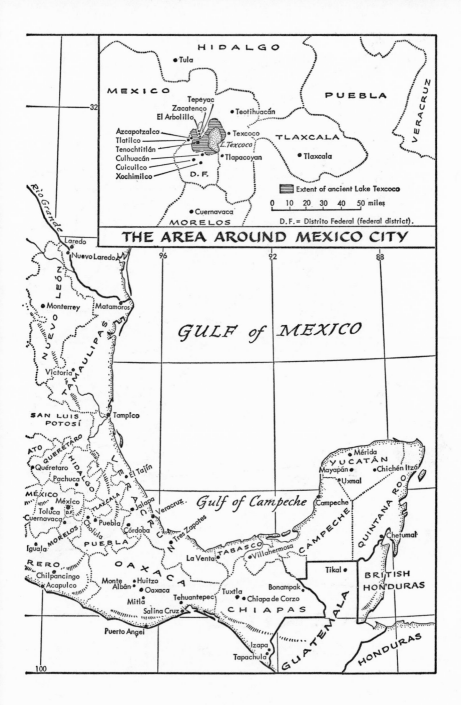

THE AREA AROUND MEXICO CITY

Extent of ancient Lake Texcoco

0 10 20 30 40 50 miles

D. F. = Distrito Federal (federal district).

GULF of MEXICO

Gulf of Campeche

MEXICO

ROBERT E. QUIRK

PRENTICE-HALL, INC. Englewood Cliffs, New Jersey

A SPECTRUM BOOK

F 1226
Q 8

Contents

Acknowledgments

Seldom does such a short volume owe so much to so many scholars —those who wrote the books, articles, dissertations, and theses cited in the bibliography, those who read papers at conferences, those colleagues at Indiana University and visitors who talked to my class on Contemporary Mexico, those friends who so generously read part or all of early drafts of the manuscript, and those graduate students who, through the years, helped assemble the bibliography and who made valuable comments on the project. I express my appreciation to all, and particularly to John F. Scott, Charles Gibson, Charles Hale, John Womack, Michael Meyer, and James W. Wilkie, who read chapters, corrected errors, and suggested changes. For the most part I bowed to their superior knowledge in the areas of their specialties. I note here three instances in which I recklessly disregarded dissenting views: Charles Hale on Mexican liberalism, John Womack on the parochialism of the Zapatistas, and James W. Wilkie on the maneuverability of the President. My associate on the *Hispanic American Historical Review*, David M. Pletcher, read the entire manuscript, ruthlessly cutting away unnecessary verbiage with his editorial broadsword. The lectures of Robert E. Scott, Juan Orrego-Salas, David D. Burks, and Merle Simmons at Indiana University gave me some understanding of subjects not close to my own discipline or research.

Constance Crowder Carter, Alan R. Scott, Thomas G. Powell, and Jeffrey Adelman provided much assistance as I prepared the book for publication. Margaret Broaddus and Betty Pace somehow managed to decipher my handwriting to type different drafts of the manuscript.

Special thanks go to Edmundo O'Gorman, Lewis Hanke, Ivan Illich, Isaac Bar-Lewaw, and John Brown. I trust that each will know the reason.

1

Mexico in Its Monuments

Mexico City, like the majority of the world's capitals, is a city of historical monuments—to the Revolution of 1910, to Independence, to great nineteenth-century liberals, to preconquest Indian heroes. But the Mexicans seem to have taken their history more seriously than the people of other countries. A leading Mexican historian, Edmundo O'Gorman, once observed that "history walks the streets of Mexico." It also seeps through the cracks of buildings and charges the atmosphere. A happening four hundred years ago can still occasion excited and heated controversy among scholars and ordinary citizens alike. The student of Mexican history would do well to consider not only the actual events but also what the people believe has occurred and their attitudes toward these events. Mexico's chief monuments provide a good starting point. To commemorate great men and their deeds Mexican governments have renamed states and towns, christened streets, plazas, and city districts, fixed national holidays, and erected statues throughout the Republic. No memorials are more significant, however, or more revealing of the Mexicans' feelings toward their past than those on the capital's broad Paseo de la Reforma.

Running generally east and west, the magnificent boulevard cuts a swath through the heart of the city. Near one end is the Plaza of the Three Cultures, symbolizing the mixture of races and the synthesis of influences which have created modern-day Mexico. The western extension of the Paseo de la Reforma bisects Chapultepec Park, the focus of Sunday diversion for Mexicans of all social classes, and it winds through the fashionable Lomas de Chapultepec among the homes of many of

1

Mexico's wealthiest and most influential citizens. To say that the Paseo de la Reforma represents the capital, let alone the great Republic would be misleading, for this is the Mexico of the American tourist and the businessman. Only the occasional Indian beggar surprises the visitor with the sudden awareness that cruel poverty can exist so near the luxury hotels and the gaudy shopwindows. Yet the broad boulevard does have a lesson to teach, and he who would understand the Mexican people and their history might well begin with a slow journey down the Paseo, allowing ample time to examine the many statues and monuments and to ponder their significance.

Traffic circles (*glorietas*), each with an elaborate monument, periodically interrupt the long Paseo, while small statues, mostly of nineteenth-century political leaders, line the sides. The concatenation of monuments is unplanned, because they were erected at different times and by governments of widely diverging views. That some logic dictates the arrangement can only mean that they do represent a wider consensus, a common Mexican outlook toward Spaniards, Indians, and foreigners, and toward the country's recent past.

A seeming anomaly is the equestrian statue of the eighteenth-century Spanish king, Charles IV, which dominates the juncture of the Paseo and the important Avenida Juárez in the city's center. A cuckold monarch and unenlightened despot in real life, the Charles of Mexico's Paseo de la Reforma appears, crowned with a laurel wreath, as the most noble Roman. It is truly a magnificent execution in bronze. But why recall Charles in the last third of the twentieth century? Probably few Mexicans today could account for the monument or even identify the mounted figure. Some who do would remove the statue and honor a more appropriate hero, such as the revolutionary peasant leader, Emiliano Zapata. But it may be that Charles IV's statue is a fitting memorial to Spanish Mexico. Most Mexicans have few good words for Spaniards or for Spanish rule in their country. The conquerors are seen as avaricious and cruel, their present-day descendants as stingy and grasping. The Spanish *gachupín* (tenderfoot) is an object of scorn, as is the cuckolded eighteenth-century king. So what better daily reminder (to the intellectuals, at least) that Mexicans mistrust Spaniards and reject their Spanish heritage? Mexico has erected no memorials to Spanish soldiers, least of all Hernán Cortés.

Further along the Paseo stands a monument to Christopher Columbus. The recognition of America's discoverer is understandable, but despite the statue the honor is less for the peerless navigator than for the continents he found. With his left hand Columbus lifts a veil which had, until 1492, obscured the New World. Mexicans, like most Latin Americans, celebrate October 12 as the Day of the Race—they honor themselves, the people of the New World, no longer Spanish, but in the words of the philosopher José Vasconcelos, the Cosmic Race, a newer and improved breed of *homo sapiens*. But the Cosmic Race is Latin American, the Iberian peoples of two continents. Mexico's national pride centers chiefly on its indigenous population—Aztecs, Mayas, Toltecs, Zapotecs, Tarascans—and the monument to its Indian heritage, with its imposing statue of Cuauhtémoc, the last Aztec emperor, is the cynosure of national attention.

Cuauhtémoc's circle, where the Paseo de la Reforma intersects Avenida Insurgentes, is the spiritual epicenter of the Republic. To the north, Insurgentes becomes the Pan American Highway to Monterrey, Nuevo Laredo and the United States; to the south, it leads to Cuernavaca, Taxco, and the Pacific coast. More than any other individual in Mexico's long history, Cuauhtémoc represents, for the Mexicans, that which has been most praiseworthy—resistance to foreign intruders. Mexico, a powerless country, has been invaded many times and has won no wars (and few battles) against outsiders. Close to the Paseo at the entrance to Chapultepec Park stands another popular monument to Mexican nationalism—the Boy Heroes who gave their lives, bravely and recklessly, defending the capital against an American army in 1847. National honor and pride are all the more sacred to a weak country that cannot boast a glorious military history. Conquered by the Spaniards, invaded by French troops, defeated by American armies, Mexico looks back with nostalgia to the splendid days of Aztec monarchs.

West of Cuauhtémoc's statue are three glorietas with monuments to Independence, to Diana, and to the Petroleum industry. The Roman huntress' graceful form recalls nothing significant in Mexican history and is associated today with the terminus of the Paseo de la Reforma's jitney service. The gilded angel of Independence, however, like the Aztec warrior, Cuauhtémoc, presides over important civic festivities—wreath-laying, florid political and patriotic oratory. The spirits invoked are of those warriors whom Spain defeated and killed—Miguel Hidalgo and José María Morelos; Agustín de Iturbide, chiefly responsible for severing Mexico's ties with the mother country, is largely ignored. As a reactionary Iturbide has been excluded from the official hagiography, while the two turncoat priests, Hidalgo and Morelos, receive honors far beyond their actual accomplishments. Since Independence, Mexico has had two traditions of history writing, the one dominant, official, liberal (in the nineteenth-century sense), and revolutionary, the other representing a small minority, to be sure, unpopular, conservative, Catholic, and pro-Spanish. A more valid picture of Mexico's past comes perhaps by combining both inexact and partisan views, as though through a stereopticon.

The last and latest monument, Los Petróleos, where the boulevard enters the Lomas de Chapultepec, commemorates President Lázaro Cárdenas' seizure of British and American oil properties in 1938. For Mexico this act implied a new assertion of independence, freedom from the domination of foreign capital, especially of the United States. And though the economic consequences of the oil nationalization had no transcendent significance, the psychological effects were incalculable, for Cárdenas' act raised Mexican self-esteem at a moment of national pessimism and helped launch the country toward industrial development. Los Petróleos is a monument to the outstanding accomplishments of the Revolution of 1910.

Mexico today is, without doubt, the most dynamic country in Latin America and a leader among the developing nations of the world. At the same time, modernizing Mexico has preserved the official policy, laid down sixty years earlier, of identifying the Revolution's aims with the needs and aspirations of its indigenous population. Mexico is revolutionary, hence ever new, yet at the same time Indian and age-old. It is also, though patriotic Mexicans tend to ignore the fact, very much Spanish and colonial. The capital's monuments continue to illuminate the complexities in Mexico's turbulent history.

2

Indian Mexico

The human history of Mexico began with the advent of primitive Indian hunting bands from the north more than ten thousand years ago. These Indians were in the paleolithic stage of human development, and with their crude stone-tipped weapons they followed and slew the great herding mammals—mammoths and mastodons, bison, and now extinct species of camels and horses. Despite fanciful theories of lost continents in the Atlantic and Pacific oceans or of early colonizing expeditions from Asia or Africa, archaeological evidence makes it abundantly clear that the ancestors of the Indians came to the New World by means of a land bridge across the Bering Strait during the late Pleistocene (Ice Age) period when ocean levels were much lower than today. About 7500 B.C. a general warming trend ensued with the result that the continental glaciers melted, the land connection with Asia was inundated, and the Indians of Mexico (as well as Central and South America) almost certainly developed their high civilizations without extra-American influences.

Though a slight possibility exists that "Kon Tiki" rafts made voyages from the Polynesian Islands and that primitive ships sailed from China, Japan, or even Africa during the first or second millennium before Christ, no such inter-continental exchanges are needed to explain any element of the Indian cultures. Archaeologists can trace the sequence of uninterrupted cultural developments in Mexico from the earliest paleolithic savage to the highly civilized Aztecs at the time of the Spanish Conquest. These archaeologists discern and describe a series of preconquest stages in which Indian groups over a wide area in Mexico and

Central America shared similar cultural developments: Paleolithic, Archaic, Formative, Classic, and Militarist.

Mexico's Old Stone Age population represented two distinct cultures. If some early Indians lived by hunting large mammals, it would seem that many, if not most, depended for their livelihood upon the scanty fare of small game—snared rabbits, rats, and birds; reptiles, snails, and mussels—and upon wild seeds, berries, nuts, and fruits. As the climate became warmer and drier after 7500 B.C., Mexico's lush grasslands disappeared, and the decreasing number of herding mammals were hunted to extinction. The future of the Mexican Indians belonged to the scroungers of the Desert Culture, rather than to the intrepid hunters. To survive, the paleolithic savage was forced to exploit his immediate environment for his food supply. Though he might move short distances with the changing seasons, he was relatively sedentary. He lived in caves and ultimately began to construct rude houses.

Most important, at some time before 5000 B.C., the Indian learned to domesticate food plants. No longer was he dependent upon the vagaries of the hunt for his sustenance. In a slow process that spanned many centuries the paleolithic savage became the neolithic agriculturist —the first and crucial step toward the creation of the great Indian civilizations of Mexico.

The Archaic Period in Mexico comprehends the four millennia from about 5200 to 1500 B.C. Archaeological evidence for this period is sparse. But it seems clear that sites were occupied in many parts of the country, although the population, limited by both the natural resources and the primitive agricultural techniques, was still small. Most of the available information has been obtained from the excavations of Richard S. MacNeish and his associates in the northeastern state of Tamaulipas and in the Tehuacán Valley, southeast of Mexico City. At Tehuacán MacNeish uncovered the oldest known domesticated maize. It was near there (between 5200 and 3400 B.C.) that man first tamed this valuable seed crop from the primitive pod-corn that grew wild in the valley. Through subsequent centuries the maize plant was improved and many varieties developed, and it remains today, as it was for the early agriculturists, the chief staple of the Mexican diet.

At Tehuacán and other Archaic sites in Mexico the Indians learned to cultivate beans, squash, pumpkins, zapotes, tomatoes, avocados, amaranth (pig weed), gourds, and sunflowers. They wove baskets and made nets of maguey fibers. They domesticated dogs and turkeys for food. About 2400 B.C. the first pottery appeared, perhaps introduced from South America. Between 3400 and 2500 B.C. family groups began to take advantage of the better growing conditions in river valleys, and they moved into more permanent settlements by establishing villages. By 1500 B.C., the end of the Archaic Period, many of the Indians were full-time agriculturists. Increased harvests and an insured food supply made possible much larger populations. They also facilitated specialization and the growth of new social classes—the potters, the weavers, and, most important, the priestly caste.

There can be little doubt that shamans played a significant role in the lives of paleolithic hunters and gatherers. Everywhere in the world early men turned to magicians to control the capriciousness of nature. The presence of grave furniture and evidences of human sacrifices in burial remains from the Paleolithic and early Archaic periods give mute testimony to the Mexican Indian's early concern for an afterlife and the propitiation of nature's forces. In an agriculturist society the shaman-priest assumed even greater importance. He advised when to plant crops, and he provided the magical incantations to invoke the spirits of rain, sun, and earth and to assure the success of the harvest. He kept track of the seasons and the passing of the years, and in so doing he made possible the construction of a calendar system. In the new society after 1500 B.C., Mexico's Formative Period, the priest became the prime mover—in religious matters, in scientific matters, in medicine, and (most probably) in politics.

The changes which took place throughout southern Mexico and Central America about 1500 B.C. may have been due to the climate's becoming wetter or to the introduction of a newer and much improved variety of maize. (MacNeish's investigations have shown that not until Formative times could maize provide significantly more energy than wild plants.) Or they may have occurred because the Indians had learned to utilize land along streams, on the banks of lakes, and in the wetter lowlands. For the first time villages grew on the shores of Lake Texcoco in the Valley of Mexico. The more fertile conditions in these locations made possible the establishment of permanent farming communities.

In the Formative Period (1500 B.C. to A.D. 250) the foundations were laid for the great accomplishments of the Indian civilizations of the Classic era. By the middle of the second millennium before Christ the area of the higher cultures on the North American continent had been delineated. The archaeologists have named it "Mesoamerica," and it extends from slightly north of the Valley of Mexico (the basin in which Mexico City lies) to present-day Guatemala, Honduras, Nicaragua, and El Salvador. It includes as well the Gulf Coast of Mexico south of Veracruz, the Pacific Coast south and east of Mazatlán, and the entire Yucatán peninsula. The chief Mayan sites were in Guatemala and Honduras. But because many important religious centers were located in what is now Mexican territory, an account of Mayan civilization can properly be introduced into a history of Mexico.

Common developments throughout Mesoamerica provided an easily discernible unity in the Formative and subsequent periods. At the same time, two distinct methods of agriculture evolved, and the differences were to have profound effects on the growth of population centers. In the lowlands of Mexico and Central America the slash-and-burn (milpa) cultivation predominated. Farmers prepared a field for planting by clearing a wooded area and burning the felled trees and bushes. They poked holes in the soil with fire-hardened sticks and pushed in the seeds. The seasonal rains then provided ample moisture for growing the crops. After two to seven years, weeds and soil exhaustion, as well as the growth of saplings, forced the farmers to abandon a plot and start the milpa cycle in a new location. Without draft animals to pull a plow, the Indian agriculturists were restricted to the simple planting stick, and large-scale field cultivation was impossible. Despite the inefficiency and waste of milpa agriculture, Indians maintained the method even after the Spaniards introduced oxen and burros and have continued it to the present day. The absence of trees in many parts of Mexico is a costly result of centuries of milpa burning. Before the Conquest the milpa plots of farm villages supported large populations in the Maya areas.

Milpa cultivation has been practiced in the highlands also since the early Formative Period. But more important for the developing population centers were other more efficient methods—terracing, irrigation, and the construction of chinampas (the Aztec "floating gardens") in Lake Texcoco. Probably because of their superior agricultural techniques, the highlands Indians were subsequently able to build true cities— Teotihuacán, Tula, and Tenochtitlán, for example. And these capitals took the lead in the creation of large "empires." The Maya states, however, with the possible exception of Tikal, were not true urban developments. The population, though dense, was never as clustered as in the highlands. Whereas highlands cities used military power to force other peoples into their sphere of domination, the lowland Mayan city-states, with dispersed populations and ample agricultural lands, remained relatively peaceful until the end of the Classic Period. No single city-state gained a hegemony over its neighbors.

Among the earliest known Formative Period villages were Chiapa de Corzo in the Mexican state of Chiapas, La Victoria and Kaminaljuyú in Guatemala, Uaxactún and Tikal in the Mayan lowlands, and Zacatenco and El Arbolillo in the Valley of Mexico. Similar Formative techniques are in evidence over the wide area of Mesoamerica and indicate trade or at least communications at great distances. There is no archaeological evidence that the Valley of Mexico was occupied during the Archaic period, so in all probability the inhabitants of these farming villages came from outside, perhaps from areas such as Tehuacán, bringing with them all of the agricultural skills of the late Archaic sites.

Subsequently, other villages (Copilco, Cuicuilco, Tlatilco) emerged on or near the shores of Lake Texcoco, as the farmers took advantage of the fertile soil and the fish and water birds that inhabited the lake. Each of these three sites is of considerable interest to archaeologists because it indicates an important step toward the creation of the urban centers of the Classic period.

Copilco, on the southern shore of the lake, is still well preserved today by a lava flow from the nearby volcano Xitle. Metates (stone querns for grinding maize) that are almost identical to those used in Mexican villages today have been unearthed at Copilco. The burials, which included pots and other grave furniture and a red substance (cinnebar) to give dead bodies the semblance of life, demonstrate a concern for the continuity of existence after death. There were no pyramids, however, or other signs of an organized religion until the middle centuries of the Formative Period, when ceremonial mounds appeared at La Venta on the Gulf Coast and Huitzo in the Valley of Oaxaca and when a well-organized fertility cult at Tlatilco, an important village on a stream west of Lake Texcoco, was established.

Tlatilco was discovered by workers in a brickyard in Mexico City, and subsequent excavations have turned up hundreds of clay figurines, some of animals, but mostly of human females. The female representations are usually small-breasted with narrow waists, bulbous legs, and rudimentary hands and feet. Many have double faces—three eyes, two noses, and two mouths, so that the full face can be seen from either side. The figurines were probably not idols, for they were widely scattered and far too numerous to be sacred objects. In all probability, they were votive offerings for a female deity venerated at Tlatilco. It may be that even at this early date (600 B.C.), peasants from other nearby villages made pilgrimages to Tlatilco.

By 500 B.C. the villagers abandoned Tlatilco and the figurine cult ceased. Perhaps a new people came into the valley from the Veracruz area—the archaeologist George Vaillant found that traders at this time brought seashells from the Gulf Coast. This new phase, called Ticomán by Vaillant, is represented in the Valley of Mexico by the sites of Ticomán, Cuicuilco, Tlapacoyan, and the Cerro de Tepalcate. Other contemporary villages, at a similar stage of development, have been discovered in river valleys in the Mexican states of Puebla, Morelos, Oaxaca, Veracruz, Michoacán, and Guanajuato, and in the Guatemalan highlands. In agriculture and in handicraft techniques the villagers of this period were not more advanced than their Zacatenco or Copilco predecessors. Principally, Ticomán was a long period of consolidation of techniques, and of increasing populations in the many villages. The chief innovation was the construction of pyramids at Cuicuilco (the oldest in Mesoamerica) and at Kaminaljuyú. In the building of a flat-topped

pyramid with its temple on the summit, we can see the first formaliza-
tion of the agriculturally oriented religion of the Mexican Indians. The
priests acquired the power to persuade or compel the villagers to per-
form the arduous tasks of hauling stones and adobe bricks and of raising
them into massive structures. And the pyramid-temple complex, such
as that at Cuicuilco, which also had a figurine cult, became the center
for the religious activities of the surrounding villages. The same lava
flow that covered the deserted Copilco also destroyed Cuicuilco. But
the custom of erecting temple-pyramids was preserved during the late
Formative Period in many parts of Mesoamerica, from Teotihuacán
near the Valley of Mexico to Monte Albán in the state of Oaxaca, La
Venta on the Gulf Coast, and Uaxactún in the Mayan lowlands.

If the general economic and social level of the Formative Period
was that of the unsophisticated agricultural village, a singular exception
was the culture of the Olmecs. These mysterious people of the Gulf
Coast built and occupied La Venta between 1000 and 600 B.C. The origin and even the identity of the Olmecs is unknown today. They may
have come from Guerrero, but to date archaeological investigation has
turned up no evidence of early Olmec culture on Mexico's southwest
coast. The American archaeologist, Michael Coe, has discovered pre-
La Venta sites along the Gulf Coast. It is possible that the Olmecs were
a Maya-speaking people, cut off from related groups in the lowlands
south of Tehuantepec. In any event, they emerged sometime before
1000 B.C. with a culture far superior to that of other early Formative
peoples. They possessed artistic skills so advanced and sophisticated as
to indicate a long period of development in Mexico or elsewhere. (There
are intriguing hints of extra-American influences, however, in their por-
trayal of what appear to be negroid or caucasoid faces.) Olmec carvings
in basalt and jade were unsurpassed by those of any other people in
preconquest America. In fact, Olmec statuary and lapidary work compares favorably with the artistic endeavors in Europe and the Middle
East in the second and first millennia before Christ.

The Olmecs built their capital on a sandy island in the middle of
a swampy river. The population was not large, though the priest-rulers
of La Venta commanded the loyalty of a great many villages in the
surrounding countryside. That it was an important ceremonial center
is shown by the construction of a massive clay mound, shaped somewhat
like a volcano, 250 feet wide and about 400 feet long. It was over 100
feet high and truncated and had a temple dedicated to the jaguar rain
god. The masons of La Venta cut columns and altars of basalt, moving
these heavy stones great distances from their quarry sites. And sculptors
carved large stone heads of helmeted males, some nearly ten feet high.
These curious objects have been excavated at La Venta and at other
Olmec sites along the coast.

The Olmec art style is most easily distinguished in the drooping or trapezoidal mouth of the jaguar, which makes Olmec influences recognizable wherever they occur in Mexico or Central America. The artists seem to have been obsessed with monstrosities—misshapen heads, hunchbacks, dwarfs, club-footed individuals. Though they occasionally portrayed women, most Olmec stone sculptors made statues of male figures, especially were-jaguars, which were probably representations of the rain deity—the earliest known ancestor of the universal rain god of Mesoamerica, Tláloc. The figures were usually without genitalia and had the faces of babies.

The Olmecs were the first Indians to use the vigesimal counting system and the calendar, later perfected by the lowland Mayas. The Long Count calendar, based on the vague year of 360 days, enabled the Olmecs and the Mayas to determine dates with great precision over several centuries. The oldest known dates using bars and dots (a bar represented the number five, the dot a unit) were at Olmec sites— 36 B.C. at Chiapa de Corzo in central Chiapas and 31 B.C. at Tres Zapotes. It seems clear that Olmec was the "mother culture" for all the higher civilizations of the Classic Period. Perhaps by means of military conquest, almost certainly by missionary and trade activity, Olmec influences were carried from La Venta to the Mexican highlands and as far south as El Salvador and Costa Rica. Olmecoid faces appear on clay figurines at Tlatilco in the Valley of Mexico; there are unmistakably Olmec finds in the Mexican states of Guerrero and Puebla; and at Monte Albán in Oaxaca early stone carvings of misshapen men (danzantes) seem to be of Olmec derivation.

La Venta was destroyed through internal insurrection or external invasion about 600 B.C. Many of the great monuments uncovered in the recent excavations show signs of deliberate mutilation. The Olmec cultural developments remained, however, to inspire other Indian groups in the Classic Period. The chief agent for transmitting Olmec culture was the town of Izapa, a large site near Tapachula on the Mexican-Guatemalan border. Izapa maintained the Long Count calendar and passed it to the Highlands Mayas of Guatemala. Kaminaljuyú in its late Formative "Miraflores" Period was definitely Izapan. At Tres Zapotes in Tabasco, Olmec and Izapan influences merged. As the Formative Period drew to a close in the first centuries of the Christian era, the lowland Mayas took over the Olmec-Izapan culture to raise the Mesoamerican Indian civilization to its apogee. In the Mexican highlands to the north, however, the Olmec scientific innovations had little permanent effect. During the Classic and Militarist Periods, though trade and sometimes military relations were maintained between north and south, the Mayan and Mexican paths diverged. The Mexicans failed to preserve the Long Count calendar, which the Mayas utilized to record the great events of their history. The inheritors of the highlands Teotihuacán culture, the Toltecs, Mixtecs, and Aztecs, had only the 52-year cycle (also used by the Mayas), which combined a 260-day ceremonial year with the 365-day solar year, a much less efficient dating device than the accurate Long Count system.

Until the Classic Period in Mexico (A.D. 250–950), life centered in the villages. But in the first two centuries after Christ populations grew, and agricultural production increased markedly, so that the priest-rulers could employ the excess labor in ever larger construction projects—terracing for agriculture, leveling of mountain tops for building sites, and the erecting of pyramids, temples, and palaces. Society was well organized, and class distinctions were maintained to separate the peasantry from an aristocracy of religious and military leaders. And an incipient middle class grew, composed of merchants, artisans, and minor priests and officials. Urban developments took place in many parts of Mexico. At Teotihuacán, about 30 miles northeast of today's Mexico City, a true city appeared, and by the sixth century A.D. it had a population of some 85,000 inhabitants. At El Tajín in the state of Veracruz, at Monte Albán near Oaxaca City, at Xochicalo near Cuernavaca, and at many sites in the Mayan area, villages were closely linked into city-states. The Classic Period was indeed a Golden Age for Mexico's Indians. Subsequent peoples respected and imitated their Classic predecessors, but they never surpassed them in their accomplishments.

Teotihuacán was initially occupied during the late Formative Period in the first century after Christ. Though the early inhabitants came from elsewhere in Mexico, perhaps from the Gulf Coast or even from the north, they carried on the traditions of the Formative villages in the Valley of Mexico. By the end of the third century, it was not only a large city, but a religious center for the Mexican highlands with a figurine cult like those of Tlatilco and Cuicuilco. The priest-rulers laid out Teotihuacán in an orderly fashion with a wide Avenue of the Dead bisecting the city from north to south. At its greatest expansion the city covered over five square miles. The principal structures were on either side of this avenue, from the Pyramid of the Moon on the north to the Ciudadela (Citadel) in the south. The most imposing structure at Teotihuacán is the great Pyramid of the Sun, which rises 210 feet above the floor of the valley. It measures nearly 700 feet on each of its four sides and contains about 1,300,000 cubic yards of stone, adobes, and rubble. The pyramid was faced with stone and stuccoed white. On its flat top the priests of Teotihuacán worshipped the sun god. In the Ciudadela is the famous Pyramid of Quetzalcóatl, the Feathered Serpent deity. Quetzalcóatl became, during the Militarist Period, a most important god and the bringer of civilization for the Toltecs, Mixtecs, and Aztecs in the Mexican highlands and for the Mayas at Chichén Itzá on the Yucatán peninsula.

The position of the temples on the flat tops of pyramids at Teotihuacán and elsewhere in Mesoamerica provides an important clue to understanding preconquest religious practices. In no sense were the Indian religions congregational in character. The pyramid tops were for ceremonies celebrated by priests within the precincts of the temple. The pyramid's steep sides (especially steep among the Mayas) precluded participation by any great number of worshippers. From the base of the pyramid it was virtually impossible to witness what took place on the top. Clearly, the rituals of the state religion at Teotihuacán, as later at Tula and Tenochtitlán, were the business of the priests. The ordinary citizen came to Teotihuacán as a pilgrim, bringing votive offerings to the city's gods, but not as an active participant in religious ceremonies. For the peasants, far more important than the veneration of Tláloc and Quetzalcóatl, were the magical rituals involved in making milpa or in curing the sick. The chthonic and healing rites endured countless changes of suzerainty through the preconquest Classic and Militarist periods, the Spanish colonial regime, and even Mexican independence into the present century. Whether the Great Master is Quetzalcóatl, Huitzilopochtli, or the Christian God is somehow of less import than the eternal verities of the agricultural cycle.

At the height of the city's power, Teotihuacán's influences reached the Mexican highlands and deep into the Mayan area. Though the cultural domination seems to have been largely peaceful, through trade rather than by conquest, military activity probably did play a role in the creation of a Teotihuacán "empire." A group from the city seized Kaminaljuyú in the Guatemalan highlands and rebuilt that site about A.D. 400 as a replica of the Mexican metropolis. And it is possible that Tikal was a trade center for Teotihuacán in the Mayan lowlands. Representations of Tláloc and Teotihuacán trade wares are in evidence at both Guatemalan sites. Teotihuacán merchants exchanged the excellent polychrome pottery from their capital for feathers and other finery from the lowlands. Since Teotihuacán traders ranged widely through Mesoamerica, there is no explanation at present for the complete absence at their city of the Long Count calendar or Mayan hieroglyphics. The priest-rulers of Teotihuacán were master builders; and their artisans made fine pottery and did excellent stone work. But in intellectual matters they were surpassed by their contemporaries to the south in the Mayan city-states.

That the spirit of Teotihuacán had become more martial in the sixth century is shown by the wall paintings of jaguars and coyotes, for these predatory animals were to be the symbols of warrior knights at Tula during the Militarist Period. Perhaps the paintings are associated with the conquest of states such as Tikal and Kaminaljuyú. But by the end of the century Teotihuacán itself had fallen to invaders, probably from the north. Some of the inhabitants fled to the shores of Lake Texcoco where they occupied Azcapotzalco to carry on the traditions of the Classic culture in the Valley of Mexico. Though the barbarian new-comers lived as squatters and buried their dead in the sacred precincts of the great city, they made no effort at further construction. In the succeeding centuries new waves of conquerors moved into the Valley of Mexico. Teotihuacán remained a dead city, however, its pyramids and temples a fitting memorial to the priest-rulers who inspired the people to such heroic feats of construction.

Contemporary with Teotihuacán was the great Zapotec citadel of Monte Albán. Its origins are to be found in the late Formative Period, and early Monte Albán art work shows unmistakable Olmec survivals. There are bar-and-dot date representations (though not the Long Count calendar) and the ubiquitous Olmec jaguar mouth. The site of Monte Albán is a leveled-off mountain top 1000 feet above the valley floor where Oaxaca City lies today. It was occupied for more than ten centuries; between A.D. 300 and 900 it received influences from both Teotihuacán and the Mayan city-states to the south. The Zapotecs never reached the intellectual heights achieved by the Mayas, and later generations seem not to have capitalized on the early use of the vigesimal counting system. Nor did the city become a great metropolis like Teotihuacán. In Mexico's years of upheaval about A.D. 900, Monte Albán was seized by aggressive Mixtec warriors from the north. The Mixtecs constructed their capital at Zaachila and inspired the beautiful religious precinct of Mitla, south of Oaxaca City. They also used the site of Monte Albán to bury their dead. They were premier goldsmiths, and excavations of Mixtec graves at Monte Albán have turned up treasures of gold orna-ments. (The Mixteca-Puebla culture, centered in Cholula, had wide influence in Mexico from the Gulf Coast to Guerrero in the west. The Mixtecs probably devised codex paintings, a means of recording his-torical information, and they seem to have passed this art, along with the vigesimal counting system and the 52-year calendar cycle, to the Aztecs and other inhabitants of the Valley of Mexico.)

Though the term "Classic" is generally used to describe the Meso-american period between A.D. 250 and 950, it is most aptly applied to the Maya Indian cultures. In the rain forests and highlands of Guatemala, Honduras, and Southern Mexico and on the limestone peninsula of Yucatán, the Maya-speaking peoples brought the preconquest civiliza-tion to an eminence unequalled by contemporary and succeeding Indian groups. They perfected the counting system of the Olmecs and devised a calendar more accurate than that used in Western European society until the late sixteenth century. They developed a writing system to record religious and secular historical information. Though their hiero-glyphics were probably ideographic rather than phonetic, the stone inscriptions and paper books served the Mayan scribes well in pre-serving the history of their city-states. Only the Maya, among the many civilized Indian peoples of the Americas, employed an arch (false, or corbeled) in their temples to increase interior space.

Mayan constructions in the ceremonial centers were neither as large nor as imposing as those of Teotihuacán, Monte Albán, or the Aztec Tenochtitlán. Like the Greeks, the Mayas sought perfection on a small scale, and their buildings overwhelm the viewer through sheer beauty rather than size and grandeur. Their pyramids were smaller and steeper than their counterparts in other areas of Mexico. Temples, as well as secular structures, were lavishly decorated and even painted vivid colors. To provide sufficient external surface for the exuberant artist and sculptor, the Maya architects topped many buildings with "roof combs." The great weight of the roof required thick walls, and despite the cor-beled vaults, the interiors were cramped and dark.

About A.D. 900, the Mayan people abandoned their ceremonial centers, returning to the simple village life of their ancestors. The rea-sons are not readily apparent today, and one can only conjecture. The pioneer American archaeologist, Sylvanus G. Morley, believed that the Mayan peasant, through his wasteful slash-and-burn cultivation, had exhausted the land, so that the maize output could no longer support the large population. Others have pointed to general climatic changes over all of Middle America at the end of the ninth century which may have decimated staple crops. Farmers would no longer labor to build pyramids and palaces for priests who could not assure rain. Another possible explanation lies in the evidence of feverish building activity in the Mayan city-states during the eighth century. Perhaps the exactions of the priest-rulers became too onerous for their subjects, causing the farmers to rebel. The "creative minority" may have become a "dominant minority," as the ruling-class sought to maintain its power and privileges through force. Certainly late Classic wall paintings at Bonampak are dominated by military activity—battles, prisoners, and sacrifices. What-ever the cause or causes, the results are indisputable—over a wide area, the Mayan people broke off their march toward an even more advanced civilization. Only on the Yucatán peninsula were the Mayan city-states preserved, and the Yucatecans kept their polities only by becoming militarists.

All over Mesoamerica the years around 900 were a "Time of Troubles" for Classic peoples. The priests were relegated to a secondary role in society, and the new age belonged to the professional soldiers, who could protect a city or destroy a neighbor—and keep a subject population in check. It was an age of fortified strong points, of barbarian invasions, and of the frequent migrations of peoples. In the highlands, the urban populations were better organized than their peasant Maya contemporaries. The new militarists used the cities as bases of power to take control of wide areas and even to create "empires."

With the coming of the Militarist Period (A.D. 950–1519), Mexico entered a historic era in which peoples, events, and even individual persons can be identified. Chronicles at the time of Cortés' arrival preserved the memory of the conquests, the wars, the internal strife, and the rise and fall of many cities and states in the course of these six centuries. A city would grow in size and importance and levy war against its neighbors, creating a brief hegemony over other states. Coalitions would be formed to defeat an aggressor or to launch an imperial conquest. Among the many new states, those of the Toltecs, the Mixtecs, and the Aztecs were the most important. Each dominated an extensive area in its time of greatness, and all were based in the central highlands in or near the Valley of Mexico.

Because the Valley of Mexico was the northernmost outpost of advanced civilization in Mesoamerica, it was vulnerable to attacks by untamed tribes beyond the frontier. The Aztecs called these barbarians Chichimecs (People of the Dog), and though there were actually many diverse tribes speaking many languages, we find the generic term useful today. All of the Chichimec people shared a common way of life; they were semi-nomadic and they lived close to subsistence level. The period of aridity in Mexico at the end of the ninth century bore most heavily on the hitherto peaceful tribes. In desperation they made incursions into the settled areas, raiding cities and wresting control of agricultural lands from the valley's inhabitants. Groups of Chichimecs probably served as mercenary soldiers for imperial cities in the highlands. Eventually the invaders settled down and adopted the culture of the peoples they had defeated. The Toltecs were a Chichimec tribe who entered the valley perhaps as early as the eighth century.

With the advent of the barbarians, war became a normal part of life in Mesoamerica. New and more ferocious gods were introduced into the common Mexican pantheon, and human sacrifices were an essential element of the Indian religion. Artists mirrored the bellicose spirit of the times with their representations of jaguars and coyotes, of eagles eating human hearts. Death heads were a popular motif in temple adornments. The Toltecs, who launched the first militarist state in Mesoamerica, set the political, religious, and artistic pattern for their successors.

During the tenth century the Toltecs founded their capital of Tula, about fifty miles north of today's Mexico City, in the state of Hidalgo. From Tula they dispatched military expeditions which ranged through Mesoamerica and as far away as the Yucatán peninsula. In the last years of the tenth century a Toltec leader called Quetzalcóatl was driven from his capital by a rival faction. It was widely believed that this godlike hero had fled to the coast and had taken a raft to the East, and that he would return to lead his people once again. As if to corroborate the Toltec myth of Quetzalcóatl, Mayan histories recorded that in 987 a Toltec warrior, Kukulcán (both names mean Feathered Serpent), seized the Yucatecan ceremonial center of Chichén Itzá. He and his followers built there a Mayanized copy of their own capital. In both cities stone columns supported temple roofs (an innovation in the Americas); the Feathered Serpent deity was the dominant motif in temple art; and human sacrifices became much more numerous than in any previous era.

On the Yucatán peninsula the incursion of the Mexican highlanders led to a Mayan renaissance and to the building or rebuilding of many cities. The most important, Uxmal and Mayapán, shared with Chichén Itzá the domination of the peninsula. Mayan histories, available to the Spaniards at the time of the Conquest, told of internecine wars among the states and of dynastic struggles within the states, as faction struggled against faction. By 1441 the Mayan cities had exhausted themselves through constant warfare. When the Spanish invaders arrived in the second decade of the sixteenth century there were no strong Mayan states left.

In the course of the twelfth century the Toltecs, too, were brought down by a new wave of Chichimec invaders. The barbarians put the torch to the city of Tula and demolished its temples and monuments. Thereafter, until the rise of Aztec power in the fifteenth century, no single state dominated the Mexican highlands. Old towns grew, and new towns, such as Azcapotzalco, Culhuacán, Tenayuca, and Texcoco, were founded on or near the shores of Lake Texcoco. Though wars were frequent, armies no longer destroyed cities. Each new barbarian group was absorbed into the population of the valley and took over the Classic culture that had been handed down by the Toltecs. Chroniclers kept alive the memory of Tula's greatness until Aztec times, and Tenochtitlán's proud nobels proclaimed themselves descendants of the storied Toltec heroes. "Nothing," said the Aztecs, "was too difficult for them!"

The Aztecs were the last significant Chichimec group to enter the Valley of Mexico. According to their historians, they had come from the north, wandering for many years before they arrived on the shores of Lake Texcoco in the thirteenth century. Though the valley was crowded, the leading states permitted the strangers to settle near the lake, on the hill of Chapultepec. The Aztecs repaid their benefactors by raiding nearby cities. As a result, Azcapotzalco and Culhuacán turned upon the Aztec settlement to reduce the barbarous newcomers to serfdom. Some refugees from Chapultepec fled to an island in the lake where they founded the city of Tenochtitlán. Protected from attack, the Aztecs then adopted the life of the farmer and trader, and they took over the religion and culture of their neighbors. During the fourteenth century Tenochtitlán grew in power and by 1425 had defeated the once dominant Azcapotzalco and Culhuacán. Forming a triple alliance with Texcoco and Tlacopan, Tenochtitlán subjected the many states in the Valley of Mexico and ultimately extended Aztec power from the Mexican highlands to the Gulf Coast and even as far south as Guatemala. By 1502, when Moctezuma II became king of the Aztecs, the tribute payments of conquered tribes, which by agreement had been divided among the three partners, were monopolized by Tenochtitlán. It would be imprecise to say that Moctezuma II ruled an organized empire, for he lacked a bureaucratic structure centered in Tenochtitlán, but no military force in Mesoamerica could match the armies of the Aztecs. Traders and soldiers from Tenochtitlán went where they pleased, and only the Tlaxcalans to the east, the Tarascans in the west, and some Mixtecs held out against a complete domination by the Aztecs.

Tenochtitlán was a great metropolis with a population in 1519 of perhaps 250,000 persons, larger than any contemporary European city. It was certainly more beautiful—a jewel of white stone buildings set in the azure waters of Lake Texcoco. The soldiers of Cortés were amazed when they first beheld it, exclaiming that it seemed like a city from one of the fanciful novels of the day. One of the soldiers, Bernal Díaz, called it the "garden of the world." The Aztec farmers grew ample crops on irrigated land or in the chinampas constructed in the lake. Great quantities of goods were carried in boats across the lake from other settlements in the valley and through the city's many canals. Spaniards who had traveled in the Mediterranean insisted that the markets of Tenochtitlán were larger and busier than those they had seen in Rome or Constantinople. Great quantities of tribute poured into the city from the conquered tribes—amaranth, maize, cotton, gold, and mantles and shields of many varieties. The king maintained a botanical garden and a zoo and aviary filled with exotic animals and birds. The military aristocratic classes had the best in housing, rare foods, perfumes, and clothing; peasants cultivated their extensive lands. Those farmers who were not bound to the private lands worked their own fields in common. Slavery existed, though the bondsmen were few and were not harshly treated. Tenochtitlán had an important middle class of traders, artisans, and state employees. Food abounded and life was not difficult for most of Tenochtitlán's citizens. The city's rule bore most heavily, of course, upon the conquered tribes, who furnished not only their annual tribute, but also war prisoners to be sacrificed to the bloodthirsty Aztec gods.

Though the people of Tenochtitlán venerated the ancient rain god,

Tláloc, and claimed as their own Quetzalcóatl, the Toltec bringer of civilization, they also worshipped newer and fiercer deities who demanded their ration of human blood: Huitzilopochtli, the Aztec's god of war; Tezcatlipoca of the Smoking Mirror; Xipe Totec, Lord of the Flayed One; and Coatlicue, the Eater of Filth and the hideous mother of the gods. In the temple to Huitzilopochtli, atop the great pyramid in the center of Tenochtitlán, Aztec priests slew countless thousands of human victims. The temple precinct, the altar, the priests themselves reeked of the blood of those sacrificed to keep Huitzilopochtli in his daily rounds as the Lord of the Sun. By means of these ritual killings, the Aztecs believed that they could ensure the orderly working of the universe. Without them all would be chaos. To secure victims for the insatiable gods, the Aztecs made war on their hapless neighbors; to be successful in battle they sacrificed war prisoners to the gods. It was indeed a vicious and tragic circle. We need not wonder at the horror of the Spanish soldiers, no strangers to violence themselves, who recoiled at the sight of the blood and the skulls of thousands of victims, and who destroyed the temples and tore down the pyramids as soon as they could.

Moctezuma II represented both the strengths and weaknesses of the Aztec system. Brave in battle against his Indian adversaries, he could not cope with the unexpected and the inexplicable. Moctezuma was superstitious, and strange happenings that he could not comprehend filled him with awe. When the Spanish ships first appeared on Mexico's Gulf Coast, his couriers brought him reports of towers that moved on the water, and of beasts larger than deer that seemed half-human and half-animal (horse and rider). In Tenochtitlán there were weird portents of disaster: a comet "like a tongue of fire"; the mysterious burning of a tower of the great temple; an unknown woman's voice crying in the night; a bird with a mirror in its forehead. As the Spaniards approached Tenochtitlán in late 1519, the Aztec ruler, it was said, feared that Cortés was Quetzalcóatl returning to assert lordship over his people. Moctezuma at first ordered Cortés to stay away from the city; after his warning was ignored, he welcomed the Spanish commander with open arms. When Cortés seized Moctezuma and held him prisoner, the Aztec submitted humbly. Because of the king's paralysis in the time of greatest danger to his city, Cortés, with fewer than 1000 men, was able to conquer a state with several million subjects. When the last Aztec king, the youth Cuauhtémoc, surrendered in 1521, the great Indian civilization ended.

Inspired by the missionary priests to eliminate the pagan cults, the conquering Spaniards demolished Indian religious centers throughout Mexico. They leveled pyramids, broke apart the temples, and used the stones to construct their own buildings. They proscribed the priest class and killed or tamed the tribal rulers. Thus Spain destroyed the formal structure of the preconquest civilization. What remained, virtually intact, was the bedrock of the Indian culture, the way of life of the people. The Europeans came as masters, and the new institutions, imported from Spain, replaced the old formal organization of society. Some European plants, animals, and technology were used, but for most Indians life went on much as before. They ate the same foods—maize, beans, and squashes. They built the same houses, used the same utensils. And they worked their fields and planted their crops in the same milpa cycle as their ancestors. Even the popular religion changed little with the imposition of Christianity.

Huitzilopochtli, Tezcatlipoca, Tláloc, and Quetzalcóatl were all dead. On the sites of their temples the Spaniards erected churches. But the orthodox Christian rituals, the sacramental system, never played an important part in the lives of most Mexican Indians. Instead of attending Mass and receiving the Holy Eucharist, they venerated the saints of their villages and took pilgrimages to holy places. It may be that the act of making a pilgrimage and venerating a saint with an Indian physiognomy is as praiseworthy as the regular partaking of the Church's sacraments. In fact, however, the Indian practices gravely weakened the hierarchical structure of the Church. Priests, sacraments, and especially bishops or popes meant little to an isolated Indian community with the tangible powers of its own saint's image. In moments of crisis, when the Church was attacked by the civil authorities, the larger part of Mexico's population was indifferent to the vicissitudes of the formal religion. The Indianization of Catholicism in Mexico helps explain much in the history of Church-State relations in that country.

During the colonial period and in the first century after Independence the ruling class exploited or neglected the Mexican Indian. Since 1910 he has been apotheosized as the hero of the Revolution. In the Revolutionary myth Mexico is today an Indian country. The Spaniards were outsiders who conquered "us Mexicans." The symbol of Mexicanity is not the Church, not the Conquistador, not the Spanish poet, philosopher, or historian, but the Indian Cuauhtémoc, who died a victim of Spanish treachery. The alleged discovery of the Aztec king's bones in 1949 provoked a furious and emotional debate. His monument in Mexico City is the site of much fervent historical oratory, and a politician seeking public favor will appear there to be photographed for the newspapers. A foreign diplomat, hoping to associate his country with Mexico's most sacred and hoary traditions, will ostentatiously place a wreath at Cuauhtémoc's feet.

In November 1964, Mexico dedicated its new Museum of Archaeology and Anthropology (designed by Pedro Ramírez Vázquez), an architectural gem of breath-taking splendor. Without doubt one of the world's greatest museums, it brings together priceless art objects from all of the country's preconquest cultures and represents the outlay of millions of hard-earned pesos. It is indeed a premier tourist attraction in the nation's capital. But the museum's chief concern is for the Mexican people. The entrance fee is lower on Sundays (one peso), when the ordinary citizen is presumably freed from his weekday toils. And as the visitor departs, after seeing the impressive displays from Indian cities such as Teotihuacán, Palenque, Tula, and Tenochtitlán, he reads this admonition inscribed in stone over the exit: "Mexican: Behold thyself in the mirror of this grandeur!"

Clearly it is not today's Indian, however, the barefooted, maize-eating campesino wearing ragged clothes, with whom Mexico identifies itself. In the 1970s the generic term "Indian" is virtually indistinguishable from a state of endemic poverty. A Mexican of the politically effective class, proud to proclaim himself an Indian, would be highly indignant to be called that by a foreigner. Rather it is the ideal Indian, the mythic Indian, the Indian on a monument, who recalls the past glories of an Aztec empire. This empire ceased to exist in 1521 and therefore contributed almost nothing to Mexico's postconquest civilization. What the Indians are today has little to do with Aztec kings. Yet what the Mexicans believe to be true is true for them. In August 1970, the anthropologist Antonio Caso, director of the National Indigenist Institute, proclaimed the Indian "lord" of the Mexican nation. "Here he was born, here he grew, and here he has created his culture," said Caso. And as long as the Revolution endures, Mexico, the modern country of sophisticated industries, of urban skyscrapers and luxury hotels and apartments, will most probably continue to be an "Indian" nation.

3

Spanish Mexico

The Catholic monarch Ferdinand of Aragón died in January 1516, bequeathing his kingdoms in Spain and Italy and his New World territories to his young grandson, Charles of Ghent. Three years later Charles became Holy Roman Emperor and added the Hapsburg lands of northern and central Europe to his domain. He ruled this conglomeration of states until 1556, when the frustrations of the Empire's insoluble problems led him to abdicate and turn over Spain and the Netherlands to his son Philip. The other Hapsburg lands devolved upon Charles' brother, Ferdinand, who succeeded him as Holy Roman Emperor. To the Spaniards, Charles was always a foreigner. And it is true that all too often the affairs of Germany—wars against France and the Turks and the stubborn revolt of the Lutheran princes—took precedence over the concerns of Spain. The Emperor squandered Castilian lives and silver in an unending series of foreign adventures. In May 1520 the townspeople of Castile rebelled against their absentee king and his alien counsellors, demanding that Charles respect the independence of Castile's parliament, the Cortes. But the cause of these Comuneros gained little support among the other social classes, and by the time Charles returned to Spain in July 1522, the royal army had crushed the revolt. Though the Cortes continued to meet on rare occasions, the townspeople of Spain were impotent to influence the policies of the King, either foreign or domestic.

In Castile Charles inherited from his grandfather a half-modernized state structure. Ferdinand and Isabella had strengthened the monarchy, taking a medieval congeries of provinces and transforming it into a united and powerful kingdom. They curbed the powers of the feudal aristocracy and the town governments, appointing corregidores as agents of royal authority in the various provinces of this kingdom. They increased the wealth and prestige of the monarchy by taking control of Castile's powerful military orders. They facilitated equal justice throughout Castile by establishing a system of royal courts or audiencias. They wrung concessions (the Patronato) from the papacy which placed the government of the Church in the hands of the monarchs. And they assured the orthodoxy and homogeneity of their Catholic kingdom by conquering the Moors and expelling the unconverted Jews from Spain. The other Spanish kingdoms, Catalonia, Aragón, and Valencia, were less touched by these royal reforms. In any event, Castile was the largest, the dominant part of Spain. It was Castile that discovered and conquered, and subsequently peopled the New World, and that gave its institutions to Spain's overseas possessions.

Though the Castilian monarchy grew in power, its Achilles heel was its system of finances. The traditional source of royal revenue were the personal estates of the monarchs together with sales taxes (the alcabala) and import-export duties (almojarifazgo). To support the Church the Crown had the tithe and the sales of indulgences (the Bulls of the Holy Crusade). In a crisis the Cortes might be summoned to vote the government a servicio, to be collected by the towns of the kingdom. But this levy was only temporary, and there was always the danger (from the royal viewpoint) that the members of the Cortes might seize the occasion to extort concessions from the Crown, The Catholic monarchs, as well as their Hapsburg successors, preferred to rely upon the parliament as little as possible and to assemble its members only in times of grave need. The tax burden fell most heavily on the townspeople, both rich and poor, because the landed aristocracy and the clergy were exempt from most levies. For this reason there was no incentive for the noble classes (the hidalgos) or the clergy to make common cause in the parliament with the townspeople. The Cortes remained weak, and the Crown lost an opportunity to unite royal interests (as the Tudors had in England) with those of the mercantile and industrial classes.

Castile's royal revenues, which sufficed in the last years of the fifteenth century to finance the War of Reconquest against the Moors in Granada, could not meet the greatly increased demands of the Hapsburg Empire. Thus the treasures of the New World seemed a godsend to the harassed Charles. But the amount of gold and silver to reach Spain from the Indies was only a trickle before the 1550s, and the Emperor was forced to borrow ever larger amounts of money from German and Italian bankers. By his profligacy, he put in hock the economy of Castile for decades to come. Had Spain been free to seek its own destiny, to concentrate its attention on the Iberian peninsula and the overseas possessions, a strong national state could have developed in the sixteenth century. Instead, Charles, as Holy Roman Emperor, wasted his heritage when he thrust Spain willy nilly into the arena of Northern European politics. Nevertheless, in the first optimistic years of his reign the conquest of Mexico appeared to promise unlimited wealth for the royal coffers and power for His Imperial Majesty.

Columbus carried out his explorations under the auspices of the queen of Castile. For Isabella the admiral sought in four voyages to reach the Indies of the East. To his deep disappointment he found little wealth and discovered only the Caribbean islands and the mainland coasts of present-day Venezuela and Central America. After the death of Isabella in 1504 Ferdinand kept some interest in these New World possessions, but as King of Aragón he turned his attention primarily to Mediterranean affairs, to the problems of securing a foothold for the Spanish monarchy in Italy. For this reason the discoveries and acquisition of new territories in the first two decades of the sixteenth century resulted largely from private enterprise. Juan de Solís explored the coast of South America; Diego de Velázquez occupied Cuba and became its governor; Vasco Nuñez de Balboa crossed the Isthmus of Panama and discovered the Pacific Ocean; and Ferdinand Magellan set out to circumnavigate the globe. But the territories claimed by Spain and effectively occupied by Spanish settlers were small and of little commercial significance. Nor could Charles, preoccupied at first with securing the imperial crown and then with putting down the Comunero revolt, manifest much interest in enlarging his overseas possessions until after 1521. It was Velázquez, as governor of Cuba, who was largely responsible for the discovery and conquest of Mexico. In 1517 and 1518 he sent out expeditions to explore the coasts west of Cuba. These expeditions to Yucatán, which were duly reported to Moctezuma in Tenochtitlán, brought back gold and other evidences of wealth. In 1519 the governor commissioned his brother-in-law, Hernán Cortés, to assemble men, weapons, horses, goods, and ships for a large-scale trading venture to these newly discovered and promising lands.

Cortés, a landowner and magistrate in Cuba, had been chafing at the tranquil life of a gentleman farmer. Proud and self-confident, he was embued with the spirit of Spain's Reconquest against the Moors. Like most of his comrades and the conquerors who came later to Peru, he was, by preference, a professional soldier. They were all poor men in Spain. But they were also filled with ambition. Bernal Díaz del Castillo, who fought at Cortés' side in Mexico, put it frankly: "We came to serve God and the king, and also to get rich!" To the men of the Reconquest, wealth and honor were to be won in battle against the infidel. Working with one's hands was degrading—the business of Jews and Moors, not of Christian gentlemen. Courageous, even foolhardy, the conquerors would suffer privations, would risk death for their king innumerable times in battle. But they all expected to be rewarded for their efforts, to acquire grants of land, to have vassals to work their estates, and to receive titles of nobility. Though their ambitions were understandable, they were doomed to frustration, because of the Crown's determination to wipe out feudalism in Spain and to prevent the growth of medieval institutions in the colonies.

Cortés had been sent to the continent to discover wealth for the governor of Cuba. He was too ambitious, however, to remain the subordinate of Velázquez. Suspicious of Cortés, the governor tried unsuccessfully to depose him even before he left the island. Once in Mexico, Cortés cut himself off from Cuba and wrote to Charles V asking that the Emperor name him governor of this rich land which he called New Spain. Some in his troop sided with Velázquez and opposed Cortés' plan to press on to Tenochtitlán. But Cortés was adamant. Starting with fewer than 500 men, he gained Indian allies as he climbed to the highlands and was able to immobilize the power of Moctezuma. When the Aztec king allowed the Spanish army to enter Tenochtitlán unmolested in November 1519, he sealed his own fate and assured the destruction of his empire. Subsequently Moctezuma died under mysterious circumstances, and Cortés and his men were driven temporarily from Tenochtitlán, but the Spanish leader never wavered in his self-confidence. He built boats to carry his men across the lake, and in May 1521 he invested the island city. The fighting lasted for three months as the Spaniards devastated the great city. To facilitate their advance they tore down the temples, the pyramids, and the palaces and filled the canals with rubble. When the young Emperor Cuauhtémoc was captured on August 13 Tenochtitlán had ceased to exist.

The destruction of Aztec power by so few Europeans was a remarkable feat. Yet the Spaniards had many military and psychological advantages—their firearms and armor, their horses and wardogs. Cortés' men went into battle to destroy their enemy, while the Indians were accustomed to a ritual warfare in which tribes fought to acquire tribute or to capture sacrificial victims for their gods. During the final assault the Aztecs were weakened by a smallpox epidemic among their population. But most important, the Spaniards had in Cortés an indomitable leader. He inspired his soldiers with his own courage and confidence. He could be ruthless and cruel; yet he was conciliatory when the time came for peace. Though he ordered the death of Cuauhtémoc, he won the hearts of the Indians whom he liberated from Aztec tyranny. Today there are no statues of Cortés in Mexico's capital. No states, cities, towns, or hamlets preserve his name. His only monument is Mexico itself, the country which he established.

With the fall of Tenochtitlán Cortés set about to pacify the outlying areas of Mexico. He dispatched his lieutenants to explore and conquer the land farther south in Guatemala and Honduras. And he ordered the construction of his new capital on the site of Tenochtitlán. Many of his men opposed this decision, maintaining that Coyoacán or some other site away from the lake would be superior. But Cortés held fast to his purpose, realizing that the religious and political prestige of the Aztec capital would pass to the new Mexico City. Subsequent events showed that Cortés' men were correct. Because the city was built in the lake, even though the Spaniards filled the canals and later drained off the waters, floods were to plague the capital's inhabitants for centuries. Buildings have shifted and cracked because of the spongy ground and the absence of firm foundations. Only in the second half of the twentieth century have Mexican architects solved the problem by devising a method of floating their structures on concrete piers.

The Spaniards in Europe and in the Indies were urban dwellers. Though they might become great landowners, they preferred to live in town and manage their properties through overseers. As a result, Spanish American populations became clustered and remain so today. One of Cortés' first important actions in Mexico was to found the city of Veracruz and to establish its government. In 1523 he asked Alonso García Bravo to draw up a plan for the construction of his new capital. Erected without protecting walls, it was one of the world's first modern cities. The architect laid out the capital with a plaza in the center and divided the city into blocks for the residences of the conquerors. Indians were to be excluded from the inner city, except when they labored for the Spaniards. On the central plaza, where the great pyramid of Huitzilopochtli had once stood, were the cathedral and Cortés' palace. (Subsequently the Conqueror's son, Martín Cortés, sold the residence to Philip II to be used as a government building.) The Spaniards' private residences were built in the traditional Mediterranean fashion—with thick stone walls flush on the street and with a patio in the center.

Since the early sixteenth century substantial Mexicans have preferred to build their houses as fortresses against an alien and dangerous world. Barred windows or high outer walls topped with shards of broken glass (because of the ubiquitous sneak thieves) contribute to the attitude of hostility toward the outsider. There has been little neighborly togetherness in the great houses of Mexico City. Each family is an isolated unit turned in on itself as it repels the outside world. The aristocratic social pattern has meant a greatly strengthened family structure, but it has also made cooperation among a city's citizens difficult. In turn, the lack of cooperation has militated against the effective organization of citizens, in political parties, for example. It is true that most Mexicans, whether poor Indians, mestizos, or whites in the colonial period or the poverty-stricken classes in today's cities and towns, have been forced to exist under overcrowded conditions. But the poor majority has always lived outside the political structure, and the politically effective citizens have preserved the aristocratic mentality of the great house.

Once the fighting was concluded, the soldiers of Cortés clamored to be recompensed for their services. Petitioning the Crown for grants of land and Indians to build their town houses and man their estates, the conquerors confidently expected to become feudal lords in the New World. A decree of Charles V in 1520 forbade the distribution of Indian vassals in the New World. Nevertheless, Cortés ignored the royal ban and awarded his men groups of Indians (encomiendas). He told the Emperor that the Indians needed to be protected from their own rulers. Moreover, he said, his men demanded encomiendas, and he had no other choice. These Indians, who continued to live on communal properties (ejidos) in their preconquest towns and villages were to provide labor for their Spanish lords. Thus an incipient feudalism struggled to emerge in the first days after the Conquest. At the same time, the Crown acted to restrict the authority of Cortés as governor of New Spain.

Cortés was a magnificent leader of men, perhaps the ablest captain to fight in the Spanish Indies. Bold and intelligent, he could act with confidence and dispatch in moments of crisis. Yet the very qualities that made him an effective military commander also made him less suitable as a civilian official. The Crown needed governors who would loyally follow bureaucratic procedures. Above all, the great distance from Spain required the naming of officials who could be counted upon to put the Crown's interests uppermost. Charles began to clip Cortés' wings by appointing bureaucrats to reduce the Conqueror's wide powers. Cortés, in a letter to the Emperor, had asked Charles not to send lawyers to New Spain. In 1524, however, two treasury officials arrived to assure that the Crown received its share of Mexico's treasures. In the same year Charles created a Council of the Indies in Spain to govern all of his newly discovered territories overseas. And two years later, a royal judge, Luis Ponce de León, came to New Spain to investigate complaints of misgovernment against Cortés. When Ponce de León removed him as governor and the Council of the Indies named an audiencia to replace him, the Conqueror returned to Spain to complain to the Court that he had been mistreated. Charles ennobled Cortés, designating him Marquis of the Valley of Oaxaca, and granted him a vast estate south of Mexico City. But thereafter Cortés had no political power. By 1530 Mexico of the conquerors was giving way to the New Spain of bureaucratic officials.

Antonio de Mendoza was a distinguished civil servant in Castile when he came to the New World in 1535 as New Spain's first viceroy.

An astute diplomat and a capable administrator, Mendoza was able to keep Cortés and the aggressive conquerors in check and at the same time to secure law and order in the colony. The viceroy built up the economy of New Spain, importing European crops—wheat, barley, rice, and fruit trees—and farm animals—horses, mules, cattle, sheep, pigs, and chickens. Mulberry trees were planted to make possible a silk industry in the colony, though the Crown later discouraged silk production because it competed with the Philippine trade. Under Mendoza the first books were printed in the New World, and schools were opened for Indians and for the children of conquerors. At his recommendation, the Crown chartered the New World's first university in Mexico City, which opened in 1553. The viceroy sent Francisco Vásquez de Coronado to explore what is now the Southwest of the United States. Mendoza laid the foundations for a system of government that his able successors were to maintain until the beginning of the nineteenth century.

Royal government, as it developed in the Indies, was a pyramid, with the Council of the Indies in Spain at the apex. The Council carried out the orders of the king. When the king absented himself from Spain, as Charles V frequently did, the council acted in the king's name. It was a legislative body, decreeing laws for the Indies. But it also served as an executive institution, appointing viceroys, bishops, and other royal officials in America and seeing that its own laws were carried out. And finally, the Council acted as a court of last appeal from decisions of royal courts abroad. It is evident that Spanish legalists made no attempt to separate the legislative, executive, and judicial powers or to institute an elaborate system of checks and balances.

In New Spain the king's authority was vested in the viceroy. Audiencias in Mexico City, Guadalajara, and Guatemala City shared some powers with the viceroy, but they served chiefly as courts of law and secondarily as local lawmaking bodies. Viceroys wielded great power and had discretion in enforcing the king's will in the colony. But the Crown, fearful that a strong viceroy might show himself too independent, encouraged the audiencia judges to correspond over his head with the Council back in Spain. The Council also appointed judges to make periodic investigations of the viceroys and other public officials. At the intermediate level, under the viceroy and the audiencias, were corregidores or governors and, at the lowest level of the pyramid, the town councils (cabildos). Some corregidores governed Indian communities, others Spanish towns. All were judges, as well as executive officials. It was only at the intermediate and lower levels, however, that the New World population was represented.

In order to insure the fidelity of royal officials in the Indies, the Crown reserved the most important offices for Spaniards born in the peninsula. To those born in the New World (the creoles) royal government came to be something alien, imposed by a system in which they had little participation. Orders flowed from the apex of the pyramid, and every public official owed his position to the king and Council in Spain or to the viceroy, who was always a Spaniard. Because the Crown never permitted a parliament in the colony, there was no legal method by which the Americans could influence royal policy in the colony.

The military conquest and political consolidation of Mexico were accompanied and reinforced by a spiritual conquest which was considered the chief justification for the Spanish presence in the New World. The papal grants upon which Spanish claims to the Indies rested held the Catholic monarchs responsible for the Christianization of these newly discovered territories. Cortés brought a priest with him to Mexico, and at one point the Conqueror risked the safety of his expedition by clearing the idols from an Indian temple and substituting an image of the Virgin. The Spaniards were not hypocrites. They had a genuine concern for the spiritual well-being of the conquered Indians. But they saw no contradiction between the European's obvious passion to enrich himself at the expense of the hapless natives and his determination to save the Indians' souls. The intimate union between Church and State in the Spanish political system mirrored a deep conviction on the part of the Spaniard that his religious life and his secular life were inseparable.

At the time of the discovery and conquest of the Indies, the Church in Castile was undergoing a reformation at the hands of Isabella's adviser, Cardinal Ximénez de Cisneros. He had improved seminary education and had insisted upon a spiritual purification of the clergy. As a result, by the 1520s the orders in Spain were in good condition to undertake the herculean task of converting the many new subjects of the Spanish Crown. The responsibility was entrusted to the mendicant orders, chiefly the Franciscans and Dominicans, who had a special dispensation from the papacy to act as parish priests. In 1524 the first contingent of missionaries arrived in Mexico, twelve Franciscans. The Indians were amazed to see the great Cortés humble himself before these simple priests. Two years later the first Dominicans came, and in 1533 the Augustinians. With much ardor and zeal the friars began to preach to the Indians, converting and baptizing the natives and building mission churches.

Church architecture in colonial Mexico reflected the current styles in Spain. The earliest churches in the cities were constructed with three aisles of equal height, and often with wood-beamed roofs. Outside the cities, however, the friars in New Spain developed a unique church structure to deal with the special problems of preaching to the heathen and uncivilized Indians. At Acolman, Actopan, and many other sites throughout Mexico south of the Chichimec frontier, they erected buildings that were at once churches and monasteries, with thick walls and parapets for defense against attack. The façade of the fortress-church had plateresque (Spanish Gothic) decorations around the entry—though the Indian laborers often worked native motifs into their carvings. The interior of the church, which was vaguely Gothic in concept, had a single large nave with no side aisles—for the sake of apostolic simplicity, said the friars, but also so that they could watch over their Indian charges. The first city churches were subsequently replaced, but the mission structures remain today as reminders of the friars' vigorous building activities during the sixteenth century.

In order to communicate the teachings of the Christian religion to the Mexican natives, the missionaries used various techniques. Many of the friars, such as Bernardino de Sahagún and Toribio de Benavente (Motolonía) with the Aztecs and Diego de Landa in Yucatán, taught themselves the Indian languages and put together dictionaries and grammars to aid other missionaries. Some constructed elaborately painted banners as mnemonic devices. Perhaps the most effective (and certainly most enjoyable to the Indians) were the religious plays written by the priests, in which the Indians themselves acted out the principal roles. Favorite dramas were the expulsion of Adam and Eve from the Garden of Eden and the battles of Christians and Moors. (The latter play is still produced annually in Mexico's countryside.) The friars baptized millions of Indians, and the natives imbibed a modicum of Christian teaching. But they also brought over into Catholicism many of their pagan beliefs and practices. They buried Tlálocs at the feet of Christian statues or inserted obsidian hearts in stone crosses. Of greatest significance, they transformed Christian hagiolatry, creating new saints in their own image—Our Lady of Guadalupe at Tepeyac and the Black Christ of Chalma. It was no coincidence that the Virgin of Guadalupe was said to have appeared to a young Indian at Tepeyac, a site holy to Tonantzín, the Aztec Earth Mother. The new European religion remained for many a veneer, while the age-old beliefs and practices kept their hold on the people.

In the first burst of enthusiasm the friars hoped to provide a Christian education for many if not most of the Indians. Pedro de Gante established a primary school for Indians in Texcoco and later in Mexico City. The most prestigious Indian academy was the Franciscan Santa Cruz de Tlatelolco founded in 1536. Among its distinguished teachers was Sahagún, who compiled an account of preconquest Mexico. At Tlatelolco the sons of Indian caciques were taught Latin and rhetoric, as were the children of the nobility in Spain. It was intended that the students at Tlatelolco become the governors of their people. The friars' hopes to educate the Indians were thwarted, however, by the problems of sheer numbers and of finances, and also because of the lay Spaniards' hostility to the program. The conquerors wanted the Indians to labor, not to be scholars or to master the arts of government. Critics charged that the students were heretical in questioning Christian dogma. For the Indians, said one, reading and writing were "as harmful as the devil." They should be taught their prayers and the Ten Commandments "and no more." Faced with open antagonism from the settlers, the friars were forced to curtail their instructional activities. Thereafter few Indians even learned Spanish. The greater part of the indigenous population continued to speak the native languages, well into the nineteenth century and thus lived beyond the pale of the Spanish-Mexican culture and institutions.

By the 1570s the original enthusiasm of the friars had begun to wane. It is usually difficult to maintain the crusading spirit beyond the first generation of missionaries. For the next century and a half a small number of clergymen (particularly the Jesuits, who came to Mexico in 1572) labored selflessly in the north, but for most priests the spiritual conquest was at an end. The secular clergy moved into the settled areas to replace the friars. Many of the friars resisted the pressures to leave lucrative and comfortable parish posts, however, and the bitter contentions among the churchmen scandalized Indians and Spaniards alike. In fact, the temptations of the good life led many priests astray during the remainder of the colonial era. In all probability most of the clergy led exemplary lives then as in other ages of Christian history, but the frequent injunctions of prelates and Church synods against clerical immorality show that it was an endemic problem and a difficult one to cure. Even in serious crimes the churchmen might escape retribution because of the clerical immunities (fueros) to civil procedures. Some priests became wealthy; some had concubines; some gambled. Like the lay Spaniards, most of them exploited the Indians in their charge.

In the first two decades after the Conquest the number and size of encomiendas continued to increase despite the Crown's prohibitions. The Indians' lands and properties were taken from them. They were forced to labor in the Spaniards' fields, to work in the silver mines, to build houses, churches, and public buildings for the conquerors. The cruel mistreatment of the Indians led to vigorous protests by clerics such as the Franciscan Juan Zumárraga, first bishop of Mexico, and Bartolomé de las Casas, later bishop of Chiapas. Zumárraga's charges against the members of the first audiencia led to its removal by the Council of the Indies. Though he worked hard to protect his newly converted charges, it was the Dominican friar Las Casas who was most vigilant in the Indians' defense, preaching, writing books, and agitating furiously for legislation to restrain the cupidity of the Spaniards. After more than twenty years in the New World, he returned to Spain in 1539 to rally support for the Indians. His propagandizing bore fruit in 1542 when Charles V issued his New Laws, by which the Emperor intended to deal a deathblow to Indian servitude and to the encomienda. The Indians were not to be enslaved; the encomienda could not be inherited. Though the Crown did not order an immediate confiscation of encomienda rights, the New Laws meant that the institution would terminate with the current holder's death.

The publication of the Emperor's decrees in the New World brought consternation, complaints, and even threats of rebellion. In Peru a civil war ensued, and the viceroy was captured and beheaded by the angry colonists. The astute Antonio de Mendoza in New Spain realized that rigid enforcement of the laws would mean the extinction of the Spanish colony, and he persuaded the Crown to modify them. Though Indian slavery was still outlawed, the encomienda could be passed on. But the possession of an encomienda was to involve only the right to collect a tribute, not to hold land or to require work from the Indians. And the encomienda, while renewable at the Crown's discretion, was not permanent. Clearly the Crown was determined to remove the encomienda's feudal implications. The issue remained alive, however, and sparks of feudal particularism were fanned by a theological debate, ostensibly on the nature of the Indians, but with a direct bearing on the encomienda question.

This controversy culminated in 1550 in a disputation between Las Casas and Juan Ginés de Sepúlveda, one of Spain's leading humanists. The learned Sepúlveda was thoroughly conversant with Aristotelian philosophy, having translated an edition of the *Politics*. Reports from the New World of the savage natives who painted their bodies and practiced human sacrifice and cannibalism inspired him to write a book utilizing the doctrines of Aristotle to defend the Spanish conquest of the Indies. He applied to the New World's inhabitants Aristotle's stricture that some men are by nature inferior and wrote in his *Democrates Alter*, which he circulated in manuscript, that the "rude nature" of the Indians compelled them to serve the civilized Spaniards, for they were "serfs by nature." If Sepúlveda could demonstrate by logical reasoning that the Indians were ontologically inferior to the Spaniards, he would provide a powerful argument for a permanent system of feudalism in America. The fiery Las Casas entered the lists to defend his Indians from the humanist's attacks.

To settle the issue the court halted the conquest and ordered the two antagonists to debate the question before a group of Spanish theologians at Valladolid. Sepúlveda presented the arguments he had used in *Democrates Alter*. Las Casas did not deny Aristotle's doctrine of natural servitude, but he sought to prove that the Indians were not by nature inferior, that they indeed possessed the qualities of civilized men. The importance of the issue is shown by the presence at Valladolid of representatives of encomenderos who had come from Mexico to convince the Crown that their demands for lands and Indians were just.

The outcome of the debate was perhaps anticlimactic, for the judges dispersed without an official decision. Las Casas continued, however, to write and to publish his books, while Sepúlveda was not allowed to print *Democrates Alter* and lost his preferment with the royal family. The conquest in the Indies now became a "pacification" or a "settlement." Whatever the theological merits of the debate, the Crown could not permit Sepúlveda's ideas to prevail. To do so would be to admit the reasonability of the encomenderos' demands that the lord-vassal relationship with the Indians be made permanent. Instead, the Crown strengthened the corregidor as the chief agent of royal government to deal with the Indians. The hopes of the conquerors and their families in New Spain were not extinguished so easily, however, and though after 1550 the intentions of the royal government were clear concerning the encomienda as a feudal institution, the issue was still to be fought out. The 1560s saw an abortive attempt on the part of the Mexican creoles to impose their own solution by force and perhaps even to win independence from Spain.

Philip II came to the throne of Spain in 1556 at the abdication of his father, the Emperor. Like many a son of a strong-willed father, Philip's character contrasted markedly with that of Charles V. Charles was a soldier, while his son preferred the quiet seclusion of the library and his state papers. Where Charles was bold, Philip vacillated, unsure of himself. The Emperor, much more pragmatic and conciliatory than his son, was willing to compromise with his enemies (the Lutheran princes, for example). Philip was more orthodox, more rigid, even, than the Pope, and he fought the dangers to the Catholic faith both at home and abroad. Intolerant and fanatical, he strengthened the Inquisition, banned foreign books, and forbade Spanish students to study abroad. Yet he continued the disastrous foreign policy of his father, leading Spain into wars with the Dutch and the English, with France, and with the Turks. And like Charles, he wasted the wealth of his country and his overseas possessions. Within a year of his accession to the throne the Spanish government declared itself bankrupt. This was the first of many financial crises for the Crown, crises which had repercussions in the colonies as well as in the peninsula.

The second viceroy of New Spain, Luis de Velasco, replaced Antonio de Mendoza in 1550. He was a worthy successor. Completely loyal to the Crown, Velasco could handle the colony's affairs with industry and vigor, and yet with understanding. Under Velasco New Spain expanded to the north, beyond the Chichimec frontier. Most significant was the opening of rich silver mines in Zacatecas, Guanajuato, and San

Luis Potosí, followed by Francisco de Ibarra's conquest of Durango. The introduction in the late 1550s of the patio process, in which silver was extracted from the ores by means of an amalgamation with quicksilver, greatly increased the production of the metal during the following decade.

The outpouring of treasure from the Mexican mines (and from the mountain of ore at Potosí in Upper Peru) brought prosperity during the 1560s and 1570s to Spain and its New World colonies. In Spain Philip began to build his new capital in Madrid and started construction of his labyrinthine palace, the Escorial. (Henceforth, he decreed, Spanish buildings would be erected in the austere style of the Escorial.) His armies defeated the French and increased the tempo of the sea wars against the Turks and the Dutch. To protect the silver from enemy attacks, Philip instituted the fleet system in 1564, and twice a year convoyed ships plied between Seville and ports in the Indies. In the viceregal capital of Mexico City the aristocratic creoles lavishly spent the fortunes which they owed to their fathers, the men of Cortés, entertaining each other on a grand scale and riding through the city streets accompanied by pages and mounted courtiers. The son of the Conqueror, Martín Cortés, set the standard for the new aristocracy. A close friend of King Philip, possessor of vast estates and of many encomiendas of Indians, he was indeed a prince in the realm created by his father.

Despite their affluence, however, the aristocrats murmured against the royal government and the king's representative in New Spain, the viceroy Velasco. Philip's wars cost money, and he found it necessary to increase taxes (notably the almojarifazgo) and to wring a forced loan from his subjects at home and abroad. The chief irritant of the creoles was the impermanence of the encomienda, which could be terminated at the king's whim. It was this uncertainty that caused a small group of their leaders to plot rebellion. But the Spanish authorities acted quickly and ruthlessly to frustrate the plot before it could get started. Two young aristocrats, the sons of the conqueror Gil González de Ávila, were sentenced to death by beheading, while Martín Cortés was arrested and sent back to Spain. Philip freed Cortés and restored his estates, but the Marquis never returned to Mexico. In New Spain restrictions continued on the encomienda, which became increasingly less desirable until it was virtually extinguished in the seventeenth century. Because the Spaniards were not willing to engage in hand labor, however, a new institution was required. To provide a work force for the mines, textile shops, and farms the Spaniards in New Spain turned to the repartimiento, a system of compulsory part-time labor.

The last two decades of the century were catastrophic for both Spain and New Spain. Yet in 1580 Philip seemed at the pinnacle of success. He was elected to the throne of Portugal to unite the Iberian peninsula for the first time since Roman days and added Portugal's overseas possessions to his own. The wealth of the New World, of Africa and the Orient, seemed limitless, and the king planned even more audacious ventures against the English and the Dutch. Philip spent ten million ducats to launch the ill-fated "Invincible Armada" against England. The destruction of the Spanish invasion fleet in 1588 began a series of national reverses. During the 1590s Dutch raids on Spanish and Portuguese shipping took a heavy toll. Taxes were increased in Castile to such an extent as to damage irreparably the country's industry and trade. In 1596 Philip suspended payments on the Crown's debts, and his government plunged into bankruptcy once more. His only recourse was to seek a forced "gift" from his hard-pressed subjects. Two years later, when Philip died, Spain, once the greatest power in Europe, was by all counts a second-class nation. Nature added yet another cruel blow in 1599, when a plague in Castile killed off perhaps fifteen percent of the population. The seventeenth century in Spain was a period of economic stagnation and decay, for the spirit of confidence that had characterized the wars against the Moors and the conquest of America had been dashed against the rocks of unceasing disasters. It was in this era of national pessimism that Miguel de Cervantes wrote *Don Quixote*.

New Spain, like the mother country, was prosperous in the 1570s and 1580s. Construction on great cathedrals began in Mexico City, Puebla, Michoacán, and Oaxaca in the new Renaissance style dictated by King Philip. Work started on a vast drainage project to remove the threat of floods from the Valley of Mexico. Expeditions explored north into New Mexico. Luxury goods came from China by way of the Philippines and Acapulco. But New Spain was now beginning to feel the effects of a calamitous population decline, brought on in part by Spanish mistreatment of the Indians, but principally by widespread epidemics in the years 1545–48 and 1576–81. It was the loss of the larger part of the Indian population to disease that pushed New Spain into a century of depression. The decline also hindered the effective operation of the repartimiento and gave impetus to the growth of large estates.

Throughout the sixteenth century it had been the policy of the Crown to restrict landholding by the Spaniards in the colonies. Royal decrees confirmed the rights of the Indians to their ancestral lands. From the beginning, however, the intentions of the Crown broke down in the face of the demands for rewards from the conquerors, and some land grants were made, notably Cortés' extensive Marquisate of the Valley of Oaxaca. Further exceptions were made in the areas of the mines in order to provide food and supplies for the new mining communities. But the Spaniards in New Spain also illegally helped themselves to lands, especially toward the end of the century when the plagues depopulated many areas. The financial exigencies of the royal government gave further impetus to the growth of large estates, as colonists purchased titles to these illicitly acquired properties from the Crown. In a society that equated social eminence with the possession of a noble title and landed estates, they could gain prestige only by becoming hacendados.

The earliest haciendas were dedicated principally to cattle and sheep raising. The Indian communities furnished most of the agricultural produce consumed in the Spanish towns and, under the repartimiento, the labor required to operate the estates and the urban sweat shops (obrajes), as well. The sharp population decline after 1570 dealt the Spaniards a double blow. As the numbers of Europeans in the colony grew through immigration and as the Indian communities were decimated, severe food shortages developed, and there was intensified competition for the labor of the remaining Indians. The repartimiento obligations were increased until the lot of the Indian, never pleasant under the best of circumstances, became intolerable. Young, old, and infirm were snatched off to work long hours for the Spaniards. The employers illegally prolonged the temporary work periods and by force prevented the laborers from returning to their homes. Moreover, the Crown, casting about for any expedient to augment royal revenues, increased the tribute tax owed by the Indians. It is not strange that large numbers of Indians deserted their villages for what appeared to them to be the more attractive life on the estates. The hacendado paid the Indians' tribute to the Crown and offered protection from the demands of the repartimiento. In turn, the hacienda Indians provided a permanent work force, which was far more satisfactory to the Spanish land owners than the temporary repartimiento. As a result, the repartimiento went the way of the encomienda. In the seventeenth century New Spain's economy was dominated by the large estate, as mercantile and industrial activities decreased during the prolonged depression.

Critics of the colonial regime in Mexico point to the harshness of the hacienda system, stressing that it tied the Indians to the estate by means of debt servitude (peonage). It is true that the hacendados encouraged an accumulating debt in Indian families through the *tienda de raya* (commissary store) and loans for fiestas and church fees. Yet in the colonial era the debts were often not onerous, and most Indians evidently preferred the security of the hacienda to the precarious village life and the excesses of repartimiento labor. After independence, when the Indians could no longer turn to the government or the Church for redress, conditions worsened measurably. It is ironic that the development of the hacienda system brought ultimately to New Spain the feudal relationship that the Spanish Crown had opposed so strenuously in the years after the Conquest. Legally free, the peons were in effect serfs, since they could not ordinarily leave the estate. As Spain itself declined in the seventeenth century, and the Crown's control of the colonies slackened, New Spain became more and more isolated from the mother country. The King's power was no longer so strong in Mexico's rural areas, and the hacendados came to assume the prerogatives of a feudal aristocracy, even to the extent of dispensing justice on their lands. Sepúlveda was proved right, after all. Given the social attitudes that prevailed among the Spaniards, the Indian and Spanish communities in the New World could not coexist without an arrangement similar to the medieval manorial regime.

The population decrease in New Spain was accompanied by a ruinous decline in the mining industry, caused in large measure by the idiotic fiscal policies of the Crown. Despite the obvious fact that the New World's treasure was indispensable to finance Spain's wars, the royal government, in searching for ever new sources of revenue, destroyed its means of support. The mining of quicksilver was a royal monopoly, and an adequate supply of the metal was essential to the production of silver. Yet the Crown was so shortsighted as to raise the price of quicksilver in order to add a few more ducats each year to the royal exchequer. As a consequence, most miners in New Spain could no longer afford to produce silver, and they took up other occupations. The last blows against the industry came in 1637 and 1639 when the Crown seized all of the silver that arrived in Seville with no compensation for the owners. Thereafter there could be little incentive to produce silver, and by 1640 it was apparent that the industry was ailing in Mexico.

The decade of the 1630s was singularly traumatic for Spain and the colonies, all the more so because the king, Philip IV, and his shrewd minister, the Count of Olivares, at first seemed capable of halting their country's plunge toward oblivion. Olivares was determined to reform the Spanish government and, above all, to bring unity to the disparate kingdoms of the Iberian peninsula. But the king's chief minister could not resist the seductive lure of imperialism, and he committed his country to new wars against the French and the Dutch. To pay for these costly ventures the king increased the impositions on his already heavily burdened subjects in Spain and in the colonies. In addition to the regular taxes, the Crown levied a charge of half a year's income against each office holder (the media anata), imposed a stamp tax on every legal transaction, sold titles of nobility and many official positions, and ordered hidalgos to provide troops for the army at their own expense. In the Indies the government terminated the encomienda and ordered Indian tributes paid directly to the royal treasury. When all legal devices failed to head off national bankruptcy, Olivares' government confiscated the national bonds held by private citizens and began to depreciate

Spain's currency. Lacking means of supporting the foreign wars, Olivares failed even to keep the peninsula united. In 1640 Aragón revolted, and the Portuguese broke away, declaring their independence under the Braganza family. Three years later the king dismissed Olivares, and with him went the last faint hope for governmental reorganization. For the rest of the century Spain's overseas commerce was beset by piratical attacks which the weak government was powerless to prevent.

The last half of the seventeenth century (the Baroque Age) saw the first stirrings of national sentiment in Mexico. Spain, in a slough of despond under the late Hapsburg monarchs, had little concern for the colonials. Cut off from Europe by the paucity of trade, New Spain became introverted. Decrees still came from the Council of the Indies, and viceroys and audiencias continued to execute royal policy in the colony. But creole power was increasingly felt on the local level. An hacendado made his own law on his estate and might occasionally defy royal officials. Creoles could purchase from the Crown the offices of corregidor and town councillor, giving themselves considerable importance as political bosses in the provinces. Creole handicraft industries, utilizing slave labor, became more efficient and prosperous. In religion, the cult of the dark Virgin of Guadalupe seemed more vital than traditional European practices. It is too early to speak of Mexican nationalism. Yet the creoles were quite aware of the differences that separated them from the Spaniards, whom they contemptuously called gachupines. The incipient creolism is best seen in Carlos Sigüenza y Góngora, a cosmopolitan scientist and man of letters and, at the same time, a proud Mexican. An avid student of Indian antiquities, he used the occasion of the installation of a new viceroy to enlighten the Spanish official concerning the virtues of the Mexican Aztec civilization. Creole architects also gave a peculiarly Mexican exuberance to the late baroque style (Churrigueresque) used in constructing such elaborate buildings as the parish churches in Taxco and Tepozotlán and the Sagrario Metropolitán in Mexico City.

Aside from Sigüenza y Góngora's writings, there is little overt evidence of the creole spirit in the seventeenth century. Certainly the sublime poetry of Sor Juana Inés de la Cruz was as much Spanish as it was Mexican. Rather, creolism can be found in attitudes and in chronic complaints about Spanish governors. So long as the feeble hand of Spain rested lightly on the colonies, the complaints did not lead to active opposition. The Indians, ground down by centuries of exploitation, were too disorganized to offer resistance. The great popular riot of 1692 in Mexico City was caused, not by the oppression of the masses, but by a severe food shortage. For most Indians, the only recourse was to escape life's harsh realities in religious fiestas and in excessive drunkenness. The mestizos could not be white and did not want to be Indian, and so they were caught between the creole aristocrats and the Indian and Negro lower classes. Discriminated against by law and by the caste system, the mestizo class was still too small and insignificant to wield any power. The creole disliked the gachupines and resented the favors reserved for the peninsular Spaniards, but they would not attack the political structure if they could ignore a royal decree or bribe a corrupt Spanish official. When, in the next century, a revivified Spanish government attempted to strengthen its hold on the colonies, a series of crises resulted in New Spain, leading in 1810 to the Revolution for Independence.

The first half of the eighteenth century was relatively peaceful, as the colony was little touched by the international rivalries and dynastic wars in Europe. For New Spain it was a period of quiet and modest growth. The piratical raids that had harried the coastal settlements during the previous century ceased, and if English privateers continued to attack Spanish treasure ships, it was on the high seas and in other parts of the world. Internal peace was secured by the establishment of a rural police force which reduced brigandage outside the cities and towns. By the end of the seventeenth century the demographic decline had been halted, and the years after 1700 saw a slow but steady population increase. The colony experienced an economic expansion brought on largely by a regeneration of the mining industry. As viceroy succeeded viceroy without incident, there were fewer scandals in government, rioting in the cities ceased, and life in New Spain continued on an even keel.

Spain, on the other hand, found itself dragged into every major European conflict, largely as a result of a dynastic change as the new century began. In 1700 Charles II died, the last product of the blighted Hapsburg dynasty in Spain. As death approached, the feeble-minded Charles, who had been incapable of siring an heir, was beset by advocates for various candidates, while the great powers hovered like vultures, anticipating the dismemberment of his empire. Shortly before he died, the bewildered king chose as his successor the French candidate, Philip of Anjou, grandson of Louis XIV. The accession of the French prince to the Spanish throne in 1701 precipitated a general war, as the English, the Dutch, and the Austrian Hapsburgs sought to prevent the French Bourbons from upsetting the balance of power in Europe. The war's end in 1713 saw Philip V confirmed in his possession of the crown of Spain, but with the stipulation that the thrones of France and Spain should never be united.

Europe's politicians need not have worried. In the succeeding decades, Spain had no consistent foreign policy, at different times supporting or opposing the cause of the French Bourbons. An unwilling participant in the scheme of international rivalries, Spain was hauled by her kings this way and that as though in an elaborately disorganized diplomatic quadrille in which partners were exchanged with bewildering frequency. Thus, the Crown had little time for American internal affairs, and New Spain was permitted to continue in relative isolation from the events in Europe. Such political and economic reforms as the Bourbons introduced from France were confined largely to Spain itself. Philip V used the threats of foreign invasions to break the independence of Aragón and Catalonia, and he imported the French institution of the intendancy to extend royal power throughout Spain. Similar reforms for the New World awaited the reign of Charles III, who assumed the throne in 1759.

Charles III was the greatest of the Spanish Bourbons, a benevolent despot formed in the mold of his contemporaries, Frederick the Great of Prussia, Joseph I of Austria, and Catherine the Great of Russia. He assembled a group of reform-minded ministers, many of whom espoused Freemasonry—in the late eighteenth century the font of liberal and enlightened ideas. Perhaps Charles and his ministers were not completely altruistic in their reform program. Charles had had the misfortune to choose the losing side in the Seven Years War, and the king's advisers believed that Spain could not regain a strong position in Europe unless they reorganized the government's structure. To strengthen the economy would mean, in turn, more income for the royal treasury. But whatever the Crown's motivations, the result was more prosperous conditions in Spain and the Indies.

To encourage commerce, most mercantilistic restrictions on trade between Spain and its colonies were eased. The office of the intendant was introduced into America in order to end the corruption and excesses of the corregidores and other royal officials and to assure the steady flow of taxes into the vice-regal coffers. And in an unprecedented attack on the Spanish Church, the Crown, in 1767, ordered the expulsion of the Jesuits from all of Spain's territories and the sequestration of the Society's properties. At the same time, Charles' anticlerical ministers persuaded him to curtail the privileges that had hitherto made priests immune from civil legal procedures. The ministers believed that the wealth of the Church, notably lands held in mortmain, and the obscurantist clergy were an obstacle to progress. The destruction of Jesuit power would free large tracts of the best land for private use and prevent the "superstitious" priests from deforming youthful minds in the Society's colleges. Actually the Jesuits' estates were among the most progressive in New Spain, and the colleges were far more up-to-date than the conservative university of Mexico City. But the Society was a convenient scapegoat for all of Spain's shortcomings, and its members were sacrificed to the political ambitions of the Crown. In New Spain the secular and religious reforms had unexpected consequences which helped bring on the Wars of Independence in the first decade of the nineteenth century.

During the last half of the eighteenth century Mexico became the most prosperous and wealthy of all the Spanish colonies. The mining industry, after a steady development through the century, spurted in the 1770s and 1780s, largely because of reform measures recommended by the royal visitor-general, José de Gálvez, who came to New Spain in 1765. Working with the viceroy, the Marquis de Croix, Gálvez remained in the colony until 1772 and suggested concessions to the mine operators that would encourage production. Royal decrees lowered the cost of quicksilver and cut taxes in order to increase profits. A mining guild was formed, and miners received legal privileges similar to those that had been taken from the clergy. (To Charles and his ministers privileges were for the "useful" classes, those contributing to the prosperity and general well-being of society—the merchants and miners, who created wealth, and the soldiers, who protected the nation.) In 1776, after Gálvez had returned to Spain to become Charles' Minister for the Indies, the intendancy system was established in New Spain. The general prosperity made possible a burst of construction activity—public buildings, hospitals, and churches, many of these designed by Francisco Tresguerras in the new, more severe, neoclassic style, characterized by simple pilasters and pediments. Gálvez was also responsible for the more effective occupation of New Spain's northernmost provinces, especially California. Principally to forestall possible Russian expansion from Alaska, a chain of missions and military presidios extended Spanish occupation as far north as San Francisco.

By 1800 Mexico was a rapidly developing country with the hope of creating a self-sufficient economy and political system. But much of the wealth, particularly the silver, continued to be siphoned off to support the unrealistic pretension of the Crown that Spain could be a strong European power. Moreover, the Bourbon reforms, which had helped bring on prosperity, had the unexpected result of making life more intolerable for the creoles. During the lax years of the late Hapsburgs and even during the first half-century of Bourbon rule, the creoles in Mexico were able to avoid the strict monopolistic controls dictated from Madrid. Despite the fleet system and bans against foreign trade, English goods, better and cheaper than the Spanish equivalents, were smuggled with ease into Mexico. If legal trade was no longer a monopoly of a few mercantile houses in Cádiz and Seville, the new, ostensibly more liberal measures meant a tightening up of trading procedures. From the creoles' viewpoint, government that was more efficient and incorruptible was also more tyrannical. For the creole who must now pay taxes or who might be prevented from exploiting Indian laborers, the introduction of the intendancy was a dubious blessing. The intendant was most likely to be a peninsular Spaniard who took away prerogatives that hacendados and corregidores had exercised for generations. It is not surprising that the voices of revolution in the Anglo-American colonies and in France sounded a siren call to many a Mexican.

The Mexico of 1800 was a society in flux. The rigid class structure of the previous three centuries was beginning to crack under the impact of economic growth and the Bourbon reforms. Power and prestige came less by virtue of aristocratic lineage than of wealth and economic position. The old social bonds were further disturbed by the introduction of new legal privileges, the fueros of miners and, especially, of the military classes. Until the time of Charles III royal control of New Spain rested on civil institutions and the Church more than on military force. After the defeat of Spain in the Seven Years War, Charles decided to strengthen his armed forces at home and abroad. In New Spain regular garrisons were augmented, and a militia was formed, officered by young creoles. In time, because of the military fuero, these officers came to consider themselves a class apart, not subject to the restrictions of the civilian society. In the Wars of Independence they served on both sides, and, after Mexico had broken away from Spain in the 1820s, they continued the praetorian tradition, dominating the country with their armies. The problem of the military and ecclesiastical fueros was to agitate Mexico for nearly half a century after Independence.

If the creoles were restless, ready to oppose Spain's continued rule in the New World, it was Old World political events that set the stage for the independence movement in Mexico. Spain had the misfortune, during the critical period of the French Revolution and the Napoleonic dictatorship, to be saddled with one of the least distinguished rulers in her history. Charles IV became King of Spain in 1788 at the death of his father, Charles III. The new king inherited his father's despotic nature, but while Charles III was enlightened, his son was degenerate. The fatuousness of the king and the royal family is depicted in the unflatteringly cruel portraits of Francisco Goya. Charles raised to the highest rank in the land a young soldier, Manuel Godoy, with whom his silly queen, María Luisa, was enamored. The heir to the throne, Ferdinand, was scarcely more accomplished than his father. When the Revolution of 1789 destroyed the French Bourbon monarchy, Godoy attempted to save Louis XVI, yet at the same time to avoid war with France. He failed in both purposes, and the invasion of Spain by French armies revealed the incapability of the Crown to defend itself. Subsequently, when Napoleon Bonaparte ousted the Directory and took power in France, Spain was drawn into the war against England, with the result that British ships seized the treasure fleet in

1804 and crippled Spanish sea power in 1805 at Trafalgar. In 1807 Charles arrested his son, accusing him of treason with the French and of conspiring against Godoy. Ferdinand was later reconciled with his father, and in the following year Charles abdicated, relinquishing his throne to Ferdinand.

The wily and ruthless Bonaparte took advantage of the unpopularity of the Spanish royal family to force both Charles and Ferdinand in 1808 to yield the throne to his own brother, Joseph. It was the deposition of the Bourbon monarchs and the accession of Joseph I that cut the dynastic ties between Spain and the colonies. In the New World local juntas met in various viceregal capitals to provide legitimate governments independent of the French usurper. Most creoles and peninsulars in the Indies professed allegiance to the deposed Ferdinand, who became a heroic figure to Spaniards everywhere.

If the royal family, imprisoned in France, acquiesced in the French dictation, the people of Spain did not. Popular opposition to the invaders continued until the defeat of Napoleon and the restoration of Ferdinand in 1814. Though French armies controlled Madrid and most of Spain's chief cities after 1808, a national junta assembled in Cádiz to assert the right of the Spanish people to govern themselves and to write a constitution. For the first time in Spanish history the Cortes had the opportunity to restrict royal despotism. In the name of Ferdinand, the parliament proclaimed a constitution in 1812 that embodied the liberal principles of the Enlightenment. The Constitution of 1812 declared that sovereignty rested in the Spanish people, at home and abroad. All Spaniards were equal regardless of race or of territory. It abolished the special legal fueros of the military and clergy and put an end to the inquisitorial courts. The constitution failed to survive the Bourbon restoration in 1814, however, and Ferdinand, determined to put down liberalism in Spain and the colonies, brought back the old regime with all of its repressiveness. By his arbitrary and short-sighted opposition to reform, Ferdinand assured the ultimate independence of his chief overseas possessions.

The first consequence of the French wars in New Spain was that the Mexicans were obliged to share in Spain's new financial crisis. Godoy's government called for additional forced "loans," and in December 1804, two months after the British capture of the treasure fleet, the Crown sequestered the charitable funds held in trust by the Church. The involuntary loans, though a pretext for a confiscation of wealth, could be borne by New Spain's taxpayers. The seizure of the charitable funds, on the other hand, represented an attack not only upon ecclesiastical wealth, but also upon the landowners' mortgage structure, for most of these funds had been lent to civilians, and their confiscation meant a forced redemption of the mortgages. Godoy's arbitrary fiscal policies further alienated the property-owning creole class, and when in 1808 word reached New Spain that Napoleon had deposed Spain's legitimate monarchy, a group of creoles in Mexico City called a national junta to provide a government for the Mexicans. The viceroy, José de Iturrigaray, joined the creole cause. Spanish officials in the capital, fearful that Iturrigaray and the creoles were planning to declare Mexico's independence, arrested the viceroy and replaced him with an aged Spanish general. During the next two years, though there was no overt revolutionary activity, groups of creoles throughout the country came together clandestinely to work for home rule for New Spain and perhaps eventually independence. Such a secret society was formed in Querétaro, north of Mexico City, under the leadership of a young creole officer, Ignacio Allende, and Miguel Hidalgo, the parish priest from the nearby village of Dolores.

Miguel Hidalgo was born in 1753 of a creole family in Valladolid (today's Morelia). Educated for the priesthood, he taught theology and later became rector at the College of San Nicolás in Valladolid. After two years as an administrator he resigned to take a succession of positions as a parish priest in western and northern Mexico. Some said that he gave up the rectorship because of financial irregularities in the college, others that he was ousted because of his penchant for gambling and his fall from celibacy. To be sure, Hidalgo sired a number of illegitimate children before he came to Dolores in 1803. His personal life, however, if not consistent with the Church's traditional code of clerical ethics, seems to have caused little comment in the lax ecclesiastical society of late eighteenth-century Mexico. The inquisitorial court investigated Father Hidalgo twice, not for personal licentiousness or theological heterodoxy, but on account of his political views. He was said to have been "afrancesado"—corrupted by the dangerous ideas of the French Enlightenment.

Hidalgo's curacy in Dolores was a sinecure. While assistants handled the religious duties in the parish, Hidalgo devoted his attention to improving the economic and social conditions of his people. He founded, among many industrial ventures, a pottery plant and encouraged the cultivation of mulberry trees and grape vines. But because the production of silk and wine was a Spanish monopoly, the viceregal government ordered Hidalgo to halt these two projects. The curate led an active social life in Dolores, playing cards and holding dances and tertulias in the parish house. His career, after he left Valladolid, differed little from that of secular well-to-do creoles. When the Spanish authorities suppressed the junta in Mexico City, he joined and soon took a leading part in the conspiracy for independence organized by the Querétaro aristocrats.

The uprising was planned for December 1810. Led by creole militiamen, the rebel forces, in the name of Ferdinand VII, would call for support from the servile classes in order to overthrow the French-dominated viceregal government. In early September, however, the conspirators were denounced to the Spanish authorities, who ordered the arrest of the leaders. Warned by a messenger from Querétaro, Hidalgo decided to act without further delay. He summoned the parishioners of Dolores and Indians from nearby villages to join the war against the hated gachupines. His call ignited the tinder of native resentment against Spanish excesses, and violent revolution flamed up in central Mexico. Increasing in size as they rolled across the countryside, Hidalgo's hordes destroyed haciendas, looted cities and towns, and killed Spaniards. Celaya, Guanajuato, Valladolid, and Guadalajara fell before the terrible onslaught. Hidalgo grandiosely proclaimed himself "Captain-General of America" and prepared to take the viceregal capital and end Spanish power in Mexico.

From the first many creoles had doubts about supporting the cause of independence, when Hidalgo's revolution appeared synonymous with rapine and disorder. Dissident voices within the revolutionary movement denounced the continued leadership of Hidalgo. The creole propertied classes, while sustaining the idea of independence from Spain, could not countenance violent social upheaval. They remembered the revolution in Haiti which had wiped out the white ruling class there. Hidalgo's movement was doomed to failure because he alienated the responsible creole citizens of Mexico. Though his armies won a last victory near Mexico City, he failed to move on the capital, for he too had qualms about turning his vengeful and undisciplined Indian troops loose in the viceregal capital. Thereupon, his movement began to disintegrate. Hidalgo, Allende, and the other leaders of the insurrection fled north, hoping to regroup their forces, but they were captured by Spanish authorities, tried and executed for treason.

As the fire of Hidalgo's revolt was extinguished in the north, new centers of revolution erupted in the west and south. With the death of Hidalgo, the leadership devolved upon another priest, José María Morelos. In 1813 and 1814 Morelos controlled important towns from near the Valley of Mexico to Oaxaca, Puebla, and Acapulco. His followers declared Mexico's independence in 1813 and, in the following year, proclaimed the country's first constitution. But like Hidalgo before him, Morelos could not command the support of the creoles. He too was captured by Spanish troops and sentenced to death. Though guerrilla bands continued to operate in the mountain fastnesses of the west, after 1815 the cause for which Hidalgo and Morelos had fought and died was irreparable. Had Allende's plan for a revolt of the creole militia prevailed, independence might well have been achieved. But it was far too early in Mexico's history for a social revolution.

By 1820, except for a few isolated spots of irregular guerrilla activity, Mexico was again firmly in Spanish hands. Independence seemed as far away as it had before Hidalgo called his Indians to battle. Yet 1820 was a year of surprises for Spain and its overseas possessions. In Cádiz a large army, preparing to embark to South America to put an end to the independence movements on that continent, revolted, proclaiming the cause of liberalism and constitutional monarchy. Ferdinand VII was forced to accept the revived Constitution of 1812, and his new ministers initiated a liberalization program for the royal government. Decrees from Madrid ended the Inquisition and special ecclesiastical fueros, as well as the entailing of landed estates. All Spanish citizens, regardless of race, were declared equal before the law. Ferdinand's ministers, many of them Masons, proposed the suppression of monastic orders and the expropriation of their properties.

The liberal reforms caused widespread dismay among Mexico's conservative classes, both Spanish and creole, who rejected these jacobin attacks upon religion and their traditional privileged position in society. Uniting behind a young creole aristocrat, Agustín de Iturbide, the leaders of the Church and the conservative elements raised the cry for Mexico's independence from the suddenly radicalized mother country. Iturbide's Plan of Iguala in 1821, the first of many such revolutionary pronunciamientos in the history of the country, called for equality of creoles and Spaniards and the preservation of the Church's privileged position. There was little opposition to Iturbide's revolution, as even guerrilla chiefs embraced the Plan of Iguala. Thus, after long, bloody, and fruitless years of revolutionary activity, the enemies of Hidalgo and Morelos reached the goal toward which the two priests had striven. Mexico began its independent career on a wave of reaction and clericalism and with an imperial government proclaimed by Agustín de Iturbide.

The achieving of independence did not, however, bring Mexico into the modern world. A people could not change so quickly, and the country felt the effects of the long colonial era for more than a hundred years after its liberation from Spain. In the nineteenth century the political, social, and economic issues raised during the Wars for Independence continued to divide Mexico. Only after the Revolution of 1910 was this colonial structure finally broken apart. As the Revolution exalts the Indian, so it also rejects in clarion tones the colonial past. Mexico's painters draw inspiration, not from New Spain's excellent artists, but from the preconquest Indians. The accomplished creole composers of the seventeenth and eighteenth centuries, many of whom compared favorably with their European contemporaries, are virtually ignored in Mexico today. Intellectuals point to a single culprit to explain modern Mexico's shortcomings—the Spanish colonial heritage.

Yet despite the disclaimers of politicians and intellectuals, the aristocratic traditions still have a strong hold on Mexican society. Even today, remnants of colonialism remain to dispute the campaign oratory of the Revolution's leaders—large properties in the countryside, great houses in the cities, a nouveau riche aristocratic class with archaic feudal pretensions. One need only visit Mexico City's Chapultepec Park on a Sunday to observe, contrasted with the teeming masses of the poorer citizens, the wealthy aristocrats, riding their horses—as Martín Cortés once did through the same city—feudal lords of all they survey. The aristocratic disdain for manual labor allows the well-to-do mistress of the household to prepare a meal but not to peel a potato, to shop in the market but not to carry a market basket. A man of the propertied classes cannot change a lightbulb in his own home without losing status. An obvious social chasm separates the middle and upper classes from their servants and other menial workers. The colonial era, wrote Fernando Benítez in 1962, "is closer to us than we think. . . . The upper classes throw their money away on much the same sort of things as in the time of the second Marqués del Valle de Oaxaca." And Lesley B. Simpson notes in his *Many Mexicos* that "the passion for holding land, with the sweet privilege of ordering one's fellows about, pervades all classes. . . . The mestizo is assuming the same marks of nobility that he formerly envied." As these astute commentators make clear, the attitudes and values of Spanish Mexico are far from dead in the last third of the twentieth century.

4

Europe, the United States, and Mexico

Mexico began its independent career in a mood of optimism and buoyancy. The economy seemed basically sound, and once the scars of the long civil war had healed, the Mexicans could look to a revival of the prosperity that had brightened the first years of the nineteenth century. The vaunted silver mines would pour out their wealth to the continued advantage of the people and their new government. Agustín de Iturbide's Plan of Iguala proclaimed a national conciliation, a great union of Spaniards and native Mexicans. Yet the obstacles to progress proved to be formidable, for the heritage of Spanish culture was as much a hindrance as a blessing. The expectations soon gave way to despair, as the new political structure collapsed and the economy stagnated. Through the succeeding decades the Mexicans looked abroad for help and inspiration in solving their social, economic, and political problems.

Few Mexicans in 1821 had had any experience in government. Under the Spanish system politics as practiced in the Anglo-Saxon nations simply did not exist. To be sure, some Mexican delegates were chosen to attend the Cortes at Cádiz, but regular elections required a parliament, educated voters, and some conception of nationhood. Mexico at independence had none of these. Rejecting the Spanish regime against which they had revolted, the country's leaders took over the British and American two-party system. Though the spirit of the first constituent congress was that of the Spanish Constitution of 1812, the new constitution was based largely on the American model. But because the leaders lacked political know-how, their initial attempts at self-government collapsed. They could not or would not subordinate themselves to the discipline of a political party. Since elections were rigged by the men in power, the leaders of a losing faction might turn to rebellion to upset the decision of the polls. The masses, more than 90 percent illiterate, played no part in the political machinations. As a result, Mexico never had a stable, orderly two-party system in the nineteenth century, and has been unable to establish one to the present.

With the success of his revolution assured, Agustín de Iturbide summoned delegates in early 1822 to a congress in Mexico City to write a constitution and establish a framework of government. Factionalism and intransigence were evident from the first sessions. Some delegates preferred a republic, others a Bourbon monarchy; a third group supported Iturbide. Faced with a constitutional impasse, the victorious military commander seized political power in May 1822 and proclaimed himself Emperor Agustín I. Many creoles favored a monarchy for its inherent stability and resistance to violent change, and had Iturbide ruled the country with wisdom, he might have inaugurated a period of peaceful growth. Instead, he proved incompetent and improvident, and in less than a year new military uprisings had driven him into exile. Out of the struggle to create a republican constitution ultimately came the ideological division of Mexico between liberalism and conservatism. And it was this division, made worse by obduracy on both sides, that doomed the country to a half-century of civil war.

Mexican liberalism was born in the first years of the Republic, during the 1820s and 1830s, from the reaction against the centralized Spanish regime. It drew its sustenance from English rationalists such as Newton and Locke, from propagandists for the French Enlightenment such as Raynal, Condorcet, and Voltaire, and from the British Utilitarians, Malthus and Bentham. The chief theoretician of the liberal cause was José María Luis Mora, who imbibed the teachings of the Enlightenment and Utilitarianism less from the original sources than through the works of the French constitutional liberal, Benjamin Constant, and the Spanish minister of Charles III, Gaspar Melchor de Jovellanos. But no single Mexican writer synthesized European liberalism for the Mexicans or modified it for Mexico's conditions. And because circumstances were often beyond the control of the liberals, their philosophy developed by leaps and starts, taking off in unexpected directions. It was never coherent, and was often illogical—while proclaiming the Rights of Man and individual freedom, the liberals could use the powers of the state to curtail or destroy the rights of their opponents. Liberals never reached complete agreement about their philosophy, but by the 1850s they had come to accept the chief elements of European liberalism.

Mexico's liberals, like the Europeans, were secularly minded; they believed that man's paramount concern was with the here and now; the matter of eternity and the soul was an unfathomable mystery, consigned to the priests and to Sunday mornings. They were optimistic about the future of mankind in general and of the Mexican people in particular. Man was perfectible on this earth and in the present life, if he followed the dictates of his reason and liberal teachings, eschewing the superstitions of the past (by which the liberal mind usually meant religious dogma). And because man was perfectible, the liberals believed in the possibility of unlimited progress, but a material progress that could be achieved by the acquisition of earthly goods. Thus, happiness was equated with affluence. They looked to the future paradise, not in eternity, not in the Christian sense, but as an earthly state in which all Mexicans would be educated and prosperous. They stressed the basic worth and dignity of the individual, denying the necessity or value of communal organizations and of corporate privileges based upon occupation—the military, for example. Following laissez-faire doctrines, the liberals rejected state interference in business activity. Economic advancement would be attained by individual effort and initiative. There was no place for mercantilism or for archaic institutions such as the village communal ejido in the liberal scheme. They advocated a polity based on federalism to assure freedom and individual responsibility.

In principle, then, there was much agreement among the Mexican liberals. In practice, they frequently disagreed. Some, the puros or radicals, wished to move ahead rapidly, often recklessly, toward the goals of their philosophy. The moderates would go more slowly, for they believed that the Mexican people, especially the economically backward Indians, were not ready for precipitate steps.

The radicals were violently anticlerical. They wished to attack, to curtail the privileges of the priests and the bishops. They charged that the Church absorbed and monopolized capital needed for private development, while resisting modernization and change. The radicals would excise the Church, as a cancerous growth, from the body politic of the Mexican people. They would force the Church into its own sphere, that of spiritual matters. Rules for the organization of society would be the concern of the state, not the Church. Public education would be secularized. Marriage would become a civil, not religious contract. The state, not the Church, would keep birth and death records and control the cemeteries, so that no person, at the whim of priest or bishop, could be refused a proper burial. If Mexicans desired a church marriage or baptism for their children, if they preferred to enroll their sons and daughters in parochial schools, or if they wished a priest to officiate at a funeral, that was their own affair. But state functions took precedence over those of the Church. The radical liberals deemed all these arrangements reasonable and logical, holding that they stemmed from natural law. There would be two spheres in society, the temporal and the spiritual; each institution would predominate in its own sphere, separate and independent of the other.

The moderate liberals in Mexico had the same vision of the future as the radicals, but they would attain the earthly paradise at a more prudent pace. Resisting the more stringent measures of the radicals, they sometimes seemed to rest at dead center, paralyzed, unwilling to take any action, lest it be wrong. In reality, they were closer to the conservatives in their immediate program than to the extremists of their own party, for they opposed separation of Church and State and toleration for other sects in Mexico. Before 1859 most Mexican liberals were moderate and were not prepared for a violent attack upon the Church.

Conservatism is essentially a negative philosophy, for its proponents more often react against than for a concrete program. The liberals in Mexico set the tone of the ideological debate in the nineteenth century by advocating specific social and economic reforms. Though the liberals had a powerful and effective propagandist in Mora, the conservatives could only criticize, resist, or attack. They invoked the long continuity of Spanish culture to justify their stand. The chief conservative spokesman was Lucas Alamán, a historian-politician who served in presidential cabinets in the 1820s and again in the 1850s. In economics Alamán was progressive, and long before the liberals he proposed the industrial and fiscal development of the country. But in matters that concerned religion, politics, and the constitution of society he championed the status quo. The Catholic faith, he said, was the "only common tie which binds together all Mexicans." Alamán advocated a strong central government that could "fulfill its obligations." The conservatives opposed separation of Church and State, the federal system, and popular checks against the national government. To preserve a society with special rights and privileges they engineered the overthrow of Valentín Gómez Farías in 1834 and revolted against the liberal Constitution of 1857. And when internal opposition did not suffice to defeat their enemies, they turned to foreign intervention, supporting the French invasion of 1862 and the Empire of Maximilian. Though adherents to both parties lived throughout the Republic, conservatism was most strongly based in Mexico City, the nation's capital. Liberalism, on the other hand, found its chief support in such provincial cities as Veracruz, Oaxaca, Zacatecas, and Guanajuato.

During the nineteenth century the Church in Mexico reflected the conservatism of the Church Universal and of Pius IX's *Syllabus of Errors* (1864). A politically impotent prisoner of Italian nationalism, the Pontiff threatened eternal damnation for those in Catholic countries who proposed significant and radical alterations in the traditional fabric of society. Pius thundered his anathemas upon the liberals in faraway Mexico: "We energetically condemn every decree that the Mexican Government has enacted against the Catholic religion. . . ." He declared the Constitution of 1857 "null and void, and without any value. . . ." Mexico's prelates threatened to excommunicate those politicians who supported the constitution. Leagued with lay conservatives and military, the bishops fought to preserve ancient prerogatives—union of Church and State, exemption from civil law, a Catholic monopoly of education, and control over the larger part of the country's arable land. Since the programs of the liberals and the Church were mutually exclusive, the intransigence on both sides made conflict inevitable.

As Mexico plunged into ideological strife, the early optimism of the liberals yielded to the harsh reality that the country was not ready for a popularly determined government. In the 1820s Masonic lodges assumed the role of political parties, and for over two decades the political scene was dominated by strong personalities such as Gómez Farías, Mora, Alamán, Lorenzo de Zavala, and, above all, Antonio López de Santa Anna. Whichever group held power, the country was controlled by a minority of the population and most often run for the benefit of the few. Neither the conservatives nor the liberals were democrats. Both preferred strong-man rule to civil strife and anarchy with consequent destruction of civilian lives and property. In the ever-recurring crises the propertied classes, liberals and conservatives alike, rallied around Santa Anna as the nation's savior.

Mexico's colonial traditions of militarism and the monopoly of public offices contributed to the persistence of revolutions throughout the half-century following independence. The country inherited from New Spain a military class upholding the principle of special fueros that exempted its members from civil laws. Most of the presidents were generals with little formal education, and they had no compunction about using their troops to crush their political opponents. Armies were the private possessions of military leaders, to be utilized for their political advantage. The first Vice-President, Nicolás Bravo, revolted against the legally elected chief executive. In 1829 President Vicente Guerrero was ousted by Vice-President Anastasio Bustamante and, in 1831, shot by Bustamante's troops. Though the presidents frequently brought important civilians into their cabinets to advise them (as Alamán served Bustamante and Mora served Gómez Farías), all too often military exigencies determined policy. Parties alternated in power, not with the concurrence of the electorate, but because of revolutions and coups d'état. The need to employ civil servants on public payrolls also encouraged Mexico's revolutionary habit. Without a developing economy, most of the intellectuals, especially lawyers, had to turn to the government for jobs. Once in office, they clung to their posts and supported the use of armed force to keep their faction in power. (The contemporary word for this practice was empleomanía.) Thanks to the army and the bureaucracy, rebellions have been endemic in Mexico until fairly recent times. Human lives counted for little, and violence and death were accepted facts of political life. The liberal historian, Lorenzo de Zavala, called for legal sanctions against this violence. The trouble with Mexico, he said, was that there were no laws against revolution.

The frequent revolutions not only kept the nation in turmoil and destroyed lives and property, but also sapped the income of the government. Mexico inherited from Spain an inadequate fiscal structure based on import-export duties and internal trade taxes. In the first decade after independence the administrations of Guadalupe Victoria and Bustamante secured extensive loans, especially from British banking houses, but the lending conditions were highly unfavorable to Mexico, with steep interest rates and heavy discounts. The monies were soon swallowed up, providing Mexico with little benefit and leaving the country saddled with debts. Not only did the revolutions cost money; at the same time they inhibited economic development which might have brought increased revenues and foreign investments. After 1831, the chronic financial troubles encouraged Mexican governments to turn avid eyes on the landed properties of the Church as a possible source of credit and revenue. Eventually, the Mexican failure to maintain its repayment schedules led to outside pressures and even to intervention. Twice, in 1838 and 1862, foreign troops occupied Veracruz to assure debt servicing from the port revenues.

Despite the glowing hopes of the first Mexican governments and of the foreign bankers, there was little economic advancement until Porfirio Díaz became president in 1876. The mining industry, which had brought affluence to New Spain in the eighteenth century, stagnated. Large and inefficient estates dominated the rural economy and produced goods chiefly for local or domestic consumption. Most well-to-do Mexicans preferred to invest their capital in land, which was safe, rather than in enterprises which were novel or which risked bankruptcy or destruction in a revolution. Moreover, a capricious and arbitrary government was less likely to confiscate private lands or buildings than the more fluid industrial capital. Thus, economic progress could come only through the large foreign loans and investments.

Lucas Alamán sought to break this impasse. As a member of Bustamante's cabinet in 1830, he initiated a program of internal development, founding a state mortgage bank (Banco de Avío) as a nucleus. He stimulated the development of a textile industry, helped organize a mining company, introduced improved brands of livestock, and worked to bring industrious artisans and craftsmen from Europe. None of his ventures had much success. His immigration program encountered religious restrictions in the Constitution of 1824, which required all immigrants to be Catholics. Further, the newcomers would have to compete with cheap Indian labor in a society that was aristocratic and even feudal. Though other Mexican governments, both liberal and conservative, subsequently encouraged immigration, Mexico was never attractive to the European workers who came in such great numbers to the United States, Argentina, Chile, and Brazil. Alamán's Banco de Avío failed after a decade, partly because of mismanagement and a lack of government support, but also because it could not compete with the lending agencies of the Catholic Church, the chief source of internal capital. The Church could offer long-term, low-interest loans to hacendados, mine operators, and merchants.

Economic development was hindered, too, by high production costs and by poor roads and travel conditions. Main highways were scarcely more than carriage ruts through the countryside, for both national and state governments neglected road-building, leaving that task to private companies. Highwaymen were a constant threat. Frances Calderón de la Barca, Scottish wife of Spain's first minister to Mexico at the end of the 1830s, has left a dramatic account of the perils of travel in rural Mexico. "Woe to the solitary horseman or unescorted carriage," she wrote. Without heavy guards, travelers might be robbed or even murdered. The inferior road system was both cause and result of Mexican fragmentation. There could be little sense of nationalism or national purpose when even one's neighbors were aliens. Mexico began its first railroad construction in the 1840s with a concession by President Santa Anna to a group of Mexican businessmen, but little could be accomplished until conditions were more settled and Mexico could attract a large amount of foreign capital. Not until the era of the Restored Republic after 1867 did serious work begin on a railway net for the country.

The revolution for independence brought no marked social change to Mexico in the nineteenth century. One ruling class replaced another, and class structures remained hierarchic, hindering social mobility. Even the liberals had no intention of disturbing the arrangement of society, and their insistence on individual property rights actually strengthened the position of the hacendados. The middle sector was small and ineffectual and could not expand without increased mercantile activity and industrial development. And the white merchants and businessmen felt more solidarity with the creole aristocrats than with the aspiring mestizos of the commercial classes. Urban workers, mestizo and Indian, lived in poverty, and beggars were a constant problem. Mme. Calderón de la Barca wrote of "lounging *léperos*, moving bundles of rags, coming to the window and begging with a most piteous, but false-sounding whine, or lying under the arches and lazily inhaling the air and the sunshine, or sitting at the doors for hours basking in the sun or under the shadow of the wall." With wages low, jobs scarce, and violence commonplace, most of Mexico's poor lived constantly on the verge of personal disaster.

The largest part of Mexico's population was in the countryside—the Indians, who in their own villages or on haciendas formed the broad base of the social structure. The Spanish system had given them protection and a measure of security—if only a meager hope for emancipation—and the conservatives strove to maintain this paternalistic arrangement in the Republic. Even upper-class liberals might proclaim their concern for "the Indian" as an abstract, but they paid scant attention to the plight of individual peons. Because all men were considered equal under the law, no man could be protected from his oppressor or exploiter. Liberal measures that ostensibly freed the Indian from tutelage and made him a citizen instead of a ward of the state in reality subjected him to increasing exactions, exploitation, and cruelty. He paid taxes and served as a soldier in armies, fighting and dying for causes that were not his. He was impressed into work gangs and flogged for seemingly petty offenses. In 1856 the liberal Ley Lerdo proclaimed the forced sale of lands held in common by Indian villages. The liberals hoped to promote, thereby, a society of small landowners. Instead, the rich hacendados and businessmen engrossed the lands, and the concentration of rural properties in the hands of the few was increased. By the first decade of the twentieth century the plight of the Indian was considerably worse than it had been a century earlier, before Independence.

The state of the Church mirrored Mexico's archaic social structure. A great disparity existed between the well-to-do prelates and the ignorant, poverty-stricken priests who lived and worked in the Indian villages. Church wealth, like rich secular possessions, benefited the few, and with large incomes bishops and archbishops could afford the luxuries of feudal princes. Mme. Calderón de la Barca penned a graphic description of Manuel de Posada y Garduño, the first Mexican to serve as Archbishop of Mexico after Independence. He enjoyed a life of "tranquility, ease, and universal adoration," she said, "a Pope without the trouble or a tenth of the responsibility." "His palace in town, his well-cushioned horses and sleek mules seem the very perfection of comfort. In fact, *comfort*, which is unknown among the profane of Mexico, has taken refuge with the Archbishop. . . . He looks like one on whom the good things of this world have fallen in a constant and benignant shower, which shower hath fallen on a rich and fertile soil." That the good life caused some prelates to relapse from celibacy is indicated in Charles Flandrau's tale of a powerful bishop in the Díaz era whose "wife" and large family of sons and daughters were "complacently taken for granted by his entire diocese."

Not even the convents escaped the corroding influence of excessive wealth. The wife of the Spanish minister visited one nunnery (it was far from exceptional) and found it to be a "palace." Most of the halls, she wrote, were "noble rooms," and each nun had a servant, some two. "The convent is rich; each novice at her entrance pays five thousand dollars into the common stock." She found the "prevailing sin" in the convent to be "pride." Convents were among the chief holders of ecclesiastical wealth, owning extensive properties in the cities and in the rural areas. If Mme. Calderón de la Barca is to be believed, the nunneries served as a last resort for women whose lack of physical charm made marriage unlikely. Once having taken their vows at an early age, the nuns, like members of monastic societies, were forced by law to stay in convents for the rest of their days. Some taught or performed charitable works; most lived in comfortable idleness.

Life in the countryside was harder, even for the priests. The village curate was often as ignorant as his Indian charges; yet he found ample opportunity to exploit the parishioners—selling holy candles, charging fees for sacraments such as baptism, Holy Matrimony, and Extreme Unction, or forcing the villagers to work for him without pay. And celibacy was undoubtedly even less observed in the rural areas than among the urban clergy. Sympathetic bishops responded with understanding to requests from parish priests for financial aid to support their illegitimate children. Foreign visitors might cluck their tongues at clerical concubinage, but the prevailing attitudes of the Mexicans was that the priest was only "a sinner like the rest of us." Perhaps the stories of immorality and high living were exaggerated; no doubt most clergymen, rich or poor, as in the colonial era, carried out their priestly duties in an exemplary fashion. But more important than the authenticity of the accounts was the fact that they were widely believed. Liberals in the nineteenth century and radicals after the Revolution of 1910 held the Church to be wealthy and corrupt and the priests to be seducers of women. Their prejudices do much to explain the anticlerical legislation in both periods.

As in making constitutions and laws, Mexico's politically effective population sought to create a new culture that was aristocratic and European. Writers, composers, artists, and architects drew their inspiration from abroad, especially from France, Italy, and England. In the middle years of the century Mexicans wrote Romantic novels like those of Sir Walter Scott, while artists such as Juan Cordero and Santiago Rebull painted religious and secular subjects similar to those of their French counterparts. Even Mexico's national monuments were more European than Mexican. Miguel Noreña's monument to Cuauhtémoc, done in the 1880s, portrays the national hero as a Roman warrior rather than a savage Aztec. By the first years of the twentieth century the cultural influence of France was in the ascendant. Novels were frankly naturalistic like those of Emile Zola. Joaquín Clausell's and Romano Guillemín's oils were impressionistic imitations of the works of Pissaro and Monet. Wealthy Mexicans sent their young men to France to be educated, and the dominant political philosophy of the Porfirian regime was the Positivism of Auguste Comte. The government of Díaz began to rebuild the national capital in the pattern of Napoleon III's Paris.

In music, too, Mexico's style-setters turned their backs on their Spanish and Indian heritage. Though the jarabes, sones, and huapangos were still preserved among the popular classes, and especially in the countryside, the aristocrats favored Italian operas, from Pergolesi to Puccini, played salon music in the French style, and danced to the rhythms of waltzes, polkas, and mazurkas. Mexicans composed operas with native stories—to be sung in Italian—and Indian maids in the national operas sang mazurkas and schottisches. Chopin's influence in the salon was overwhelming, as aristocratic amateur music writers emulated his short pieces. By the end of the century Mexico had produced a number of highly proficient, but Europeanized composers, the most successful being Juventino Rosas, who died in 1894 at the age of 26. Rosas published an outstanding set of waltzes that included the internationally famous "Over the Waves." Ricardo Castro, who died in 1907, wrote concertos for the violoncello and piano and composed an opera with a French libretto.

If the native was apotheosized in operas, statuary, and poetry, the stage Indian and the stone Cuauhtémoc on a pedestal were aliens who bore little relationship to the flesh-and-blood Indians laboring on haciendas or in the textile factories. Whatever they might proclaim in speeches from the congressional rostrum, in the public press, or in their literature, the Mexicans who guided the country's destiny in the nineteenth century, whether liberal or conservative, did not care much what happened to their indigenous brothers or to their culture. As the Mexican governments commissioned statues of Aztec kings, they left the archaeological exploration of preconquest sites to foreigners. Concrete acts of concern for the Indian population and for the native culture awaited the advent of the nationalistic Revolution of 1910.

Though French tastes predominated in the arts and letters, the influence of the United States was heavy in politics and diplomacy. Little was known in Mexico about the northern neighbor during the first half of the century, since few Mexicans traveled to the United States or were acquainted with American literature. If the Mexican constitution-makers adopted a federal system in 1824, it was not because they had read *The Federalist*, but rather because they wished to destroy Spanish centralism. They admired and took over the mechanics of the American government without its informing spirit, which was Lockean and Protestant. But the westward expansion of the United States meant an ineluctable clash between the two countries. Two armed conflicts were fought in the nineteenth century—the Texan War for Independence and the War of 1846–1848. In the 1870s war again threatened over border problems. In its dealings with the United States the Mexican Republic seemed fated to pay the price of being the weak neighbor of a powerful and expanding nation.

Yet there was scant indication in the first days of Independence that the two young nations had embarked upon a collision course. Mexico and the United States, said the new Emperor, were "destined to be united in the bonds of the most intimate and cordial fraternity." But personal contacts between nationals of the two countries were infrequent, as poor communications created a barrier to easy communications. The few Americans visiting Mexico were, in the main, favorably impressed. Joel R. Poinsett, from South Carolina, wrote to friends in late 1822: "The gentlemen with whom I have associated are intelligent men. . . . The Creoles in general possess good natural talents and great facility of acquiring knowledge. They are extremely mild and courteous in their manner, kind and benevolent towards each other, and hospitable to strangers." Poinsett found the laboring classes "sober and industrious," though "ignorant and superstitious." He pointed out Mexico's shortcomings—and these he attributed chiefly to the Catholic Church. But he was neither harsh nor insulting in his criticism of Mexico. In May 1825 Poinsett returned to Mexico City as the first American minister. On his staff was a young man, Edward T. Tayloe, who shared the minister's keen interest in Mexican history. Like Poinsett's letters, Tayloe's reports on Mexico were filled with a sense of interest and wonder. He was never condescending, nor did he resort to ridicule. Within a decade, however, sentiments had begun to change in both countries. It was the events in Texas and the contacts between Americans and Mexicans in the Southwest that determined the Americans' attitudes toward their southern neighbors during the rest of the nineteenth century. The Mexican, who had been admired by Poinsett and Tayloe, became the "greaser," an object of disdain and ridicule. And the Mexicans, stung by defeat, returned the contempt with their own epithet—"gringo."

National self-esteem is comparative; it requires a scale to relate itself to other peoples. American nationalism grew and measured itself against the Mexicans in the 1830s and 1840s, tending to depreciate them, while, at the same time, exalting those qualities that the west-ward-pushing pioneer discovered in himself. To the Americans the Mexican was cruel and cowardly—he had, after all, killed the brave American defenders of the Alamo and at Goliad in cold blood. He was, or so the traders in the Southwest reported, dirty, lazy, and untrustworthy. Mexican women were little more than painted strumpets who deserved to be treated as such. Most Americans knew little of the civilized life of Mexico City. They saw or heard about only the poor and shabby outposts of Mexican life in Texas, New Mexico, Arizona, and California. And it was in this frontier confrontation of two diverse cultures that the stereotypes of the Mexican and of the American pioneer took shape. To the confident, expanding United States, its heroes were Davy Crockett, Sam Houston, and Jim Bowie. These pioneers epitomized the American, Anglo-Saxon virtues of self-reliance, generosity, and bravery. Americans readily accepted the view that the shiftless Mexicans had no right to the vast territories which they claimed as their Spanish heritage.

American readers in the years before the Mexican War were stirred by George Wilkins Kendall's description of the cruelty and duplicity of the Mexicans in his vivid account of the ill-fated expedition sent in 1841 to Santa Fe by Texas President Mirabeau Lamar. William H. Prescott published his *History of the Conquest of Mexico* in 1843. Though he had never been in Mexico, he readily accepted the popular view of the Mexicans' shortcomings. Contrasting the present-day people with their Aztec ancestors, he wrote: "Those familiar with the modern Mexicans will find it difficult to conceive that the nation should ever have been capable of devising the enlightened polity which we have been considering. But they should remember that in the Mexicans of our day they see only a conquered race. . . ." To Prescott "the Mexican's outward form, his complexion, his lineaments are substantially the same. But too many characteristics of the nation, all that constituted its individuality as a race, are effaced forever." John L. Stephens' *Incidents of Travel in Yucatan*, published in the same year, was equally popular with stay-at-home Americans. Stephens had first-hand experience in Mexico, and his observations were more specific than those of Prescott. Gambling was "the bane and scourge of all ranks of society," he wrote. He was repelled by the cruelty of bullfights, by the pomp and wealth of religious ceremonies. 1843 saw also the publication of Mme. Calderón de la Barca's *Life in Mexico*, based on letters to relatives and friends. Though she had a Protestant background, she came to love Mexico and the Mexicans. Yet she too reacted against their supposed vices. Of the servants, she wrote: "We hear of their addiction to stealing, their laziness, drunkenness, dirtiness. . . ."

When war came three years later Americans were prepared to accept and to justify it. The United States was on the crest of a wave of expansion to the West, an expansion that could halt only at California's shores. If Mexico's claims to these lands barred the way, the claims must be overridden. Newspaper editorials, particularly in the Democratic dailies of the Northeast and the Northwest, hailed the expansionists as apostles of civilization who would "regenerate the backward peoples of the continent." The House Committee on Foreign Affairs agreed with President James K. Polk that the United States had been "forced into a conflict with a semi-barbarian people." James Russell Lowell in his popular doggerel gave voice to the justification for the war. The Mexicans, he wrote, were "a sort of folks a chap could kill an' never dream on't arter." Before the war was over, some Americans were calling for the annexation of all of Mexico.

The Mexicans too felt themselves the aggrieved party in the conflict. They had never reconciled themselves to the loss of Texas, and now the Americans were seen as the aggressors, attacking Mexicans on Mexico's own soil. The early attestations of friendship and admiration, which had led Mexico to emulate American political institutions, gave way to bitterness and hatred as forces of the United States cut deep into Mexican territory. The corridos, Mexico's popular ballads, breathed defiance and militancy, demanding death for the "cowardly" invaders. The Mexicans must emulate the Boy Heroes of Chapultepec, who died vainly resisting the American assault on Mexico City. The conservative periodical *El Tiempo*, wrote: "We are not a people of merchants and adventurers, scum and refuse of all countries." Americans were materialists who cared only for money and soft living.

Many Mexican liberals, even during the war, were ambivalent in their attitude toward the invaders. It was a love-hate relationship, and some Mexicans half-hoped that the United States would keep an occupation army to enforce order and stability. Travelers such as Guillermo Prieto and Justo Sierra O'Reilly continued, after the war, to praise American institutions. But the popular attitudes of hostility endured in both countries. Corrido singers in Mexico kept alive memories of the invading Yankee soldiers. And in the United States dime novel writers took up the hue and cry against the Mexicans of the Southwest. In the last half of the nineteenth century generations grew up in both countries accepting the stereotypes created in the years before and during the War of 1846. Such prejudices were to help mold relations between the two countries well into the twentieth century.

It is clear that the dime novels mirrored (and perhaps even shaped) expanding America's view of itself and the world. Like the ubiquitous *McGuffey Readers*, they exalted a spirit of adventure and rugged individualism. More respectably, the *Readers* taught young Americans the morality of the new middle class, the Protestant virtues of thrift, industry, and hard labor. They exhorted the children of America to be honest, temperate, and punctual and not to be wasteful. The dime novels were read—furtively, perhaps, but certainly with more pleasure than *McGuffey's Readers*—by the larger part of America's youth. Here in this plebeian literature the eternal battle raged between good and evil. The hero—the pioneer, the frontiersman, the Indian fighter—won out because of his "shrewdness, his pluck, his dogged courage and determination, his individual prowess." In contrast, dime-novel Mexicans were always "greasers"; they were cowardly "yellow bellies," who would steal anything not nailed down. Jeremiah Clemens in *Bernard Lile* portrayed the Mexican as a born thief, who "counts the stealage as the best part of his wages. . . . He would murder his brother for a peso, and betray anything but his priest for half the money." American nationalism, even more than in the period before the War of 1846, disparaged the Mexican, but now also the Indian, the Negro, and the foreign immigrant. Before the end of the century many men prominent in American political and intellectual life were to give voice to the prevailing racial attitudes of the dime novelists. The late Richard Hofstadter showed the age of reform, of populism and progressivism, to be also a period of growing intolerant nationalism in the United States. Across the political spectrum Americans reacted against the foreigners in their midst. The xenophobic attitudes displayed in the low-brow dime novels gained a measure of dignity when shared by aristocrats such as Henry and Brooks Adams, Theodore Roosevelt, William Howard Taft, Henry Cabot Lodge, John Hay, and Albert J. Beveridge. There can be little doubt that American statesmen regarded Mexico as a menial nation, because they believed firmly that Mexicans were inferior people. And social philosophers such as David Starr Jordan and Edward A. Ross, lent their scholarly credentials to the depreciation of their southern neighbors. Both men were Progressives, Social Darwinists, and distinguished educators.

David Starr Jordan, president of Indiana University and then first president of Stanford University, brought to California his midwestern racial prejudices. For Jordan the United States should be an Anglo-Saxon nation—Protestant, hard-working, provident, and thrifty. The Mexicans, he wrote, were "ignorant, superstitious, ill-nurtured, with little self-control and no conception of industry or thrift—lacking indeed in most of our Anglo-Saxon virtues." Though Ross, a sociologist, insisted that Darwinism had exaggerated racial factors in accounting for the inferiority of some people, it is clear that he took more from Darwin than he rejected. In an address to the American Academy of Political and Social Science in 1901, he heaped praise upon the American characteristics which he believed to be racially determined. Americans, he said, had self reliance (the "Daniel Boone type"), foresight, and stability of character. In contrast, the Mexicans, "largely of Indian breed," had no "compelling view of the future." They were occupied, he said, "in obtaining food and amusement for the passing hour without either hope or desire for a better future."

A noted nineteenth-century ornithologist, Elliott Coues, who had traveled widely through the West and Southwest of the United States, used the occasion of a bird description to offer Mexicans a gratuitous insult. Of the house finch or burion, he wrote: "It is a pleasant feature in the dirty Mexican settlements, which with questionable taste it selects as its abode, and where the air is vocal all day long with its delightful melody. They are seldom molested by the worthless population, who have only just energy enough to bask by day in the sun rolling cigarettes, and cheat each other at cards by night." Justin H. Smith set about in the closing years of the Díaz regime to write a history of the 1846 War with Mexico, which would "gratify patriotic Americans." The Mexicans before the war, he said, "spent their energy in debauchery and gambling." There was "little in the material, mental and moral spheres" that was really sound in the Mexico of 1845. "The lower orders of the people lay deep in ignorance, laziness, and vice, the upper class, if we ignore exceptions, were soft, superficial, indolent and lax, urbane, plausible, and eloquent, apathetic, but passionate, amiable, and kind though cruel when excited, generous but untrustworthy, wasteful but athirst for gain, suspicious and subtle, but not sagacious, personally inclined to be pompous and nationally afflicted with a provincial vanity, greatly enamored of the formalities of life, greatly wanting in the cool, steely resolution for which occasional obstinacy is a poor substitute, and still more wanting in that simple, straightforward, sober and solid common sense which is the true foundation of personal and national strength." By the first decade of the twentieth century many leading Mexicans had come to share the Americans' gloomy Darwinian view of their countrymen. And once more they looked to a foreign cure for Mexico's ills.

The long dictatorship of Porfirio Díaz (1876–1911) was a profitable period for American business interests. For the first time in Mexico's independent history, travel was safe throughout the Republic. Mexico was solidly on the gold standard, and the national budgets were balanced. President Theodore Roosevelt was a frank admirer of the old dictator. Díaz, he wrote, was "the greatest statesman now living." The architects of the new Mexico, embued with the practical philosophy of Positivism, looked to the United States as their model. They believed that the Mexicans, especially the Indians, were racially inferior to the more advanced Anglo-Saxon. If Mexico was to survive the struggle among nations, she must emulate the United States, must make "gringos" of her people. As one critic of the Porfirian regime put it, Mexico became "the mother of foreigners and the stepmother of the Mexicans."

In the fall of 1867, Benito Juárez' Minister of Education appointed a committee, with Dr. Gabino Barreda as chairman, to consider the reorganization of Mexico's public education system. Barreda had studied medicine in France and had fallen under the influence of the French philosopher Comte. Believing that the exact methods of science formed the basis for all knowledge, Barreda rejected "revealed" truth and metaphysical speculation. Truth could be demonstrated only through experiments, and since experiments dealt solely with phenomena, there was no point in going beyond the material into the unknown and unknowable realm of the spiritual. With Comte, Barreda believed that mankind passed through three discrete stages in its historical development: the theological, the metaphysical, and the Positivistic. In each stage explanations of phenomena were made in terms of the dominant philosophical outlook. In the first stage the gods or God had been held responsible for events. In the second, the philosophers had delved for a supposed reality behind the appearances of things. And in the third or highest stage science was the key to knowledge. Barreda equated these stages in Mexico with the colonial era, the period of liberalism, and the new era of science and progress. As the chairman of the committee, Barreda dominated the deliberations, and his Comtian principles controlled the report to the Minister of Education. On the basis of Barreda's report, the government reorganized the national system of education. After 1867 the new generation of Mexicans learned the creed of the French Positivists. Although Positivism was the offspring of the liberal philosophy, it came to reject its own parentage, and Barreda's reforms helped transform Mexico from a liberal, federal republic into a centralized dictatorship.

Mexican Positivism was a middle- and upper-class phenomenon. It appealed to the oligarchs, to the property owners and businessmen, because it seemed practical and scientific. It was attuned to the materialistic temper of the times. The Positivists mixed Comtism with ingredients from Herbert Spencer and from the Social Darwinists to exalt their group as the rightful rulers of Mexico. Where the liberals had been essentially optimistic, holding out hope for the perfectibility of the Mexicans through education, the Positivists expected none in the foreseeable future. They turned against their liberal forebears, because they deemed them too utopian in view of the actual backwardness of the majority of the Mexican people. The Positivists saw in society an organism, which must grow slowly, must evolve. They condemned revolutions as precipitate, as destructive of orderly advance. All civil strife must be avoided or stamped out like a plague. The Positivists did not deny progress. They did deny, however, that the nation could be transformed in any given moment. Nor did they permanently refuse their own privileged status to the lower classes—except for the Indians. The Positivists asked only for patience until Mexican society was ready for more privileges. Improvements would come in time; until then the propertied classes must remain the dominant group of Mexico. Under the intellectual leadership of Gabino Barreda, and later of Justo Sierra and Porfirio Parra, the devotees of the new science used their influence with the government to guarantee the ascendant position of their own classes.

The well-to-do of Mexico sought a government that would prevent any violent or revolutionary change such as might menace their interests or destroy order. In the 1870s they called for the rule of a strong man, not the weak parliamentarian regime of the liberals. They found their hero in Porfirio Díaz—a local caudillo who could overcome all other local chiefs, who could end the lawlessness and enforce a national conciliation. Acting for the property owners, the Positivists exchanged the ephemeral political liberties of the liberals for economic security, individual freedom with anarchy for order and progress under a despot. They formed a political alliance to support Díaz, called derisively by his critics the "Partido Científico." But the party was stillborn, because Díaz permitted no real political institutions. For each election temporary alliances of interests secured the permanence in office of the dictator. Stability was assured, not by the parties, but by the person of Díaz. In return for the Científicos' support, Díaz offered them an opportunity to enrich themselves and their friends. By 1900 Positivism was a sturdy bulwark of the Porfirian dictatorship. For the influential the regime brought riches; for most Mexicans it meant misery compounded.

In the Revolution of 1910 the Mexicans tried to end the subservience and imitation of foreign ways that had characterized the century after Hidalgo's rebellion. The Revolution was a new declaration of independence, offering native solutions to Mexico's grave social and economic problems. No longer would Mexicans servilely ape the customs and manners of European aristocrats and American businessmen. In 1910 a new era for Mexico began, one in which the Mexicans were determined to stand on their own feet, proud of being Mexicans, proud of their Indian heritage, proud of their cultural emancipation. It remained to be seen whether Mexico could carry out the Revolution's aims free of foreign influences and intervention.

5

Federalism, Centralism, and Dictatorship

The ideological contention in Mexico during the nineteenth century was accompanied by a struggle between two rival political theories. Most liberals advocated a federal system in order to protect the rights of individuals from an arbitrary national government. Those who would maintain traditional privileges demanded a unitary or centralist regime with power concentrated in Mexico City. In the federal system each state was an entity, controlling its own electoral procedures. Moreover, the executive was deliberately weakened, with more power going to the legislative branch. Conversely, the conservatives wrote constitutions with long-term presidencies and with state or provincial governors appointed and dominated by the national executive. By the end of the century the federal principle had won out on the field of battle, but Mexico was in the tight grip of a dictatorship—centralism in fact, if not in law.

The struggle between federalism and centralism began in 1823 with the overthrow of Agustín de Iturbide's empire. In the same year a constituent congress assembled in Mexico City to provide a constitution for the new Republic. A priest, Miguel Ramos Arizpe led the federalist majority. Ramos Arizpe, from the northern province of Coahuila, had served as a delegate to the Spanish Cortes in Cádiz and was imprisoned by the restored authoritarian regime of Ferdinand VII. His chief opponent in the republican congress was another priest, the Dominican friar, José Servando Teresa de Mier. Father Mier had also brought the wrath of the Spanish government on his head, more for his theological errors, however, than for his political activities. He had had the temerity to question the authenticity of Our Lady of Guadalupe, and he had been confined to jails or monasteries at various times in Spain, France, Italy, and Portugal. Though he was not a conservative, he made an eloquent plea in the constituent congress, urging the security and continuity of centralist rule. But the delegates had had enough of Spanish institutions, and they overwhelmingly adopted a federal system. For the next half-century Mexico was torn between these two extremes, and the Constitutions of 1824, 1836, 1843, and 1857 mirrored this political contestation.

Except for federalism, Mexico's first constitution was moderate. It established Roman Catholicism as the cult of the state, and denied toleration to other sects. The government assumed the powers of the Patronato, which were held to be inherent in the state's sovereignty. Military and ecclesiastical fueros continued unchanged from the Spanish regime, and legal procedures included no trial by jury. Superficially, however, the constitution resembled that of the United States, providing for separate legislative, judicial, and executive branches. State governors were to be locally elected, while the state legislators would choose the national president and vice-president for four-year terms. Guadalupe Victoria, a hero of the Wars of Independence and a federalist, became Mexico's first chief executive, with a centralist, Nicolás Bravo, also a guerrilla leader, as his vice-president.

Victoria named a distinguished cabinet which included Lucas Alamán and Ramos Arizpe, but internal peace proved to be fragile indeed, for dissension in the cabinet led to Alamán's resignation. The Church refused to recognize the government's claims to the Patronato, and Pope Leo XII called upon the Mexican clergy to support the cause of Ferdinand VII. Worst for the political stability of the country was the hostility of the centralist vice-president. Bravo revolted against the government, and though his army was defeated by forces loyal to Victoria, the vice-presidency remained a threat in a number of administrations. In 1828 supporters of Vicente Guerrero took to the field to overturn the legally elected chief executive, Manuel Gómez Pedraza.

Guerrero served for less than a year. He held on briefly by leading a popular attack against the Spanish in Mexico. Spain, which had not as yet recognized Mexico's independence, retaliated by invading the port of Tampico, but the Spanish troops soon surrendered to a young army officer, Antonio López de Santa Anna, who thereby became a national hero. Within a year, the inept Guerrero was in turn ousted by his own vice-president, Anastasio Bustamante, who, like Bravo, was a centralist.

Under Bustamante the Conservative Party began to emerge from the faction that had fought for a centralist regime. Many liberals, including Mora, at first welcomed Bustamante's coup, hoping that he could provide a strong, vigorous government. The President named Lucas Alamán head of his cabinet, and Alamán initiated his neo-mercantilistic program of economic development. But if Alamán was ahead of his time in his notions of economic progress, he lagged behind in his politics. The Bustamante government suppressed the federalist opposition and restricted the country's newspapers, for Alamán feared that a free press would subvert the people from their traditional loyalties to the Catholic religion. He also saw a danger in the penetration of Texas by colonists from the United States, and his government tried to end American immigration while encouraging European Catholics to come to the northern province. Bustamante's cruel and repressive measures brought a series of federalist uprisings against his regime and led to his overthrow in 1832. Entering national politics for the first time, Santa Anna became president in the next year, with Valentín Gómez Farías as his vice-president.

Now as always, Santa Anna cared more for military glory, personal aggrandizement, power, and spoils than for the administration of the country. His conscience, wrote the historian H. H. Bancroft, "was elastic and numb, never disturbed by actions that would have troubled most men." He retired to his Veracruz estate of Manga de Clavo, leaving the government in the hands of Gómez Farías. In 1833 Mexico experienced its first convulsions of liberal reform. Gómez Farías was a doctrinaire and radical liberal, determined to curtail the political and economic power of the Church. He brought José María Luis Mora into his cabinet as Minister of Education. In October 1833 Gómez Farías' government ended the obligatory tithe. Thereafter, if a Mexican wished to contribute money to the Church, it was by his own volition. Monastic vows too were made voluntary. Gómez Farías closed the Pontifical University in Mexico City as a hotbed of clericalism and encouraged the establishment of secular institutions in the provincial capitals. Mora and other liberal advisers proposed more severe measures against Church properties and prerogatives—the confiscation of mortgage funds of the monasteries, civil registry, and civil matrimony and cemeteries. But Mexico was not ready for anticlerical legislation, and the conservatives, the military, and the Church united in opposition to Gómez Farías' government. Santa Anna emerged from seclusion at Manga de Clavo to lead the new conservative coalition against his vice-president. He exiled Gómez Farías, nullified the radical legislation, and initiated a period of conservative rule in Mexico. Twenty years passed before Gómez Farías' program could be implemented in the constitution and the reform legislation of the 1850s.

Anastasio Bustamante returned to the presidency in 1836 with a new makeshift constitution of seven statutes (*Siete Leyes*). This conservative document concentrated power in the national regime by abolishing the old state governments and creating a system of departments, with department governors appointed by the president. Property qualifications were established for voting and for officeholding. The president was to be chosen for an eight-year term by an elaborate method of indirect election, and he could be reelected. By this means, the conservatives hoped to bring stability and peace to the strife-torn country. They were grievously disappointed. Liberal revolutions erupted in the year before the constitution went into effect and continued intermittently for the next two decades. But the most serious blow to the new conservative regime and to Mexican national honor was the loss of Texas.

American penetration of Texas begun in the last years of Spanish rule in Mexico through an agreement between the viceroy and Moses Austin. Though Spain had claimed and occupied the northern province, few Spanish settlers had come to Texas. There were no gold or silver deposits, and the Indian population was sparse, untamed, and not amenable to exploitation. Austin's contract had stipulated that only American Catholics "of good moral character" might emigrate to Texas, but during the 1820s large numbers of illegal colonists crossed into Mexican territory, many of them Protestants. These squatters posed a problem for the Mexican authorities, for the Constitution of 1824 barred non-Catholics and permitted only Catholic education in the nation's schools. Mexico's federal system and the difficulty of communications with the northern frontier gave Texas considerable freedom, however, and the Americans had few serious complaints before Bustamante's government moved in 1830 to ban immigration from the United States.

The resurgence of centralism in 1834 brought the Texas problem to a head. The Americans in Texas took advantage of Mexico's unsettled conditions in 1835 to begin to organize their own state government. Thereafter, there could be no turning back for the Texans. Between the adamant position of the centralists that all of the Republic be ruled from Mexico City and the desires of the Americans for home rule and the preservation of their own institutions and culture there could be no compromise. The cruelty of the Mexicans—shooting prisoners at the Alamo and Goliad and (from the American viewpoint) the inhumane practice of burning the bodies of the enemy dead—hardened the Texans in their resolve to separate themselves from Mexico. The defeat and capture of Santa Anna at San Jacinto assured Texan independence, though the fact was not recognized by the Mexican government until almost a decade later.

The years before the War of 1846 were chaotic for Mexico. Internal strife persisted between liberals and conservatives. French troops invaded the country in 1838 to enforce claims of damages by French nationals against the Mexican government. Santa Anna retrieved the popularity he had forfeited in Texas by losing a leg in a farcical defense of Veracruz. He heard the huzzahs of the fickle Mexican public as he saved Bustamante's government from rebel attacks in 1839 and 1840 and again when he ejected the president in 1841. Santa Anna brought back Nicolás Bravo as president with a centralist constitution (1843). (Later, when Santa Anna fell once more from favor, a mob overturned his statue in the capital, dug up his leg, and dragged it through the streets.) As the Republic rent itself, many Mexicans despaired of representative institutions, whether federalist or centralist. An erstwhile liberal aristocrat, José María Gutiérrez de Estrada, called for a monarchy in 1840. If the Mexicans did not change their ways, he warned, they would one day see the flag of the United States "waving over the National Palace." Gutiérrez Estrada was exiled for his treasonous publication, but the idea of a monarchy continued to have allure in Mexico.

The war between the United States and Mexico seemed to grow, as had the Texan Revolution, from an inexorable succession of events. Border conflicts are as old as the human race, for men have always been wont to take up arms to defend disputed territory. Once Texas joined the United States, the Mexicans would treat the annexation as a hostile act. Nor did the United States shrink from war. The plain fact is that the Americans were embarked upon an expansionist crusade that would carry them to the Pacific Coast, while the Mexican nation was stagnant. Yet, in its weakness, Mexico too dreamed of glory—with an unrealistic belief in the superiority of its military traditions. President James K. Polk wanted war; the Mexican government did not seek to avoid it. Hostilities broke out when General Zachary Taylor's troops marched to the Rio Grande and were fired upon by Mexican soldiers.

Fighting the war was a traumatic experience for both nations. The American soldiers were poorly equipped and ill supplied; morale broke, and some troops fled the field of battle. But the superior officer corps and artillery gave the American armies a great advantage. The Mexican cause was lost from the beginning, for the country was poor, and liberals and conservatives seemed more bent on fighting among themselves than in presenting a common front against the foreign invaders. In the midst of the conflict conservatives in Mexico, aided by funds of the Catholic Church, rebelled against President Gómez Farías, because his government proposed to use Church wealth to finance the war effort. Some conservatives worked actively for a monarchy. The American troops might have been undisciplined, but the United States was too powerful to be defeated by Mexico. The army of General Winfield Scott occupied Mexico City in September 1847, and in the following February the defeated Mexican government signed the Treaty of Guadalupe Hidalgo, which gave the United States California and the southwestern states. Mexico received $15 million in compensation. Even such an overwhelming national disaster could not bring unity to Mexico. Political instability continued to plague the country as before the war, and Mexico had five presidents between 1848 and 1853. In the War of the Castes the Indians of Yucatán drove out their oppressors and won virtual independence from the government in Mexico City. Other rebellions kept the country in turmoil, and the money paid by the United States was soon dissipated. By 1853 many in the propertied classes, and even some liberals, were ready to recall Santa Anna to power, feeling that only he could impose order in the stricken country. But at the same time, and in the midst of political disorder, a new spirit emerged like a phoenix from the ashes of defeat and national humiliation. It was an occasion of national self-assessment, a time to explain Mexico's weaknesses and to propose remedies for its ills. On the one hand, conservatives such as Lucas Alamán stressed once more the need to preserve and strengthen the Spanish heritage. On the other, a new Liberal Party grew in the states, proclaiming ever more stridently the principles enunciated two decades earlier by Mora, Zavala, and Gómez Farías. Now the ideological conflict between the contending parties crystallized.

The new liberals, trained in the provincial institutions, were mostly lawyers. Benito Juárez, a full-blooded Zapotec Indian, became governor of Oaxaca. Melchor Ocampo was elected governor of Michoacán. Miguel Lerdo de Tejada, from Veracruz, became president of Mexico City's ayuntamiento. Ignacio Ramírez, "the Necromancer," was an editor, Guillermo Prieto a liberal poet-politician. Both Juárez and Lerdo were relatively moderate. Juárez, though an Indian by birth, was white and middle class in his political and social outlook. As governor he would bring social progress to his people gradually, through education and by building roads. Lerdo joined the dictatorial government of Santa Anna in the Ministry of Development (Fomento). Melchor Ocampo, perhaps inadvertently, gained a national reputation for radicalism by leading an attack on the Church in his state. When a poor man was denied a Christian burial because his family could not afford the required fees, Ocampo engaged in a bitter polemic with the Bishop of Michoacán, Clemente de Jesús Munguía. It was to halt the spread of this dangerous anticlericalism (and also to bring political calm) that the conservatives summoned Santa Anna back from exile. Alamán wrote to Santa Anna in despair: "We are yearning for your quick return in order to put an end to such errors."

Santa Anna became president once more in 1853 with Lucas Alamán as head of his cabinet. Alamán had no illusions about the president's failings, realizing that Santa Anna preferred cockfights and gambling to the onerous duties of political office. But the conservative minister believed that he could manage the government through his position in the cabinet and give the anchorless country stability and purpose. He moved with dispatch to set up a centralist administration, disbanding state legislatures and town governments and naming political chiefs (jefes políticos) in their places as agents of presidential authority in the states. Other presidential decrees clamped down on the opposition press and exiled many of the leading liberals. The Jesuits were brought back to lead a reformation of the country's educational system. But forty-three days after the new government assumed power Lucas Alamán died, and the regime lost its sense of direction. Now corruption and extravagance were the order of the day. Perhaps carried away by his own dreams of grandeur, the President imposed monarchical trappings on the Mexican government, styling himself "His Most Serene Highness," while the supine Council of State (which had replaced the national congress) made him "perpetual dictator." Like Iturbide before him, Santa Anna wasted the government's resources with his courtly extravagances and public display. To finance the large outlays of revenues, Santa Anna resorted to all manner of nuisance taxes, and he was finally reduced to selling off national territory in the North to the United States (Gadsden Purchase).

The liberal reaction came on March 1, 1854, in the western state of Guerrero when partisans of the local caudillo, Juan Álvarez, proclaimed their Plan of Ayutla. Ignacio Comonfort commanded troops in Guerrero. Benito Juárez returned from New Orleans to join Álvarez' camp as a civilian adviser. Though he had little popular support throughout the country, Santa Anna hung on until July 1855, when the garrison in Mexico City declared for the revolution; then he once more followed the well-worn path into exile. He never returned to power. His day was past, and the destinies of Mexico seemed to belong to the new liberals who assumed control of the national government.

With the victory of the Plan of Ayutla began the period known in Mexico as La Reforma, an epoch of significant and radical change in the country's political structure. Álvarez sounded the call for a constituent congress to write a new liberal constitution. In the meantime, the provisional government began to implement the revolution's program by executive decree. On November 22, 1855, Álvarez proclaimed the Ley Juárez (Benito Juárez was his Minister of Justice and Ecclesiastical Affairs), which abolished special merchants' courts and suppressed the ecclesiastical and military fueros. Thereafter, all Mexicans would be subject to the same judicial procedures. Of even more far-reaching significance was the Ley Lerdo, decreed on June 25, 1856, by President Comonfort (who replaced Juan Álvarez) and written by

Miguel Lerdo de Tejada, the Minister of the Treasury. The decree put an end to communal landholdings, whether of the Church or of Indian villages, by obliging the owners to sell their properties to the occupants. Though the intent of the liberal agrarian legislation was praiseworthy— to create a nation of small landholders—the result proved ultimately catastrophic. The forced sales only increased the size and number of haciendas and reinforced latifundism in Mexico. And many sales of ecclesiastical properties were fictitious, so that the Church continued to hold lands illegally.

Because these laws were presidential decrees, however, they were of doubtful legality until confirmed by the Congress or incorporated into the new constitution. The Constituent Congress met in Mexico City in February 1856, and the liberal document began to take shape, as the delegates debated each new article. The spirit of liberalism was evident from the first article, which recognized that the Mexican people had all those rights that were the "Natural Rights of Man." There was little dispute about the federal system for Mexico. Santa Anna's dictatorship was much in mind as the Congress voted more powers to the states and sought to limit the president's authority through a semi-parliamentarian device of cabinet responsibility. Though the constitution provided for broad suffrage, democracy was inhibited by means of indirect election procedures. The Senate, which had been too conservative, was eliminated in favor of a unicameral legislature. The laws of Juárez and Lerdo were accepted with little opposition, and other articles provided for freedom of speech and the press. The delegates voted to abrogate the decree of Santa Anna which had permitted the return of the Jesuit order, for the Jesuits were too powerful, too insidious, they believed, and represented a threat to the government and to society. Public education was secularized (though private parochial schools were still permitted), and compulsory monastic vows were terminated.

Yet this was as far as most delegates would go. The moderates, as well as the radicals, favored in principle some regulation of ecclesiastical affairs in order to confine the activities of the Church to the spiritual sphere, but they failed to follow the principle to its logical consequence —the legal separation of Church and State. Nor could the moderates bring themselves to take a stand on toleration—lest the country see an influx of "Mohammedans, idolators, and even Mormons." The result was that the Congress nearly foundered in the shoals of indecision, and in the end voted to make no statement in the constitution on either toleration or separation of Church and State. At one juncture, with the Congress in complete frustration, the delegates, by the narrowest margin, avoided a decision to reject the proposed document in favor of a return to the Constitution of 1824.

The restoration of peace by the liberals was brief indeed. Though the moderate view had prevailed in the Congress, the Constitution of 1857 was still unacceptable to the Catholic clergy, for it sanctioned the forced sale of the Church lands and ended the traditional privileges of the priests and bishops and their immunity from civil control. In public statements the prelates condemned the new constitution. The president and his cabinet were barred from the cathedral in Mexico City unless they retracted their oaths of office. When on December 17, 1857, the conservatives raised the banner of rebellion against the constitution and the liberal government, the bishops offered to lift the threats of excommunication for all those who would support the conservative pronouncement.

President Ignacio Comonfort, among the more conservative of the moderates, was at first inclined to accept the Plan of Tacubaya. In the end, however, he resigned and turned over the presidency to Benito Juárez, who had become head of the Supreme Court and was his legal successor (under the constitution there was no vice-president). Comonfort went into exile, while Juárez directed the liberal resistance to the conservative armies. From late 1857 until early 1860 Mexico was once more wracked by bloody civil strife—called by Mexicans the War of the Reform. From the outset the conservatives had the upper hand, for they controlled most of the armies and the national capital. Juárez took refuge in Veracruz where his government collected the all-important revenues to finance the resistance against the conservatives in the rest of the Republic. As in most Mexican wars, the participants stopped at no cruelty, shooting prisoners, plundering towns and cities, and attacking the civil population, as well as enemy troops. By the end of 1859 the liberals had raised new armies, equipped them, and finally defeated the conservative forces. In January 1861 Juárez returned to Mexico City in triumph.

It was a new Juárez who took control of the nation, for the years of adversity in Veracruz had steeled his resolve. As governor of Oaxaca, he had worked in cooperation with the clergy of his state. After 1858 he was one of the most radical liberals, for he could not forget the support that the priests and bishops had given his enemies. The most violent phase of Mexican anticlericalism in the nineteenth century had its beginnings in Veracruz with the enactments of Juárez' liberal government.

During the summer of 1859, with the liberal cause in apparent dire straits and with the American government pressing Juárez for railroad and territorial concessions, Juárez launched a series of attacks upon the Church to obtain new sources of credit and revenue for his regime. On July 12, 1859, the first of the so-called Reform Laws was promulgated by Juárez. (Because there was no congress in Veracruz, all of the laws were created by presidential decree.) Church and State were now officially separated. The President outlawed all monastic orders and obliged the regular clergy to join the seculars. The provisions of the decree concerning nunneries were less severe; these would continue unmolested, though no more novices could be admitted in the future. The sharpest attack upon the Church came in the article that nationalized all Church capital and properties (in addition to the rural estates already banned under the Ley Lerdo)—the buildings, the objects within, any tangible thing held by the Church as an institution. These properties would be sold at public auction. Miguel Lerdo de Tejada, Juárez' Minister of the Treasury, planned to use this vast wealth to secure credits in the United States. In this hope Lerdo was disappointed, for the American government, wanting to exact the utmost concession from Juárez, saw to it that his financial agents failed to get the loans.

These first Reform Laws were followed in late 1859 and in 1860 by additional presidential decrees that secularized cemeteries, made marriage a civil contract, reduced the number of religious feast days, and restricted public religious processions. Juárez was determined to punish the recalcitrant clergy and to limit the Church's control over the Mexican people. By decreeing these laws, however, Juárez and the liberals sowed the dragon's teeth of even more bitter Church-State conflict. The harvest was reaped in the Revolution of 1910.

The military victory over the conservatives did not assure peace and stability, and armed bands remained a menace—a conservative guerrilla commander seized Melchor Ocampo and shot him summarily. But Juárez' greatest problem was fiscal, for the war had exhausted the national treasury. In desperation Juárez ordered a moratorium on the country's foreign debt payments. The French emperor, Napoleon III, seized upon this act as a pretext for intervention, and so the great conflict was renewed, now with the soldiers of France fighting alongside the conservative forces. Because the United States was embroiled in the Civil War, the French emperor was able to intrude in Mexican affairs with impunity, despite the Monroe Doctrine. Unable to gain victory with their own military forces, members of the conservative oligarchy welcomed the invaders in yet another attempt to restore centralism and clericalism to Mexico. The conservatives encouraged Napoleon's intrigues and the Hapsburg Maximilian's vain dreams of imperial glory. Goaded by the Reform Laws and by the loss of its wealth, the Church gave active assistance to the conservative faction and to the French troops who entered Mexico in 1862. Bishop Pelagio Antonio de Labastida y Dávalos of Puebla, Archbishop-elect of Mexico City, was a member of the triumvirate who acted as regents to prepare the way for the new Emperor.

Maximilian arrived in 1864 to accept the throne. But the conservatives and the bishops soon learned that they had made a dubious bargain. Maximilian came from a country that did not permit its Church to dominate secular affairs, and he was also far more liberal than the Mexicans had suspected. The Emperor disappointed the Catholics by refusing to restore confiscated Church properties and by pursuing a conciliatory policy toward the liberals. Though Catholicism continued as the State religion, he decreed toleration for other sects and secularized public education. Maximilian asserted his right to forbid the publication of papal communications in Mexico and proposed to the Vatican a concordat that would have recognized the liberalization of Church-State relations. But he succeeded only in alienating the conservatives and the clerics, without ever winning the support of Juárez' faction.

The armies of the Emperor, both French and conservative, could hold and control only those areas that they effectively occupied. To pacify the entire country proved to be an impossible task, for Juárez maintained a government in Paso del Norte (now Ciudad Juárez), and the implacable opposition of the liberals assured the downfall of the empire as soon as the French armies should leave. At the end of the American Civil War in 1865 the United States brought pressure on the French to withdraw from Mexico. Napoleon stalled, but in the following year France was embarrassed during the Austro-Prussian War by a diplomatic crisis with Prussia. And because the Mexican adventure proved to be more expensive than he had expected, Napoleon began to withdraw his troops early in 1867, leaving Maximilian and the conservatives to fend for themselves. The French commander advised the Emperor to abdicate and return to Europe, but conservatives, seconded by the Prussian minister in Mexico, assured him that he would be safe. The wily Bismarck did not want Maximilian to return to Austria where he might revive the moribund Hapsburg cause in Germany. In the last analysis, however, Maximilian was too proud to run away. Liberal forces captured him in Querétaro, and after a perfunctory trial he was executed by the command of Benito Juárez. With the death of the Emperor—and by the same *coup de grâce*, as it were—the Conservative Party died as a political force in Mexico. Thereafter, no political faction dared call itself conservative, for the name was stigmatized by association with traitors and foreign invaders. Mexico's conservatives confined their public activities to business and the army, leaving the field of politics to their victorious enemies.

The liberals governed Mexico from 1867 to 1876—a period called by Mexicans the Restored Republic. Though the country was exhausted by the decade and a half of intestine warfare, the defeat of Maximilian gave the Mexican people a new sense of national purpose. Under Juárez and his successor, Sebastián Lerdo de Tejada, the Mexicans began to modernize and to industrialize. Moreover, because of the intervention, the government no longer felt an obligation to pay off the loans, and the incubus of foreign indebtedness was removed. Juárez was more moderate than he had been in Veracruz, and he made no attempt to enforce the Reform Laws. It was left to Sebastián Lerdo de Tejada to secure congressional sanction for the decrees.

Though he had led his country through a decade of war, Juárez was a thorough-going civilian at heart. To prevent the intermission of the military into civic affairs, he broke up the armies and dismissed the troops—without pensions. The former soldiers remained a source of trouble for the government, as they complained of shabby treatment at the hands of the President. Some turned to banditry or even insurrection. Juárez fought a running battle with the Congress over the constitutional restrictions on the president's powers, and when he asked the Chamber of Deputies for legislation to strengthen his position, he was accused of dictatorial methods. As if to corroborate the charges of his political opponents, Juárez was forced to use strong-arm tactics to achieve his own reelection in 1871 and the election of his supporters to public office. But he died before he could take office, and Lerdo, the head of the Supreme Court, succeeded him as President.

Lerdo was an intellectual and a brilliant, eloquent orator, but too intolerant and uncompromising to make a good politician. Though he experienced the same difficulties with Congress as Juárez, he did bring the constitution into accord with liberal doctrines by legalizing Juárez' Reform Laws. And the Senate was restored as a check against the Chamber of Deputies. Other presidential decrees placed further restrictions upon the public activities of the clergy. Lerdo suppressed religious holidays and banned public religious processions. The ringing of Church bells, whose clangorous messages assailed the ears of Mexicans long before daybreak each morning, was restricted. Priests were forbidden to inherit property from any except direct relatives, and they could not wear their clerical garb in public. Thereafter these liberal measures were an integral part of Mexico's legal system. As modified and intensified in the Constitution of 1917, they remain the law of the land today.

Despite their many plans and pronouncements and their constitution, the liberals failed ultimately to provide Mexico with a satisfactory system of government. In principle, federalism should have insured individual liberty and protected local rights from the tyranny of an all-powerful national regime. In practice, however, federalism promoted anarchy, encouraged local jealousies, and fostered the rule of petty caudillos in the various states. Federalism was an artificiality in Mexico, for there was no tradition of responsible local government upon which to build a federal system. Whatever the liberals might believe, after a half-century of revolutionary turmoil, Mexico needed a vigorous hand at the helm and an era of uninterrupted peace and stability in order to further her industrial development. Even after Maximilian's defeat and death, and the destruction of the Conservative Party, there was no peace in Mexico. With no political or military opposition, the liberals fell out among themselves and quarrelled over the spoils of national and local office. Elections were as fraudulent as under the conservatives, and the imposition of official candidates was all too frequently followed by the revolt of the defeated opposition. Juárez' and Lerdo's highhandedness alienated the legislators, without strengthening the executive powers. As a result of the continued civil strife, many members of the responsible propertied classes became disenchanted with the Restored Republic, and they longed for a system that would protect, not destroy, property. Many erstwhile liberals turned their backs on Juárez and Lerdo and the idealistic principles that had long guided the Liberal Party. Because the Conservative Party was dead, they looked elsewhere for inspiration; they found their creed in the scientific philosophy of Positivism and their strong man in Porfirio Díaz.

A prominent liberal general, Díaz had served the cause of Juárez well during the intervention, winning battles against the French and the conservative forces. After 1867 he returned to his native state, Oaxaca, to enter politics. In 1871 he was a candidate for the presidency against Benito Juárez and in 1876 against Sebastián Lerdo de Tejada. Revolting in 1872, he failed because he gained little support outside his own area. But by 1876 Mexico had grown weary of imposed elections. When it became clear in early 1876 that Lerdo would succeed himself, Díaz' partisans launched a revolution with the Plan of Tuxtepec, calling for "no reelection." With the success of his revolution, Díaz was elected president. He fulfilled the pledge of Tuxtepec in 1880 and maneuvered the election of Manuel González. (Díaz stayed in the national government, however, as Minister of Fomento.) Four years later, he returned to the presidency and ruled Mexico for twenty-six more years—as a dictator.

Díaz was never a Positivist; it is doubtful if he had any political philosophy. But he accepted the support of the Científicos because the Positivists helped sustain his regime. In the last quarter of the nineteenth century the Mexican economy grew apace, as Díaz gave Mexico, for the first time in its independent history, an extended period of peace, free from revolt, free from internal dissension, free from foreign intervention. He achieved and maintained his power by playing off one local caudillo against another, by reorganizing the army, by controlling elections, and by creating a centralized regime. The dictatorship did not need to abolish the federal structure provided in the constitution; it was merely pushed aside and ignored. For the provinces Díaz appointed jefes políticos, whose job was to emasculate local independence. The ayuntamientos continued to function, but, dominated by the jefes políticos, these town governments had little authority. The educational system of Mexico was also centralized. The liberals had insisted on local autonomy for the public schools, but the Positivists used the national regime to gain control of the country's educational processes.

With Porfirio Díaz securely in the presidency, the self-seekers, both foreign and national, were attracted to that fount of dispensation, and the Científicos grouped themselves around Díaz to direct the flow of favors. A leading Positivist, José Limantour, became the Minister of the Treasury. Friends of the government received large tracts of land. The ruthless application of the Ley Lerdo and of an additional land law in 1883 deprived the Indian villages of their remaining communal holdings. Foreign concessionaires received rich oil lands for next to nothing. Railroads were built and mines developed with foreign capital. The capitalists and financiers of the United States and Britain saw in the Mexico of Porfirio Díaz a "Golden Era"—a period of stability and huge profits. It is true that the economic development of Mexico would have been impossible without foreign capital. But it is equally true that foreign investors were granted concessions of dubious legality.

By 1910, under the guidance of Limantour, the government of Mexico resembled an efficient, prosperous business. The budget was balanced and even showed a surplus. Mexico had been put firmly on the gold standard, and the peso had achieved a stability unknown in the nineteenth century. The federal army and the rural police pacified the country, keeping malcontents in check by means of ruthless terrorism. It was indeed a safe country for travelers and investors. Díaz had found Mexico in confusion and in danger of falling apart and had brought it well on the road to modernization. Under the Positivists, however, the benefits of the modernization accrued to the select few, the landowners and businessmen of Mexico, and the foreign investors. The majority of the Mexicans lived in peonage or beggary. Robbed of their lands, the Indians were legally tied to the rural estates, and few could ever escape the debts owed the hacendados. Reckoned in buying power, rural wages were only a quarter as large as wages in the colonial period, and the peon received payment, not in cash but in vales—tokens redeemable only in the hacienda store, where prices were highly inflated. For his food, his clothing, his tools, his seeds, even for his church wedding or a family funeral, the peon was perpetually in debt to the landowner. It was virtually impossible to flee from the haciendas, as the efficient rurales hunted down the fugitives and returned them to their masters. Nor was there surcease in death, for the children inherited the debts of their fathers.

If the regime of Porfirio Díaz was a dictatorship, it was certainly not totalitarian, for within the framework of oppression there often remained a surprising amount of freedom. The President and his government came under much criticism, particularly during the periodic farcical elections that gave legal sanction to the regime. Newspapers and magazines needled members of the government, and even the President, for the constant imposition of government candidates in the elections. But the criticism dealt with personalities, not institutions. Men were relatively free to talk—but not to act. When workers in Orizaba called a strike to gain higher wages and better working conditions, the army crushed the strike with great cruelty and much loss of life. Only at the risk of prison or death could a Mexican advocate basic changes in the social, economic, or political structure of his country. Consequently, most critics suggested reforms which would not disturb the status quo, or proposed them for some vague, unspecified time in the future.

One such critic was Andrés Molina Enríquez, whose book, *Los Grandes Problemas de México*, offered a mild indictment of the gross inequalities between the few rich hacendados and the masses of the peons. Molina Enríquez was neither a visionary nor a socialist, but a liberal in the nineteenth-century sense who advocated a sturdy peasantry owning small parcels of private land. Although he pointed out the glaring faults of the land system under the Díaz regime, he prudently did not call for a revolution, conceding that the government should remain dictatorial for the time being. The Catholic Church too in the first decade of the twentieth century increasingly criticized the condition of workers, both rural and urban. Laymen and bishops organized national congresses, in the spirit of Leo XIII's *Rerum Novarum*, to study means of reforming society through Catholic social action. But the Catholic reformers too were careful not to attack the Porfirian regime directly— as long as the government was willing to overlook the anticlerical articles of the constitution.

In strong contrast were the reforms demanded by the Mexican Liberal Party of Camilo Arriaga and the brothers Jesús and Ricardo Flores Magón. This party belied its name, for it was more radical than liberal. Some of the leaders, including Ricardo Flores Magón, were anarchists or syndicalists, who formed an alliance with the I.W.W. syndicalists in the United States. The Mexican government outlawed their publication, *Regeneración*, and to escape imprisonment, the party leaders fled to the United States, where they continued their agitation against the Díaz regime. American authorities subsequently brought Ricardo Flores Magón to trial for his revolutionary activity, and he was sentenced to a term in Leavenworth Prison. From St. Louis, Missouri, on July 1, 1906, the party issued its manifesto for the reform of Mexico. The Liberals called for a general distribution of land through the breaking up of large estates. For the industrial workers (the chief concern of the syndicalists) the party proposed minimum wage and maximum hours legislation, an end to child labor, and the outlawing of company stores, with wages to be paid in cash, not chits. The plan demanded the closing of all Catholic schools and their replacement with lay institutions. Though the propagandizing activities of the Floresmagonistas may have influenced small-scale local revolts and strikes between 1906 and 1908, they failed to ignite a spontaneous popular uprising. Instead, the voice of the Mexican Liberal Party sounded from the wilderness a message of reform to come in the Revolution of 1910.

In September 1910 Mexico celebrated the centennial of its Independence movement. Dignitaries of Church and State from all over the world congregated in Mexico City to render homage to Porfirio Díaz for the great advances made under his regime. There were sumptuous banquets and florid speeches. Porfirio Díaz, now an octagenarian, presided over the festivities with the benign assurance of continued prosperity and peace. From foreign ambassadors, in grateful recognition for favors granted, he accepted yet more medals to pin on his much-decorated military tunic. But the political stability of Mexico was illusory. The capital was a Potemkin village which obscured true conditions in the rest of the Republic—the grinding poverty of the masses, the illiteracy, the cruelty and oppression of the dictatorial government. Further, Mexico had experienced economic dislocation after the Panic of 1907, which caused some businessmen and hacendados to become disaffected from the regime. Above all, the festivities obscured the passions that were soon to erupt in revolution—the seething anger of Morelos peasants dispossessed by the state's sugar barons, the bitter resentment of young intellectuals who found their careers stymied by government preferment, the desperation of railroad workers and of laborers in the mines and textile mills who worked at low wages and under hazardous conditions. Before the month was out Mexico was to see the beginning of Francisco I. Madero's revolutionary movement which toppled the regime of Porfirio Díaz and ultimately brought the country great economic, political, and social reforms.

6

Revolutionary Mexico

"Mexico has had one Revolution—not more than one. It started in 1910 and is still going on." This pronouncement, made in 1926 by a Mexican educator, Moisés Sáenz, might well have highlighted any campaign speech in the succeeding four decades. The one official party has been the Party of Revolutionary Institutions. Again and again public officials invoke the magic of the Revolution to justify the current policies of a national government. Despite much cynicism from the intellectuals and apathy from the popular classes, the idea of the single, monolithic Revolution—always spelled with a capital R—endures. Like the Aztec chieftain, Cuauhtémoc, the Revolution has become the inviolate symbol of Mexico's struggle for national identity and self-esteem. The Revolution's military commanders, Venustiano Carranza, Álvaro Obregón, Emiliano Zapata, and even Francisco Villa, are enshrined in the pantheon of national honor. Official textbooks, prescribed by the federal government, hymn the Revolution's praises for generations of young scholars, though it is not always clear who fought whom and for what reasons. Other Latin American countries, especially Peru, have looked to Mexico and to its Revolution as an example of reform and modernization, carried out largely through native endeavors, and as an alternative to the Communist Cuban Revolution or to Brazil's and Argentina's military regimes.

Generalizations, though seldom wholly true, have great merit in inspiring a people to noble endeavors. The aura of the Revolutionary myth has been very useful in the half-century since 1910. But the campaign oratory and the official textbooks obscure more than they illuminate. In fact, the Revolution is an exceedingly complex movement, many diverse revolutions comprehended by a single name—a political revolt against dictatorship; an economic revolt against Científicos, hacendados, and foreign capitalists; a nationalistic revolt against the suborners of Mexico's birthright (gringos and gachupines); a philosophic revolt against foreign influences in music and the arts; a religious revolt against a conservative and antiquated Church; and a social revolt of the masses against the propertied classes. Revolutionaries fought against the Old Regime of Porfirio Díaz. They also fell out among themselves and disputed the fruits of victory in years of civil war. Some took up arms to enrich themselves at the expense of the aristocrats and foreigners; others fought for the high cause of popular economic and social redemption. Yet within this seeming disarray of conflicting motives, causes, and factions, two clear-cut principles emerge. One is nineteenth-century liberalism revived, the other a native radicalism, looking to new and even socialistic solutions to the age-old problems of Mexico.

While Positivism and the Porfirian regime may have represented the triumph of middle-class, business values in Mexico, a great part of the middle class had been excluded from the benefits of the increased prosperity. In the Revolution lawyers, engineers, school teachers, shopkeepers, small farmers, and small businessmen, especially in the northern states, forgetting the anarchy that had preceded Díaz, looked to a revival of what seemed to them the halcyon days of Juárez and Lerdo. Because of their proximity to the United States, the northerners were exposed to the advantages of liberal democracy. Most opposed violent social upheaval and expected that if social change came, it would be slowly and through legal procedures. After 1910 liberalism meant much the same as a half-century earlier—separation of Church and State, secular education, laissez faire, and a federal system with considerable autonomy for local governments. In the early days of the Revolution those who espoused the liberal cause followed Francisco I. Madero. After Madero's death Venustiano Carranza and his civilian coterie took up the banner of liberalism and led the Constitutionalist armies in the fight against militarism and dictatorship.

Many revolutionaries considered the political philosophy of Madero and Carranza obsolete. They demanded and fought for precipitate changes in Mexico's social structure—land for the landless (by direct action, if necessary) and legislation to protect the workers and their families. Some were syndicalists or anarchists, influenced by the Flores Magóns' Mexican Liberal Party. But most were pragmatic radicals with no ready-made ideology, and because they were not fanatics or puritans, they brought no reign of terror to the Revolution. They preferred a vigorous state or national government committed to genuine economic, social, and political reforms. The radicals were usually antagonistic toward the Church and would hamstring it with harsh and restrictive legislation. Priests should play no part in the education of Mexico's young; rather, the public schools should mold the child's character, free from "superstition" and "prejudice." Radicals such as Emiliano Zapata and Francisco Villa supported Madero's revolution, but later turned against Carranza when they saw that his principles and policies were retrogressive. Many moderate radicals, notably Álvaro Obregón, stuck with Carranza, however, because they preferred legality to the rapine and destruction of Villa's and Zapata's armies.

Revolutionary liberalism gained a victory in the years after 1910 and determined the shape of the Constitution of 1917. The presidential term of Venustiano Carranza, 1917–20, represented a high point for liberalism and federalism (and a low point for the Mexican nation). Radicals influenced the constitution's formation by modifying key articles—those dealing with education, land, the factories, and the Church. After 1920, in the presidency of Obregón, radicalism marked the course of the Revolution, reaching its apogee during the 1930s with Lázaro Cárdenas. Beginning in 1940, however, the momentum of social change slowed down, and though the official party and public officials preserved the myth of the radical revolution, the voice most clearly heard in influencing government decisions was that of the businessman, still a staunch nationalist but no longer a nineteenth-century liberal.

As the strength of the national government grew, the temptations of personal aggrandizement proved to be irresistible to politicians in all levels of government. From Obregón on, Mexico's presidents used their privileged positions to accumulate wealth and properties. By the 1950s and 1960s official corruption was endemic, and the chief executives were among the nation's richest men. The supreme irony was the invoking of Emiliano Zapata's spirit to bless and justify the policies of the capitalist revolutionaries. As a result, disillusioned and cynical Mexicans tended to deny the obvious and genuine accomplishments of the Revolution. And by the end of the 1960s many concerned citizens in Mexico looked to new directions for what they considered the outmoded principles of the once great and popular cause.

The Revolution burst forth in 1910 in the most inauspicious circumstances and under unlikely leadership. Francisco I. Madero, an hacendado from the northern state of Coahuila, had entered local politics in the last years of the Porfirian regime, but without success. Educated in France and the United States, he looked to liberal, limited democracy as the chief hope for a solution to Mexico's problems. And he was a spiritist, wont to seek extramundane advice during moments of crisis. In 1908 Porfirio Díaz told a correspondent for an American periodical, *Pearson's Magazine*, that Mexico was ready for democracy and that the next president would be popularly chosen. Subsequently, Madero published a book, *The Presidential Succession of 1910*, calling for free elections. He opposed revolutions as destructive of law and order, and did not attack the Church, for he felt that the Reform Laws had eliminated the religious problem from Mexico. The book outlined a moderate program in the hallowed tradition of Juárez, Ocampo, and Lerdo. In 1910 Madero entered the political lists once more, now as a challenger for the presidency against the octagenarian Porfirio Díaz.

The popular enthusiasm evoked by Madero's candidacy alarmed Díaz and his Científico supporters, and, ignoring his promise of free balloting, the President jailed his opponent until after the elections. From Mexico City the aspect seemed propitious for Díaz' government as the nation celebrated the hundredth anniversary of its Independence movement. Within the month, Madero escaped confinement and went to San Antonio, Texas, to plot with other Mexican exiles the overthrow of Díaz' government. It was a moment of decision. The temperate Madero had not heretofore dreamed of leading a military rebellion, but there seemed no other recourse—revolution or six more years of dictatorship. Madero proclaimed his Plan of San Luis Potosí and designated Sunday, November 20 as the day of revolution. He proposed a moderate program that called chiefly for political reforms—"Effective Suffrage and No Reelection." Only a single vaguely worded paragraph dealt with the agrarian problem. The revolution, said Madero, would restore those lands illegally taken from the villages. Throughout the Republic support for Madero's plan mushroomed, as revolutionary bands, among them the soldiers of Emiliano Zapata in the South and Francisco Villa and Pascual Orozco in the state of Chihuahua, took to the field to attack their oppressors. Though the movement lacked coordination, it was soon apparent that Díaz could no longer control Mexico. José Limantour, the Minister of the Treasury, had gone to Paris to negotiate a new loan from French bankers. Alarmed at the sudden deterioration of his government's position, he returned to Mexico to arrange a settlement with Madero. Representatives of the Díaz government conferred with Madero in May 1911 at Ciudad Juárez, across the Rio Grande from El Paso, Texas.

The *arreglos* of Ciudad Juárez spared Mexico a blood-letting. But the deal with the Old Regime also proved to be a Pandora's Box of mischief for Madero. Limantour agreed to exile Díaz to Europe, while Francisco León de la Barra, the Foreign Minister, succeeded him as interim president until a new election could be held. Presumably Madero would become the constitutional president later in the year. Madero returned to Mexico City in triumph, as the nation rejoiced at its sudden liberation from dictatorship. Madero believed naively that once his revolution had succeeded and he had become Mexico's president, he could turn off the revolutionary fervor like water in a spigot.

But many Mexicans, particularly the Zapatistas, mistrusted the arrangement made at Ciudad Juárez. They resolved to keep their armed forces intact until the new government demonstrated its willingness to carry out prompt and effective agrarian reform.

Madero became president in probably the freest election in the nation's history, with José María Pino Suárez as his vice president. As he took office in the fall of 1911, he proposed to give Mexico a vigorous government. But good intentions could not suffice. The new chief executive was bumbling and inept, a dreamer and a utopian, not a practical man of affairs. He surrounded himself with members of his own family —because he could trust them, he said. Madero faced the perennial dilemma of the successful revolutionary—whether to throw the rascals out and bring untried bureaucrats into his government or to leave the Porfiristas entrenched in their positions where they might sabotage his program. In choosing the latter course he confirmed the suspicions that he had betrayed the revolution at Ciudad Juárez, and his budgetary recommendations to the Congress in 1912 showed that he proposed to continue the fiscal policies of the Díaz regime.

The new President launched his administration full of hope for the future. With all good will he attempted to reach an accord with the Zapatistas. The country was free to organize new and more representative political parties, and the Catholic Church initiated an ambitious program of Social Action. Promising social amelioration based on Christian principles, the nascent Catholic Party gained control of the legislature of Jalisco and elected strong delegations from several states to the national congress. Mexico's artists and writers threw off the shackles of Positivistic cultural domination. In the Ateneo de la Juventud (Athenaeum of Youth) fledgling intellectuals such as José Vasconcelos, Alfonso Reyes, and Antonio Caso rejected the materialism of Comte in favor of a more spiritual or aesthetic (hence, Mexican) approach to philosophy. Young artists, among them José Clemente Orozco, David Siqueiros, and Gerardo Murillo (called Dr. Atl from the Aztec word for volcano), developed Mexican themes taken from the country's indigenous past. The National University in the capital was to be the focus of the new nationalism. But Madero's honeymoon days were few indeed. He did not recognize that Mexico needed more than free elections, that his liberal principles were hopelessly out of date. Above all, he failed to see the need for substantial economic and social reform, and he sought to halt the illegal seizures of haciendas by revolutionaries throughout the Republic. Opposition appeared from all quarters to threaten the government's existence and the success of Madero's revolution.

In the north Pascual Orozco rebelled, protesting that the President had withheld funds from his irregular Colorado troops. Orozco charged that Madero had failed to implement even the modest reforms promised in the Plan of San Luis Potosí. Madero was forced to call upon General Victoriano Huerta and the federal army to put down his fellow-revolutionaries. In Veracruz, Félix Díaz, nephew of the dictator, sustained a short-lived cuartelazo. Captured and brought to the capital, where he was lodged in the penitentiary, Díaz continued to conspire against Madero with Bernardo Reyes, an ex-Porfirista, who was also imprisoned in Mexico City. To the south, in the mountains and valleys of Morelos, Emiliano Zapata's Liberation Army defied Madero as it had Porfirio Díaz.

Morelos, the heart of Cortés' baronial estates during the colonial period, had always been largely Indian in physiognomy and rural in character. During the nineteenth century the villages lost much of their land through the Ley Lerdo, and this spoliation accelerated under Díaz, as the sugar-raising hacendados crowded out the peasants and forced them to work at low wages in a capitalistic economy. Consequently, malcontent and even violence were chronic in the first decade of the twentieth century. By 1910 Emiliano Zapata had emerged as the natural leader of peasant protesters. During the early days of the Revolution he spoke for the state's free campesinos, not the peons, and, in a sense, his movement was counterrevolutionary. The Zapatistas demanded, not the parcelling of hacienda properties, but the forced restoration of village lands to which they had age-old titles. It was this violent, direct action which the hacendado president could not accept. In November 1911 Zapata proclaimed his own Plan of Ayala supporting Orozco. And despite the disapproval of the federal government, he continued to confiscate lands.

The national Senate, which had not been reformed in the congressional election of 1912, owed its allegiance to Porfirio Díaz, while the Chamber of Deputies was hopelessly split by factional disputes. The sizable Catholic Party worked actively against the President and his liberal program. And the ambassador of the United States to Mexico, Henry Lane Wilson, was an unrelenting foe, undermining Madero's position in unfavorable dispatches to the Department of State. Meanwhile, the new freedom of the press allowed scurrilous attacks on the President, his family, and his government in the conservative newspapers of the capital. In the end, however, it was the federal army that broke Madero. Nominally loyal to the President, it was a potential source of treason, and the troops could be used against Zapatistas, Orozquistas, and Felicistas only with great peril to Madero himself.

When reactionary conspirators freed Félix Díaz and Bernardo Reyes from their prison cells on February 9, 1913, and marched upon the National Palace, Madero erred grievously by calling upon General Huerta for protection. Though Huerta had earlier served the President well in campaigns against Orozco and Zapata, he now plotted with his ostensible enemy, Félix Díaz, to overthrow Madero's government. Under the aegis of Henry Lane Wilson—a fact that Mexico's historians will not forget—Huerta and Díaz agreed to end the fighting in Mexico City and to depose the hapless president. On the night of February 22 Madero and Pino Suárez, having been forced to resign, were shot by General Huerta's officers. Victoriano Huerta, the "bloody usurper" in Mexico's revolutionary tradition, assumed the provisional presidency, while the martyred Madero became the symbol for the continued struggle against military dictatorship—the first "apostle" of the Revolution.

Many responsible citizens hailed the restoration of a vigorous central government with relief, weary of the two troubled years since Díaz' overthrow. De la Barra had no compunctions about joining Huerta's cabinet. Pascual Orozco, once defeated by Huerta, now made peace with the new president and ranged his Colorado troops alongside the federal forces. Most of the state governors and senators placed expediency above their loyalty to the legally constituted government of Madero. Many of the Maderista deputies (they called themselves *Renovadores*) temporized, preferring to remain in the Chamber to ascertain which direction the new government would take. The Catholic Party forsook its forward-looking program of Social Action to ally itself with Huerta. And in the nation's capital a *Te Deum* celebrated the supposed pacification of Mexico. The central government was now completely conservative and frankly military in character.

Yet Huerta was not master of all the Republic. In the mountains half-ringing the capital to the south and west, Zapatista Mexico continued its stubborn resistance; Zapata emended His Plan of Ayala to take into account the coup d'état of Huerta and Orozco's defection. Huerta's cruel repressions in Morelos drove peon laborers into Zapata's camp and helped radicalize the Zapatista movement. No longer were the Zapatistas content to regain their lost village lands. Instead they began to seize the large sugar estates and forcibly eject the hacendados. Zapata attracted many radical intellectuals to his cause, notably the socialist, Rafael Pérez Taylor, and the anarchist, Antonio Díaz Soto y Gama, a former associate of the Floresmagonistas. But the earthy Zapatistas considered the intellectuals extra baggage in their military camp, and policies were set by Zapata and his peasant chiefs.

Although his movement was still confined primarily to the small state of Morelos, Zapata claimed to lead the entire revolution. But his knowledge of the rest of Mexico was extremely limited. He was a national leader only in his own mind and in the minds of his exuberant peasant lieutenants. His forces lacked equipment and discipline, and, like guerrilla fighters, they lived off the land, getting their arms and supplies by raiding the enemy. The southern commanders, even Zapata, possessed only the barest rudiments of military science. Although the Plan of Ayala proclaimed land for the landless everywhere in Mexico, the Zapatistas showed little concern for areas other than their own. Their political horizon was circumscribed by the mountains of Morelos, and the revolution of Zapata was never a national movement. It could not defeat Huerta without the help and cooperation of chiefs in other parts of Mexico.

The principal threat against the new national regime came from the North, where many followers of Madero refused to accept Huerta's coup. The leader of these Constitutionalist forces was Venustiano Carranza, a senator during the Díaz era and later governor of Coahuila. Like Madero, Carranza was a reluctant revolutionary. When Huerta seized power, he hesitated, evidently hoping to arrange a deal with the new president. A month passed before Carranza proclaimed the Plan of Guadalupe, calling for a coalition of northern leaders under the banner of Constitutionalism with himself as First Chief. Carranza was older than most of the revolution's leaders—54 in 1913—and he could recall, however, vaguely, the pre-Porfirian days of Juárez and Lerdo. Like the assassinated president, he was a man of property, of middle-class mentality. Aloof, he surrounded himself with a barrier of lawyers, engineers, and educators. He could be admired or hated; he was too detached from his fellow citizens to be loved. Mexico's intellectuals looked to Villa and Zapata for leadership, not to the Constitutionalist First Chief. He was impeccably honest and insufferably aware of his own rectitude. He allowed others to give mouth to his political inclinations, and said, wrote, perhaps even thought, little that was important or worth remembering. Carranza was bourgeois mediocrity incarnate.

In the mining and ranching state of Chihuahua the new revolution coalesced around Francisco Villa. Unable to read or write until he was an adult, and then only partly literate, he was in his heyday Mexico's mightiest caudillo. A product of the northern frontier society, Villa lived outside the law for most of his life. He fashioned his own personal code of behavior, whether as a youthful firebrand, avenging a ravished sister, or a mature general of world renown. With no higher law to stay his hand, Villa took what he pleased, whether it was a herd of cattle, a human life, or a beautiful woman. Fanatically loyal to his friends, he was an implacable enemy to those who crossed him, rarely forgetting or forgiving a slight. He was all that Carranza was not: virile (in Mexico *muy macho*), earthy, and passionate, given to emotional outbursts. Like Zapata, Villa was rural Mexico, as Carranza was her educated, city-dwelling, middle class. Villa was a poor subordinate; he followed his own military strategy, without regard to the overall leadership exercised by Carranza. Often he waxed sarcastic about the pompous First Chief, refusing to attend banquets at which Carranza harangued his listeners with vague promises of social reform. As Villa put it, he would not "fool around with pantywaists" like Carranza. The two northern chiefs came to distrust, hate, and contemn each other. Villa formed a powerful Division of the North, which began, by early 1914, to win battles in Chihuahua against Huerta's federal forces in a drive along the railroad line from Ciudad Juárez to Mexico City. Two other commanders took charge of army corps in Sonora and Tamaulipas, Pablo González and Álvaro Obregón. González, a timorous general, made up for his lack of military skill with an unwavering allegiance to the First Chief. Obregón too, in the early days of the Constitutionalist revolution, was completely loyal to Carranza. As a result of Villa's insolence, Carranza favored Obregón and González, working to prevent the Division of the North from reaching the national capital before the two Army Corps of the Northeast and Northwest. Even prior to the defeat of Huerta a dangerous breach appeared in the ranks of the Constitutionalist armies, when the First Chief withheld coal and military supplies from Villa's Division.

As Huerta contended with revolutionary armies in the south and the north, he maneuvered on the diplomatic front to gain recognition for his provisional government. But he found an inflexible enemy in the new American president, Woodrow Wilson, who demanded the establishment of a freely elected government in Mexico. Wilson, an enlightened but dogmatic liberal, was offended by the brutality of Huerta's coup. Always the pedagogue, even in the White House, Wilson vowed that he would teach the Mexicans a lesson. Yet Huerta was caught on a constitutional dilemma. Though he had agreed in February 1913 that Félix Díaz should follow him in the presidency, he subsequently changed his mind. But the constitution barred a provisional president from succeeding himself, so if Huerta permitted a genuine election, he must give up his office.

When diplomatic pressures failed to force Huerta from power, President Wilson sanctioned the seizure of Veracruz in April 1914—ostensibly to uphold American honor. Federal forces in Tampico had inadvertently arrested a boatload of sailors from the U.S.S. *Dolphin*, and when Huerta refused to give an official apology, the American president took the opportunity to choke off Huerta's arms and supplies by holding Mexico's chief port. By July a combination of Wilson's intervention and revolutionary military victories had destroyed Huerta's power, and he prudently went into exile, leaving Mexico City to the troops of Álvaro Obregón and Venustiano Carranza.

In his dealings with his revolutionary allies as well as with the American president, Carranza exhibited the tenacity of a bull terrier. Like Juárez before him, the First Chief believed that civilians should govern when peace was restored. It was soon apparent that he had no intention of carrying out social reforms in Mexico. He took over the outposts around Mexico City that Huerta had maintained against Zapata's army. He was equally hostile toward the contumacious Villa. And when Woodrow Wilson offered to turn over Veracruz to the Constitutionalists if they would guarantee no reprisals against Mexicans who had worked for the occupation government, Carranza refused the American offer. He would not bend to the will of the most powerful military chief or of the American president. Though Carranza acceded to the request of his lieutenants that he summon a group of military leaders to Mexico City, he insisted that it was no more than a "junta," which could give his government advice, but not make decisions. And he kept the designation First Chief instead of Provisional President, for he wanted to become Constitutional President at the next election.

The assembled military chiefs were in no mood, however, to halt the march of the revolution, now that hostilities had ceased. They took control from Carranza's civilian advisers, voting to call their body a Sovereign Convention and to invite Zapatistas and Villistas to join them in Aguascalientes (which was considered neutral territory). When the lawyer Luis Cabrera protested against the exclusion of civilians, Obregón spoke for those who had fought and suffered for social reform. After Madero was murdered by Huerta, he said, the civilians stayed comfortably at home. "They pleaded: 'I'm neutral.' 'I have too many children.' Or 'It would hurt my business.' We, on the other hand, have restored, or tried to restore, their liberties. Now we are going to represent them again. The people are behind us."

The members of the Convention gathered in Aguascalientes' Morelos Theater on October 10, 1914. Though Villa sent a large delegation, the Carrancista chiefs held a substantial majority. Nor did the arrival of 26 Zapatistas, led by Díaz Soto y Gama and Paulino Martínez, give Carranza's enemies control of the Convention. Nonetheless, the delegates warmly applauded Martínez' attack on the liberal Plans of San Luis Potosí and Guadalupe. The real needs of the people, he insisted, were for "bread and justice." The Zapatistas, he said, had fought to get "a home for every family and a piece of bread for all those who have been deprived of their heritage." At the Zapatistas' invitation, the assembly joined to embrace the Plan of Ayala "in principle." When Carranza protested in Mexico City against the Convention's independence and announced that he was "inclined" to resign as First Chief of the Constitutionalist forces, the delegates quickly accepted his "resignation" and designated a minor military chief, Eulalio Gutiérrez, as Provisional President. Thereupon, Carranza declared the Convention in rebellion and ordered his representatives to withdraw from Aguascalientes. Some refused and joined with Villa and Zapata to oppose the First Chief. Obregón found himself in a quandary. He had insisted in Mexico City that the military take control of the revolution and had proposed Gutiérrez' candidacy as provisional president. But he could not abide Villa's lawlessness, and when he was forced in late 1914 to choose between Carranza and Villa, he reluctantly declared his support for the First Chief. This was a most fateful decision in the history of the Revolution, for Obregón proved to be Mexico's greatest military commander.

As the year ended, the victorious Revolution turned upon itself. Great and bloody battles were fought, more destructive than any others in Mexico's history. At first Villa and Zapata held an overwhelming military advantage. Carranza was forced to move his headquarters to Veracruz and to give the Americans the guarantees that he had earlier refused. The Sovereign Convention, now made up principally of Villistas and Zapatistas, began in Mexico City to write a program of reform based on the Plan of Ayala. Carranza, seeking national support for his Constitutionalist government, decreed his own emendations of the Plan of Guadalupe, promising the restoration of village lands illegally taken during the Díaz regime.

Meanwhile, Villa and Zapata met at Xochimilco near Mexico City to plan their military campaign. With fraternal cordiality they agreed to join forces in a mighty coalition against the armies of Carranza. But the accord between north and south at Xochimilco failed to bear fruit. Both chiefs returned to their own bailiwicks, and, as their fortunes waned in 1915, each complained bitterly about the perfidy of the other. In Mexico City the Convention split along a similar fault—the Zapatistas and Villistas could not cooperate even to complete the reform program. At the same time, the Constitutionalist armies, supplied from Veracruz, began to win battles. In April 1915 Obregón twice defeated Villa's Division of the North at Celaya. And on August 2, after the capital had changed hands several times, Pablo González' troops occupied Mexico City. Though Zapata continued to control Morelos, and Villa operated with impunity in the north, it was clear by late 1915 that Carranza had won. Reluctantly, Woodrow Wilson's government accepted the fait accompli and extended diplomatic recognition to the First Chief's regime.

Angered by the support given to his enemies, Villa turned savagely on the United States, killing American civilians and raiding an American border town, Columbus, New Mexico. President Wilson's reaction was immediate and forceful; he ordered troops under General John J. Pershing into Mexico to run down Villa and bring him to justice. But the advance of the Punitive Expedition was more like a Keystone Cops scenario than a serious military campaign. Supply trucks and airplanes broke down, and although Pershing's troops cut deep into Mexican territory, they never succeeded in bringing Villa to bay. Nor did Venustiano Carranza welcome the American assistance against Villa, for he insisted that the guerrilla was a Mexican problem to be solved by the Mexicans themselves. He threatened war against the United States and flirted with Imperial Germany, permitting the Germans to set up propaganda and espionage stations in Mexico. As the United States came closer to war in Europe, Wilson was forced to disentangle himself from the Mexican intervention. The chief accomplishment of Pershing's expedition was that its failure pointed up the shortcomings of the American army. During his second term Wilson had little time to concern himself with Mexican affairs.

Once again in Mexico City and in charge of a national government, Venustiano Carranza kept the title of First Chief. There had been no true elections in the country since 1912, and he continued to govern by executive order, as he had in Veracruz. But Carranza's agrarian reform decrees, which had been issued in extremis, were now forgotten. For the First Chief, municipal freedom (eliminating the jefes políticos) and a divorce law were more important than the ending of peonage. Still, he could not maintain indefinitely the extra-constitutional position of First Chief without a congress and courts. At the same time, few revolutionaries would return to the Constitution of 1857, which had imposed debilitating restrictions on the chief executive. Through the first months of 1916 Carranza's civilian advisers campaigned in the Republic's newspapers for a new constitution to strengthen the president's hand in dealing with the Congress. Félix F. Palavicini, an engineer, wrote that the executive power's weakness had compelled both Juárez and Díaz to resort to dictatorial rule. Carranza agreed; moreover, he needed a new constitution to give legal sanction to the measures he had decreed as First Chief.

In September 1916 the First Chief convoked an election for a Constituent Congress, and balloting took place in October. It was to be a revolutionary assembly, made up solely of representatives from the Constitutionalist faction; there would be no Porfiristas, Huertistas, Zapatistas, Villistas, or Catholic delegates. The balloting was relatively free, however, and Carrancistas of many different political views were elected to the assembly. If the First Chief had wanted to control the delegates, he should have imposed candidates on the voters. But he believed, naively as it turned out, that the Mexican populace would prefer his own brand of constitutionalism. Yet when the congress met in Querétaro on December 1, the radical delegates quickly took control of the proceedings, naming the presiding officers and the committees charged with reforming each article. An acrimonious wrangling ensued over the presence of Maderista deputies (*Renovadores*), who had stayed in the Chamber under Huerta. After Carranza intervened personally on their behalf, however, the Congress agreed to seat the liberal delegates.

The First Chief presented the Congress with a ready-made Constitution, which had been prepared by his civilian advisers, chiefly José N. Macías. Except for those sections that strengthened the executive power, it was essentially a liberal document, differing little from the Constitution of 1857. The Congress accepted most of the articles intact, thus continuing the federal system in Mexico. But a committee headed by Francisco J. Múgica drastically revised several key articles to make possible radical social reforms and to give the country a completely new type of constitution. No longer were the rights of the Mexican people anchored firmly to the bedrock of Natural Law; rather, they were subject to the shifting sands of legislative caprice. Mexicans possessed those rights "guaranteed in this Constitution"; but Congress and the states could easily amend the Constitution, and in the next half-century did so more than a hundred times, often to the detriment of individual liberties.

The most heated debate in the Congress took place with the introduction by Múgica's committee of a reformed Article 3, dealing with education. The radicals proposed to exclude the Church from all elementary instruction—which meant, in effect, virtually all education in Mexico before the 1920s. Carranza came to Querétaro to manifest his disapproval of this restriction, and Carrancista delegates, such as Palavicini, spoke eloquently and at great length for the religious freedoms of nineteenth-century liberalism. But the liberals' impassioned oratory was in vain, and even the glowering Olympian presence of the First Chief failed to deter the majority from their radical aims—to cripple the Church and to protect Mexican women and children from priestly influences. Álvaro Obregón, Carranza's powerful Minister of War, sent a message to the Congress, commending the delegates' radicalism. At one point the Congress came close to imposing a married clergy on the Church in Mexico and ending oral confession (which gave the priests, the delegates felt, a heaven-sent opportunity to seduce women in the confessional). After many coarse jests at clerical concupiscence (Why should we be "procurers of fresh meat for the priests?" asked a Yucatecan.), the Congress rejected this proposal and turned to more serious measures. But after the delegates accepted Article 3, there was little difficulty with other recommendations from Múgica's committee. The liberals saw which way the ideological winds blew, and they realized that further resistance was useless.

In Article 27 the Congress provided a legal basis for agrarian reform and for the nationalization of Mexico's natural resources—chiefly the oil industry. (The delegates understood that this land reform was based on Carranza's earlier Veracruz decrees.) Article 123 gave Mexico a charter of freedom for labor, providing for the legalization of unions, for hours and wages legislation, and for the protection of women and children in industry. Article 130 was a grabbag of restrictions on the Catholic Church. No longer were Church and State to be independent. Instead, the government would take clear jurisdiction over all religious affairs in the Republic. Religious political parties were banned; priests could not discuss political matters in the pulpit, and they were forbidden to wear their clerical garb outside the churches; there could be no public religious processions; and each state had the power to limit the number of priests, according to the "needs of the people."

In the Constitution of 1917 the basic principles of the Floresmagonistas and of Villa and Zapata won a victory denied the Convention's troops on the field of battle. But where the Zapatistas had imposed a parliamentary system with a weak presidency on the Convention in Mexico City, the delegates to Querétaro recognized the need for a strong executive. Thus, the military triumph of Carranza's Constitutionalists assured civilian government in Mexico under a federal system, but made possible extensive reforms whenever the President should decide to use his powers. Carranza promulgated the new constitution on February 5, to take effect on May 5—the anniversary of the French defeat at Puebla in 1862. And under the constitution, Carranza now assumed office as legal president with a four-year term.

The reforming articles of the Constitution brought protests both inside and outside the Republic. Churchmen vowed opposition to Articles 3 and 130, and the bishops issued a pastoral letter (prudently from San Antonio, where many were in exile), declaring that they could never accept the restrictions imposed in the Constitution. The American oil companies expressed alarm at the possibility of expropriation, and the United States Senate, controlled by the Republicans, launched an investigation of Mexican affairs. A subcommittee headed by Albert B. Fall of New Mexico (who had landholdings in Mexico) called for military intervention if the Mexican government should implement Article 27 to attack American properties.

Though Carranza had not wanted the radical articles, he had to accept the constitution. He could not, however, be forced to implement them. Each article required enabling legislation from the Congress, and no laws appeared during the remaining years of Carranza's administration. Although he had urged a strengthened executive on the Constituent Congress in 1916, in office he proved as inept as Madero, and his flaccid leadership allowed the country to slip perilously close to anarchy. Military chiefs governed the states and carved out independent satrapies, enriching themselves at the expense of the Revolution's enemies. A new word was coined to describe conditions in Mexico—*carrancear*—meaning to steal. Not that Carranza was dishonest, but he could not restrain his subordinates. Travel was unsafe and trains required military escorts. Villa maintained his guerrilla forces in the north, and though a government agent assassinated Zapata in 1919, Morelos was still controlled by the southern chief's followers. Public education deteriorated, as Carranza's government turned the schools over to town ayuntamientos, which had no funds to support them. (In 1919 the education budget was only a tenth of that proposed by Huerta seven years earlier.) By 1920 Mexico was near collapse—the consequence of ten years of disorder, of the federal system, and of a weak chief executive.

As the presidential elections approached, Carranza promised continued civilian control of the federal government. He proposed as the official candidate, Ignacio Bonillas, a nonentity without a revolutionary background, while Álvaro Obregón entered the campaign as an opposition candidate. When it became apparent that Carranza's Minister of Gobernación (Interior) would control the elections and impose Bonillas on the country, Obregón turned to revolution once more, proclaiming his Plan of Agua Prieta. Widespread military support for Obregón assured the defeat of Carranza. Fleeing Mexico City, the President was captured and shot by army officers loyal to Obregón. The death of Carranza ended an era for Mexico. He had defeated Huerta, Villa, and Zapata, had held off the United States, and had brought the Mexican nation a new constitution. But the President was a troglodyte in the twentieth century, truly Mexico's "last liberal." The future belonged to the younger and more radical revolutionaries, above all to Álvaro Obregón and the military commanders of the northwest.

Obregón's presidency brought peace and stability to the war-wracked country and made possible a nationalistic renaissance in literature and the arts. Mexico had undergone a cataclysmic social change in the ten years since the overthrow of Porfirio Díaz. The population dropped more than 800,000 in that period, because of war casualties, malnutrition, or actual starvation, and the exiling or expatriation of Mexicans in all social classes. Landowners lost their properties, more through direct seizures by military chiefs than by legal procedures under the constitution. An important segment of Mexico's professional classes was replaced—in the bureaucracy, the army, the universities, and industry. Realizing that the moment was ripe for a national conciliation, for an end to revolutionary enmities and the start of reconstruction, Obregón proclaimed an amnesty throughout the Republic and brought Villistas and Zapatistas into his government. The Revolution's exiled enemies— the Catholic prelates, Porfiristas, and Huertistas—were free to return to Mexico. And Obregón's pacification facilitated the growth of a labor organization (CROM) and the beginnings of legal agrarian reform.

Obregón's most significant accomplishment was the creation of a national system of education. He named as his Minister of Public Instruction, José Vasconcelos, a philosopher-revolutionary who had served briefly in the Conventionist cabinet of Eulalio Gutiérrez. With great confidence, Vasconcelos turned to the formidable task of regenerating Mexico through educational reforms. In the manner of the sixteenth-century spiritual conquerors, he sent forth cultural missions that would bring modern education to every hamlet in Mexico. If his accomplishments failed to match his enthusiasm, at least Vasconcelos set the educational pattern for decades to come. The rural schoolteacher became a modern-day apostle, carrying to the peasant classes the Revolution's redeeming message.

Through his patronage of the arts, Vasconcelos brought to the public the revolutionary ideals of social change. He commissioned Diego Rivera, José Clemente Orozco, David Siqueiros, and other artists to ornament the walls of the nation's public buildings. Mexicans who could not read or write would be taught the truths of the Revolution by these magnificent murals. The nationalistic artists exalted the Mexican, and especially the Indian, at the expense of gachupines and other foreigners. In his own writings, Vasconcelos rejected the current social Darwinism of Madison Grant, Edward A. Ross, and other American writers to proclaim the excellence of the Latin Americans—the "Cosmic Race," the hope for the future of mankind. With Mariano Azuela and Martín Luis Guzmán, the revolutionary novel emerged, stressing, somewhat sardonically perhaps, the shortcomings of military chieftains and the need for personal reformation in the Revolution. Composers such as Silvestre Revueltas and Carlos Chávez looked to indigenous, and especially preconquest music for inspiration. Encouraged by Vasconcelos, Chávez wrote a Mexican ballet, El Fuego Nuevo. And the painter, Dr. Atl, sought to generate interest in folk culture by publishing in 1922 his Popular Arts in Mexico. In the early 1920s educators, writers, and artists demonstrated the need for self-esteem among the Mexicans and the Revolution's admiration of the Indian and of the indigenous culture.

Obregón's conciliation policy allowed the Catholic Church, after a false start in the Madero era, to develop its program of Social Action. Because Pius IX's Syllabus of Errors had rejected all modern secular answers to the "Social Question," there was no place for Catholic action to seek inspiration except from the Middle Ages. What the Mexican Catholics strove for in the 1920s was the reconstruction of the medieval polity. They found in the centuries before the Renaissance and Reformation a golden age, an era of unity, of love, of orthodoxy. With the guild they hoped to reestablish the system of labor management relations which they felt had been so successful during the Middle Ages. They condemned the Revolution for its advocacy of class conflict and rejected radical overtures toward a classless society or toward a society dominated by the proletariat. The Church held that society was by nature a fellowship of classes, which must be hierarchically organized. God made some men to lead, others to follow. The lower classes must know their place; at the same time the ruling classes should heed their duties toward their inferiors. Christian lovingkindness would guide the relations among the various classes. All of the organizations formed by the Social Action movement in the 1920s were based on the medieval ideal of ruler and ruled. And at the apex of the social pyramid stood the princes of the Church, for the prelates made clear that they would exercise close control over Social Action and, through the movement, over society itself. Laymen held titular positions, but the clergy controlled key offices in the workers' circles, the agrarian groups, and even Damas Católicas.

If the intentions of Social Action were pious, the methods proposed by the Catholics could not succeed in a land convinced of class antagonisms—and in which few men were regular church-goers. The priests relied too much on the Christian spirit. In the rural areas the hacendado would act as a big brother to his inferiors. In the guilds of bosses and workers the wolf was to labor with the sheep. Social Action in Mexico offered reforms—land for the landless and decent laboring conditions in factories—but so slowly as to be virtually unattainable by the present generation. Mexican peasants and urban workers could not wait. It was the secular unions and the government agrarian program that promised here-and-now success. In the end, the Social Action program came to naught, and an open clash in 1926 between the revolutionary government and the Catholic Church destroyed all hope of Christian reform.

The victory of revolutionary reform was also more apparent than real in the early 1920s, for the new radical spirit did little to improve the condition of the poorer classes. Though Obregón had supported the reformers at Querétaro, he was no doctrinaire radical. He favored compromise whenever possible. And the immediate problems of his administration were fiscal and political. His coming to power coincided with the world-wide recession at the end of World War I, and Mexico's economy, badly damaged in the years of revolution, was hard hit by the slump in the silver, copper, and lead markets. The government could not take forcible reform measures without money, and increased revenues depended upon a sound tax structure. At the same time, the country had no true parties, for the long dictatorship had destroyed the Liberal Party of the nineteenth century, and in the ten years of civil war there had been no opportunity to construct a party system. During the campaigns of 1917 and 1920 the parties had been personalistic, jerrybuilt for the sole purpose of electing Carranza and Obregón. Through the decade of the 1920s the national administrations found it impossible to put together congressional coalitions that could carry out the revolutionary program.

For most of his presidency Obregón faced the threat of hostility from the United States, which refused to recognize him lest he apply Article 27 to American-owned property. Woodrow Wilson had withheld recognition from Huerta in 1913 because of his part in the murder of Madero. It was a moral act by a highly moralistic president. The Harding administration justified its refusal to recognize Obregón on the same grounds—the death of the constitutional president. But in fact Washington was more concerned with protecting American business interests in Mexico, especially the valuable petroleum properties. (The subsequent Teapot Dome scandal showed that the influence of the oil industry reached to the highest levels of the American government.) For nearly three years the two countries discussed recognition and American damage claims before the Mexican negotiators caved in under the relentless American pressure, agreeing that the restrictions on foreign oil holdings would not be retroactive. As Washington and Mexico City appointed new ambassadors, a serious revolt imperiled Obregón's government. When the President named Plutarco Elías Calles as his successor, a disgruntled candidate, Adolfo de la Huerta, proclaimed a revolution and took many leading generals into the field with him. American recognition and arms support came at an opportune time for Obregón. He was able to beat down the challenge and restore peace in time to hand the reins of government to Calles. But he had had no chance in his four-year term to bring tangible reform to Mexico, and he passed on his political and fiscal problems to his successor.

Like Obregón, the new chief executive was a revolutionary general from Sonora. He had played only a small part in the military conflicts, however, and he owed his position to Obregón's determination to continue the domination of the northern dynasty. Calles had served effectively in Obregón's cabinet as Minister of Gobernación. Under Calles the corruption that had characterized the previous administration became even more blatant. The President acquired estates in all parts of the Republic, while his associates in the government, and even the head of the national labor union, Luis Morones, had ample opportunity to accumulate wealth. Calles was a cynical, ruthless politician who could destroy his enemies with no qualms of conscience. He was also a confirmed anticleric. While Obregón had preferred to restrain the priests through a reasonable compromise, Calles would demolish the Church structure and eliminate religious influences from Mexican society. Mexico has had little reason since the 1920s to honor the spirit of Calles, for one does not willingly erect statues to cynicism. Yet Calles did make positive contributions to Mexico's political and economic development, and his administration laid the foundation for Lázaro Cárdenas' radical reforms in the next decade and for the stability enjoyed in Mexico after 1940.

For nearly two years the Calles government devoted its attention to fiscal matters—reforming the tax structure, repairing the economic damages suffered during the revolt of 1923, and founding national and agricultural banks. It introduced the first real income and industrial taxes. Calles imposed national civilian control over the armed forces, which had been fiercely loyal to regional chiefs. He initiated road-building and irrigation programs. And the Congress, in the last months of 1925, took the first tentative steps to implement those articles of the Constitution dealing with agrarian reform, factory regulation, and foreign oil holdings. But even a strong chief executive such as Calles could not induce or compel the Congress to pass effective reform laws. There were too many parties, and factions within parties, all of them undisciplined. A minority could stymie legislation by leaving the Chamber or Senate, thus breaking the legal quorum. When Calles indicated that he intended to impose Obregón as his successor, the legislators proved to be even more recalcitrant. Only with great difficulty could Calles persuade Congress to amend the Constitution to allow the reelection of the former president. At the same time, the presidential term was extended to six years. The weakness of the political system was not remedied until 1929 when Calles summoned a national convention to create a united revolutionary party.

As Calles moved in late 1925 to enforce the reform articles of the constitution, he brought to a head two crucial problems—the petroleum and Church questions—and these two problems occupied the government for the last two years of his administration. The foreign oil companies resisted a decree that required them to exchange their titles for 50-year leases, regarding it as a delayed expropriation of their properties. The American Department of State worked energetically to induce the Mexican government to abrogate the decree, and the tocsin of military intervention was sounded once more in the United States. Benjamin L. Fairchild, a New York Congressman, likened Mexico to a "sore fist thrust up into the very bowels of the United States," while Secretary of State Frank B. Kellogg condemned the "bolshevik" government in Mexico City. Instead of troops, however, Calvin Coolidge sent Dwight Morrow, a Wall Street financier, as ambassador to Mexico to deal with the oil question. With tact and skill, Morrow persuaded Calles to modify his government's stand, and the compliant Mexican Supreme Court decided that the lease decree was not retroactive. Those companies that had taken positive steps to exploit their holdings might keep them. The problem of the Church was not so easily solved, however, even by such a skilled mediator as Ambassador Morrow.

The Constitution of 1917, if enforced, endangered the existence of the Catholic Church in Mexico. The failure of Congress to implement the offending articles and the conciliatory policies of Álvaro Obregón postponed the inevitable showdown between Church and State, but through the early 1920s tensions built up on both sides. The Catholic Action leaders condemned the Revolution's reform program and the secular school system, and the bishops threatened excommunication against those who accepted lands under the agrarian laws. Calles, while Minister of Gobernación, ordered the expulsion of the Vatican's apostolic delegate in 1923 and, in the following year, severely restricted the activities of a Mexican Eucharistic Congress. As a result, Catholic laymen formed a militant national organization to "protect religious liberties."

In early 1926 an enterprising reporter for a Mexico City newspaper, *El Universal*, asked José Mora y del Río, the Archbishop of Mexico, if the prelates maintained their opposition to the Constitution of 1917. The publication of the archbishop's affirmative reply drew thunderbolts of condemnation from Calles. As though he had been awaiting the opportunity to strike at the Church, he issued decrees to implement key sections of the Constitution. In the succeeding months, Calles ordered the expulsion of foreign clergy and nuns, an end to religious education, and the forced registration of priests in charge of the churches (which were considered state properties). The bishops retaliated by withdrawing the priests from churches—in effect declaring a Church strike. They hoped that the Mexican people, deprived of masses and sacraments, would force the government to back down. At the same time, the lay leaders proclaimed a national economic boycott of local Catholics, and in various parts of the Republic Catholics took up arms, seeking to overturn the revolutionary regime by military action.

In the United States Catholic bishops and laymen launched a campaign to aid the beleaguered Catholics of Mexico. The Knights of Columbus voted to amass a "war chest" of $1,000,000 for their Mexican coreligionists. Michael J. Curley, Archbishop of Baltimore, denounced the "bolsheviks" in Mexico, and Francis C. Kelley, Bishop of Oklahoma, called upon Calvin Coolidge to break diplomatic relations with the Calles regime. Congressman John J. Boylan of New York demanded that the United States government "take prompt steps to protect its citizens in Mexico." But the anguished protests of American Catholics brought no echoes of popular support in the United States in an era of widespread anti-Catholicism when the Ku Klux Klan was influential even in the northern states. Most American Protestants felt that the Catholic Church in Mexico deserved its fate. Catholic laymen such as William F. Buckley used the oil controversy to drum up support for an attack on the Calles government. (Buckley had extensive Mexican oil properties.) But the settlement of that issue by Morrow meant that the Church crisis would be resolved in Mexico, and by the Mexicans. Though the Church strike dragged on for three years, it was evident from the beginning that the Catholics could not win their battle. The absence of priests meant little to Mexicans for whom the image of a saint was more important than a sacrament or a mass. The economic boycott failed because it received little national support. To buy no more than the bare necessities of life was already the custom of most Mexicans. And the Catholic rebels—called Cristeros from their battle cry, "Long live Christ the King!"—were too poorly armed and led to defeat the regular army troops. Ambassador Morrow brought representatives of both sides together, and, after lengthy negotiations, the prelates agreed in 1929 to register the priests as Calles had demanded, while the government consented to the teaching of religious classes within the churches.

In 1927, at the height of the Cristero insurgency, Álvaro Obregón began his presidential campaign. Two generals, Francisco Serrano and Arnulfo R. Gómez, opposed his candidacy. Because Obregón was more conciliatory than Calles, many Catholics looked forward to a rapprochement between the Church and the revolutionary government. Though neither of the opposition candidates could hope to win, Calles took no chances. He accused Gómez and Serrano of plotting a rebellion, and the two generals were seized and shot without a trial—ostensibly while "trying to escape." The unopposed election of Obregón in 1928 seemed to presage six more years of strong revolutionary rule in Mexico. But before he could take office, the victorious candidate was shot and killed by a young Catholic fanatic. As a result, the Church was forced to pass under the yoke of Calles' demands. Many politicians believed that Calles would impose his own candidacy in a new election. He did not do so, however, for he was content to run the show as Jefe Máximo behind the scenes, pulling the strings for a succession of puppet chief executives—Emilio Portes Gil, Pascual Ortiz Rubio, and Abelardo Rodríguez. In 1929 Calles formed a grand coalition of his supporters into the National Revolutionary Party (PNR), which, with two reorganizations and changes in name, has governed Mexico since that date.

The presidential campaign of 1929 pitted Ortiz Rubio, a revolutionary general, against José Vasconcelos, who had given up his allegiance to the Revolution. Vasconcelos toured the countryside, attacking the corruption of the Calles regime. In the rigged elections he received only a handful of votes. The defeated candidate retired to the United States, hoping for a new revolution which never came. Embittered by defeat and rejection, the educator-philosopher became increasingly anti-American, antisemitic, and conservative. In the semifictional autobiography, *Ulises Criollo*, he poured out his venom on his fellow revolutionaries. He wrote a history of Mexico, attributing his country's ills to Jewish Wall Street capitalists. And in 1940 he edited a pro-Nazi journal, *El Timón*, that was financed by the German embassy in Mexico City. Vasconcelos' fall from revolutionary grace could not obscure his educational accomplishments in the early 1920s, however, and he remains for Mexicans one of the towering figures in the nation's literary history.

By the early 1930s the revolutionary spirit seemed to have fallen prey to the corruption and cynicism of Calles' strong-arm rule. Politicians and unscrupulous labor union leaders flaunted their wealth. Agrarian reform and factory legislation appeared to be lost causes. (Calles' attacks on the Church continued, however, despite the modus vivendi of 1929, with crippling restrictions on the numbers of priests who could function in the various states.) But a new generation, which had grown up since the Revolution of 1910, called for a national reformation, for a return to the ideals of Zapata and the radical revolutionaries. Many were Marxists who pressed for an overthrow of the capitalistic system in Mexico. To still dissent within the party and the government, Calles moved, in 1933, to erect a façade of revolutionary change. Article 3 of the Constitution was revised to eliminate the Church from secondary as well as primary education and to provide for, not merely secular but "socialistic" instruction in the nation's schools. And the Jefe Máximo designated a darkhorse candidate, Lázaro Cárdenas, for the presidential campaign of 1934.

Though Cárdenas' victory was assured, he campaigned vigorously throughout the Republic, and as President he continued to seek popular support for his policies. Cárdenas had served as a revolutionary commander in the campaigns against Villa, and he maintained his loyalty to Obregón and Calles during the 1920s, obtaining as his reward the governorship of his native state, Michoacán. Cárdenas had received only a primary school education, and he never grasped the complexities of national administration or of international relations. The eternal rustic, even in the highest office, Cárdenas favored agrarian and industrial socialism—small-scale enterprises, held communally by local groups. At the same time, he saw clearly the need for immediate and drastic reform and for enhancing Mexico's self-esteem. Samuel Ramos, a Mexican philosopher, described his people's malaise in *Profile of Man and Culture in Mexico* as a national "inferiority complex." This spiritual uncertainty grew worse in the 1930s with the onset of the Great Depression. Cárdenas set about to improve the nation's vigor and confidence. To give his government popular support, he encouraged parades and patriotic demonstrations in the cities and towns.

Calles had thought that he could manipulate the new president, as he had controlled Ortiz Rubio and Rodríguez, but Cárdenas, having assured himself of the army's loyalty, moved with dispatch to exile the Jefe Máximo. For the first time in Mexican history a strong populist executive committed his administration to effective social reform. Cárdenas formed a national peasant confederation and distributed more arable land to peasant villages than all of his predecessors together and more than any president since. He fostered a new labor confederation (CTM), headed by Vicente Lombardo Toledano, to supplant the corrupt organization of Luis Morones. He remodeled the official party to give it a popular base, and he brought religious peace to the country by restoring the modus vivendi of 1929. Thereafter, the Church did not openly oppose the Constitution; at the same time, a succession of chief executives winked at obvious violations of the national charter. Church schools, monasteries, and nunneries continued, despite legal prohibitions.

Cárdenas' most heralded accomplishments were the seizure of the nation's railways and the expropriation of most of the foreign oil holdings. Neither act was premeditated, and both were consequences of a labor-relations crisis. The nationalization of the oil properties led to the rupture of diplomatic relations between Mexico and Great Britain and threatened possible American intervention. Mexico stood firm, however, and the American ambassador, Josephus Daniels, helped bring about an equitable settlement. If the immediate economic impact of expropriation was insignificant, the effect on Mexico's confidence was considerable. Despite dire predictions of catastrophe, the government oil company, Petróleos Mexicanos, proved (after a shaky start) to be an outstanding success. With reason the Mexicans built the monument to the expropriation on the Paseo de la Reforma, for it symbolized the pride of a newly vigorous nation. The industrial transformation of Mexico began in 1938 as Cárdenas took over these foreign properties.

When Cárdenas' term of office ended in 1940, Mexico reached a crucial moment in its revolutionary history. As though spent by six furious years of radical enthusiasm, the Revolution collapsed. The workers and peasants who had benefitted by Cárdenas' reforms hoped to consolidate their gains. General Francisco J. Múgica, the radical hero of the constitutional congress of 1916–17, had aspired to be the official candidate for the presidency. Instead, Cárdenas chose his Secretary of War, Manuel Ávila Camacho, a conservative general of no great distinction. Dissident factions supported Juan Andrew Almazán, a protean revolutionary, who at different times in his career had supported Orozco, Huerta, Zapata, Obregón, and Calles. The campaign was violent, the oratory vituperative, but Ávila Camacho's victory was a foregone conclusion. Almazán, from the sanctuary of American territory, proclaimed the election fraudulent and called for a military revolt, but his voice went unheeded in Mexico, and the Franklin D. Roosevelt administration demonstrated its backing for Ávila Camacho by sending Vice-President Henry Wallace to his inauguration.

With Ávila Camacho the Revolution veered to the right. Though the old slogans remained and could be used to good effect in political oratory, economic growth and especially industrial development became the chief aims of the Mexican government. As the old revolutionaries died off, a new generation pushed its way to the front—young lawyers and engineers and practical men of business, educated in the nation's universities and technological institutions. Though Mexico's political leaders wielded great power, they were no longer formed in the Revolution's heroic mold. Mountains of statistics and a constantly rising GNP, not military victories, became the mark of success in Mexico. And with its new generation of technicians Mexico emerged as one of the most dynamic and progressive of the world's developing nations. Maintaining a balanced budget and an excellent credit rating, the government, in the eyes of many critics, had come full circle to the values espoused during the Porfirian regime—material progress for the propertied classes. The Revolution, they lamented, had died. The Mexicans who ran and supported the government, however, said that it had merely been "institutionalized."

7

The Revolution Institutionalized

Between 1940 and 1970 Mexico's political leaders presided over the transformation of their country from a weak, insecure nation into one of the most stable and economically sound republics in the Western Hemisphere. Five chief executives—Manuel Ávila Camacho, Miguel Alemán, Adolfo Ruiz Cortines, Adolfo López Mateos, and Gustavo Díaz Ordaz—dedicated their administrations to Mexico's economic growth, for they felt that unless the country industrialized it must remain a backward colonial nation. Though each president gave lip service to agrarian reform, the largest part of the federal government's annual expenditures went to promote the development of basic industries (steel, iron, petroleum, and concrete) and, ultimately, the production of consumer goods. During the three decades the population more than doubled. By the late 1960s the Gross National Product increased at the rate of at least 6% a year. The results were obvious in the Republic's cities—new factories, office and apartment buildings, department stores and supermarkets, and a plethora of automobiles. Mexico paid a stiff price for this rapid industrialization—the country could not afford factories and, at the same time, high wages for urban and rural laborers. Lázaro Cárdenas lived on into the new era, and became a partisan of Castro's Cuban Revolution, but by the time of his death in 1970 his voice counted for little in a Mexico which had long since passed him by. Yet it was Cárdenas who, perhaps unwittingly, had marked out the new direction by forcing the selection of Ávila Camacho as his successor thirty years earlier.

Born in Puebla in 1897, Ávila Camacho was too young to have

played an important role in the first decade of the Revolution. But because he had enlisted in the Constitutionalist Army while still in his teens, he could lay claim to the magical title of Revolutionary, an important requirement for the presidency in 1940. Ávila Camacho rose to the rank of general during the 1920s and commanded government troops in the desultory campaign against Cristero rebels in the state of Colima before serving as Cárdenas' Secretary of War. By the time he assumed the presidency, Ávila Camacho had become a wealthy man, conservative in his social and religious outlook. "I am a believer!" he proclaimed in a campaign speech. During his administration the storms of anticlericalism abated, as the Congress modified the most radical provisions of Article 3. Teaching in the Mexican schools need no longer be "socialistic." Ávila Camacho's Secretary of Education, Jaime Torres Bodet, promoted a nationwide campaign against illiteracy. Increasingly, however, after 1940 the government turned its attention to industrial development.

Participation in World War II helped Mexico along its new economic path. The Ávila Camacho government broke relations with the Axis powers soon after the Japanese attack on Pearl Harbor and in 1942, when a German submarine sank a Mexican tanker, declared war against the enemies of the United States. Mexico's military contributions were slight—doctors and an air squadron participated in the Philippine campaign. Even more important was the decision to unite Mexican and American interests, to accept at face value Franklin D. Roosevelt's Good Neighbor Policy, and to forget or overlook century-old enmities between the two countries. Mexico agreed to supply minerals and agricultural products needed in the war effort. For its part, the United States aided in the development of native Mexican industries. By 1946 Mexico was well committed to industrialization, and thereafter there could be no turning back.

By reforming the official party Ávila Camacho confirmed the shift in emphasis and priorities. Where Cárdenas had balanced the influences of the military, the labor unions, the agrarian groups, and the "popular sectors" (government employees and private citizens), Ávila Camacho downgraded the army, removing the military from the political arena. As a consequence, Mexico became a demilitarized nation (a rarity in Latin America), with a relatively small army that posed no threat to the rule of civilian administrators. Even small Guatemala, because of United States military assistance, had more up-to-date weaponry than the Mexicans.

The new political grouping became the Party of Revolutionary Institutions (PRI), a juggernaut which thereafter crushed its opposition in every national election. Despite the constitutional guarantees and the campaign oratory, few believed that balloting was free. The Secretary of

Gobernación, charged with maintaining internal peace, wielded great power in the official party, and he dictated the outcome of elections at all levels, national and local. It was not without significance that after 1940 every presidential candidate but one (Adolfo López Mateos) had worked for his predecessor as Secretary of Gobernación. In the 1940s and 1950s opposition parties took shape, but because the outcome of elections was predetermined, these parties served only as democratic window dressing. Most and probably all of the parties drew some form of subsidy from the national government. The Party of National Action (PAN) represented the conservative, Catholic interests in Mexico. The Partido Popular (PP, and later Partido Popular Socialista, PPS), headed by Vicente Lombardo Toledano, was vaguely Marxist and allowed the critical left in Mexico a measure of respectability. The Authentic Party of the Mexican Revolution (PARM) gave voice to the discontent of Carrancista old-timers, who deserted the official party. Of these parties only PAN gained much popular support, and candidates from any of them took office solely through the acquiescence of PRI and the Secretary of Gobernación.

The election of Miguel Alemán in 1946 signified the exclusion of the soldier-politician from the presidency. The first civilian president of Mexico since Venustiano Carranza, Alemán put like-minded lawyers and technicians into positions of influence in his government. And though business had no organized representation in the official party, the President increasingly turned his ear to the advice, cajoleries, and blandishments of the new industrialists. Alemán used the considerable powers of the presidency to stimulate industrialization through preferential tariffs, import restrictions, and the allocation of raw materials and credits. He facilitated a resumption of foreign investments and promoted dam-building for irrigation and electrical power. At the same time, he began a campaign (expanded by his successors) to force the partial Mexicanization of important foreign businesses. His administration encouraged agricultural production by modifying the agrarian reform laws to allow moderately sized landholdings. Though the industrial growth of the country brought a marked rise in Mexico's standard of living in the succeeding decades, it also gave politicians unprecedented opportunities to acquire wealth. The administration of Alemán epitomized the corrupting influences of high office under a successful revolutionary government.

While official corruption was difficult to authenticate with facts and figures, few Mexicans denied its prevalence. In Mexico rumor and innuendo pass for coin of the realm, and it is unlikely that historians of the future will ever be able to document adequately stories of political intrigue or official peculation. Confiscating haciendas and dipping into the public tills, as in the days of Obregón and Calles, were forms of corruption outmoded in the more sophisticated fifties and sixties. A president or a cabinet minister who awarded a contract stood to gain personally through the transaction. When the chief executive could decide which automobiles might be produced in Mexico and which could not, it was hardly surprising to learn in the 1960s that a president had received half-interest in a foreign motor firm. Miguel Alemán came from a family with modest means and spent his adult years, before he became president, in public offices. Yet after six years as Chief Executive he could be counted among the most affluent of Mexicans.

If investment opportunities marked the path of high government and party officials, the public activities of minor bureaucrats presented similar, though less lucrative, opportunities. The bribe (in Mexico *mordida* or "bite") had long been an accustomed and accepted means of conducting public affairs. Now it became even more widespread. A businessman bought off a cabinet member, a defendant in a court case the judge, an erring motorist the traffic policeman, a tourist the border guard, a ship captain the port officials. There could be little doubt that a judicious *mordida* expedited transactions of all kinds and avoided the Kafkian maze of bureaucratic procedures. But the custom also corroded public regard for elected and appointed officials. Alemán's successor, Adolfo Ruiz Cortines, promised in his campaign speeches to end government corruption. Yet even this austere and honest president could not push back the sea. At the end of the 1960s the problem showed no signs of abating.

The campaign of 1952 was one of the most scurrilous and bitterly fought in Mexico's history. With corruption the chief issue the opposition parties outdid each other in attacking the Alemán regime and the government's candidate. The choice of Ruiz Cortines caused a group to break off from PRI to support the candidacy of General Miguel Henríquez Guzmán. The Henriquistas ridiculed Ruiz Cortines, calling him "The Mummy," because of his advanced age, and casting doubts on his virility. They charged that his selection was a plot to continue Alemán in power as another Jefe Máximo. Tanks and army planes assured peace as the Mexicans went to the polls in July. All opposition parties greeted the public announcement of Ruiz Cortines' victory with cries of fraud, and in the aftermath of the election several Henriquistas were killed in Mexico City. But the new president took firm charge of the government and subsequently outlawed the Henriquista party. He proved to be his own master, and though Miguel Alemán retained his influence in the official party, Ruiz Cortines gave the country vigorous leadership. To assure growing business profits he held down wages, and his government kept labor in check by controlling the union leaders and preventing strikes. Mexico devalued the peso in 1954 to encourage exports, reduce imports, and expand the profitable tourist trade. In his concern to build an industrial economy, Ruiz Cortines played down agrarian reform and handed on to his successor the critical problem of rural poverty.

A spectacular outburst of literary activity accompanied the economic growth of the 1950s, as novelists, poets, essayists, and philosophers searched for new modes of expression and in the process turned their attention inward, hoping to discover in themselves the essence of what was truly Mexican. The crisis of national self-awareness came at the end of World War II, because Mexico's leaders had brought their country into the orbit of the world's political and economic affairs. Mexico's young intellectuals—artists and writers alike—could no longer be satisfied by mere descriptions of revolutionary conditions in novels such as Martín Luis Guzmán's *Eagle and the Serpent* and Gregorio López y Fuentes' *Indian,* and by the bombastic murals and kitsch oil paintings of Diego Rivera. As a new generation of confident, civilian politicians took control of the Revolution, so the young intellectuals looked for assurances of their own and their nation's worth.

This search owed much to the awareness that Alemán and the new technocrats, like the Científicos a half-century earlier, seemed to be gringoizing Mexico. American material, and perhaps intellectual, culture threatened to engulf the country. The more Mexicans imitated and adopted Yankee ways—drinking Coca-Cola, eating Ritz Crackers and Kellogg's Corn Flakes, sleeping on Simmons mattresses, using white bread instead of tortillas, listening to American melodies on the radio rather than *ranchera* music, preferring a quick lunch to a large midday dinner at home, followed by a siesta—the more they denied the value of that which was Mexican. The republication of Ramos' *Profile of Man and Culture,* with its emphasis on Mexico's "inferiority complex," drove home the point that Americans had long depreciated the Mexican people. But the new movement also owed much to liberal refugees from the Spanish Civil War, especially José Gaos, teaching at the Colegio de México, who introduced his students to Ortega y Gasset and to the German philosophers, Husserl and Heidegger. In the fifties young Mexican intellectuals intoxicated themselves with heady brews of existentialism, phenomenology, Marxism, historicism, and anti-Americanism. The chief acolyte of the new cult was the Mexican philosopher, Leopoldo Zea, and the most important literary work was Octavio Paz' *Labyrinth of Solitude.*

A poet and quondam Marxist, Paz lived in the United States for two years on a Guggenheim Fellowship in the 1940s. Like Vasconcelos before him, Paz reacted against the blatant assumption of American superiority. In the plight of the Mexican-American "Pachucos" he discovered the key to the intellectual and psychological malaise of his own country. But where Vasconcelos stressed the physical superiority of the mestizo "race," Paz turned from the corporeal to the spiritual, and the magic mirror showed the Mexican to be fairest of all. In his *Labyrinth of Solitude* Paz both accepted and rejected Ramos' "inferiority complex." He recognized the obvious differences between the people of the United States and those of Mexico, in their values, their outlooks, and their ultimate aims in life. Because the traditional Mexican ways were different, he concluded that they were superior—more real, more eternal, reaching to the roots of things. If his countrymen appeared to have an inferiority complex, it was because of their suspicions of others. They wanted to protect themselves, to be "alone" and not "opened up." The man who allowed the outside world to penetrate his defenses felt himself emasculated—no longer *macho*. In his self-imposed isolation the Mexican probed for a sense of identity. But for Paz this was not enough. The Mexican must ultimately "open himself up" to the world, must find a "universal validity" in his situation, must stretch out his hands to other solitary peoples. To find the essence of *mexicanidad* was to discover the universal: World history had become "everyone's task," and the Mexican's labyrinth "the labyrinth of all mankind."

Paz' essay burst on the Mexican intellectual landscape like a brilliant fireworks display whose sparks and explosions touched off new essays, novels, short stories, and historical and philosophical writings. Though the Revolution continued to set the fictional pattern in Mexico, the novelists left Azuela and Guzmán far behind. Juan Rulfo, in *Pedro Páramo* (1955), focused on a revolutionary caudillo, but not in realistic, everyday terms. Time no longer had any meaning, nor did life and death, as characters inexplicably passed back and forth over the boundaries of the material and spiritual worlds. In *Where the Air Is Clear* (1958) and *The Death of Artemio Cruz* (1962) Carlos Fuentes also dealt with old caudillos, bitterly condemning the widespread cynicism and the corruption of the Revolution's true values. Both Rulfo and Fuentes tried to reach beyond the Mexican experience to give their writings universal relevance, for, in their eyes, the corruption in Mexico only reflected the decadence of bourgeois liberalism elsewhere in the world. But despite their attempts to extend Mexico's experience to the world, both remained Mexican and essentially inward-looking.

Leopoldo Zea made his mark more as a writer about philosophy and a literary entrepreneur, than as a practicing philosopher. A prolific author, Zea published two histories of Mexican thought, *Positivism in Mexico* (1943) and *Apogee and Decadence of Positivism in Mexico* (1944), before turning to studies of philosophy in Latin America. As he ticked off the Positivists' sins, he established the orthodox revolutionary view of Comtism during the Porfirian era. After World War II Zea became increasingly concerned with the crisis in Western Culture, for he believed that Mexico and the other Latin American countries could provide new answers to the chronic problems of civilization. But the philosophers, he felt, like the novelists, must first turn inward to discover that which was Mexican. In 1952 he launched an ambitious publication program with his series, *México y lo Mexicano*, small books to be written by his country's leading essayists, historians, and philosophers. Using Ramos as a point of departure, writers such as Emilio Uranga, Alfonso García Ruiz, and Jorge Carrión laid Mexico on the analyst's couch for a prolonged and intense examination of the nation's psyche. By reaching deep into the past, by discovering the causes of old traumas, Mexicans could be liberated, could shed the feelings of inferiority, insecurity, and resentment.

Mexico's great revolutionaries—Zapata, Villa, Obregón, and Cárdenas—had been self-made; they were men of action, not intellectuals. They created the Revolution by their deeds, without contemplation and agonizing rationalizations. And after 1940 the significant accomplishments, which determined the destinies of the Mexican people, were those of the hard-headed, practical men of business and the technocrats in the government. Unable to accept the modernization of their country's culture, unable to match the deeds of their fathers, the young intellectuals turned a national assessment into self-analysis, projecting their own doubts onto the psyche of the Mexican people. If they composed brilliant essays, full of scintillating insights, they were thinkers, not doers, speculators, not performers. Many became Marxists, though their Marxism was dilettantish, not violent or revolutionary. Eschewing palliatives that would leave the corrupt system intact, they dreamed of future cataclysms followed by miraculous personal redemptions. While they proclaimed the universality of Mexico's experience in self-analysis, they retreated ever deeper into self-isolation.

Thus, the intellectuals of the 1950s and early 1960s were, in the main, provincial. Their teachers and professors, even in the great National University, were almost all Mexicans—educated in the same institutions of higher learning. They studied and wrote only Mexican history. They had little interest in the leavening of foreign ideas through exchanges with universities abroad. An intellectual cactus curtain protected their country from the alien and dangerous influences north of the Río Bravo. Yet no amount of oratory or books could prevent the constant economic and cultural pressures of the United States. The contiguity of the two nations was an inescapable and undeniable fact of life for Mexico.

By the 1950s the great crises between the two countries had disappeared in the wake of the Good Neighbor Policy and the wartime cooperation against Germany and Japan. Thereafter, minor issues might trouble the diplomatic waters—shrimp fishing, bracero laborers, cotton prices, tomato imports, the salinization of the Colorado River—but all could be, and were eventually, settled by patient, if at times anguished, negotiations. If the Mexican economy grew spectacularly, the growth was due to the heroic endeavors of Mexico's political and business leaders, but also to the proximity of the United States—as a market (for cotton, sugar, cattle, seafood, and minerals), as a source of capital, as an escape valve for Mexican unemployment (the bracero program), and as a perpetual wellspring of tourism. Few countries in the world have taken tourism as seriously as Mexico, with advertising campaigns in the United States and an imaginative program of hotel construction and recreation facilities. The number of foreign tourists visiting Mexico annually, chiefly Americans, reached 700,000 by the end of the 1950s and in the following decade more than doubled. The money spent by tourists (perhaps $800,000,000 a year in the late 1960s) meant the difference between a balanced national budget and a chronic deficit.

At the same time, the diplomatic issues, which seemed picayune when viewed from Washington's world-wide perspective, were magnified in Mexico City. A minor change of policy, made by the American government for purely domestic reasons, could have considerable impact south of the Rio Grande. The dumping of surplus cotton on the international market to decrease American stocks forced down prices to the detriment of the Mexican producers. The reduction of the duty-free privileges in 1965 to $100 disturbed Mexico by reducing tourist spending. In 1969, at the instigation of Florida tomato growers, the Department of Agriculture restricted the importation of Mexican vine-ripened tomatoes—while Governor Nelson Rockefeller was visiting Mexico to determine how the Richard M. Nixon administration could improve relations with the Latin American nations. In the same year, the American Attorney-General's "Operation Intercept" subjected thousands of Americans and Mexicans crossing the border to prolonged delays and thorough searches in an effort to curtail illicit drug traffic from Mexico. And old dime-novel stereotypes lived on in the United States, as American television commercials featured Mexican cornchip bandits and lazy cigarette-smoking revolutionaries.

Not surprisingly, Mexicans became increasingly touchy as their country emerged into the 1960s from its period of introspection, defending its economic integrity and, simultaneously, reacting vigorously against slights and criticisms from the United States and from American citizens. The director of the Fondo de Cultura Económica, the largest and most prestigious publishing firm in Latin America, was forced out by the Mexican government in 1965 because he had issued a Spanish-language edition of Oscar Lewis' *Children of Sánchez*. Government censors refused permission to film Lewis' book in Mexico, because it denigrated the Mexican people. Frank Sinatra was barred from entering the country after one of his movies allegedly insulted Mexicans. Even

Mexican films came under the censor's ban, and, as Mexico prepared in the mid-1960s for the Olympic games and strove to create a favorable impression abroad, it was no longer possible to fashion such brilliant cinematic gems of social comment as "Los Olvidados" and "Yanco." A spokesman for the industry announced that Mexican films must give an "exact image of our country." In 1966 a well-meaning American industrialist collected tons of food and supplies for "famished" Tarahumara Indians in northwest Mexico. The Mexicans proudly spurned outside interference in what was considered an internal problem, however, and a train carrying the gifts was turned back at the border. The sensitivity extended to academic scholarship, as the government discouraged sociological research, which might call attention to continuing social problems in the country, and political science investigation into Mexico's electoral procedures.

The presidential election of 1958 contrasted strongly with that six years earlier, for the comparative austerity of Ruiz Cortines' administration had removed the issue of corruption from the campaigning. PRI chose as the official candidate Adolfo López Mateos, a middle-of-the-roader, who was acceptable both to the party's right, headed by former President Alemán, and to the left, which looked to Lázaro Cárdenas for leadership. López Mateos had served Ruiz Cortines as Minister of Labor and had been largely responsible for controlling the restive labor unions. The PRI candidate waged a strenuous campaign, but the absence of major issues gave the electioneering a lackluster quality shared by the opposition candidates. Like Cárdenas, López Mateos became a popular chief executive. An effective public speaker, he visited all sections of the country, dedicating a new dam or bridge, opening new schools or factories, and awarding to the campesinos land expropriated under the agrarian reform laws. Though many of the lands were non-productive, especially in the desert north, the López Mateos administration's agrarian program was more extensive than any since Cárdenas' days. The government also gained public approbation by negotiating the Mexicanization of the telephone and electric industries. In contrast to Ávila Camacho, Alemán, and Ruiz Cortines, López Mateos had a genuine interest in social reform. But his government's return to the policies of Cárdenas also reflected a serious economic crisis in the last months of 1961.

By 1960, as Mexico celebrated a half-century of revolution, the economic development achieved by the Alemán and Ruiz Cortines administrations had begun to lose its momentum. The annual growth rate, at times five or six percent through the 1950s, slipped to three percent—about equal to the yearly population increase. Prices, which had been favorable for exports after the peso's devaluation in 1954, climbed steadily without a compensatory increase in wages, and a decline in tourism in the last months of 1961 hit Mexico hard. The economic recession of 1961 coincided with two new pressures that made strong government action imperative—the revolution of rising expectations, as Mexicans demanded more consumer goods, and the Castro revolution in Cuba. After January 1, 1959, no responsible Latin American government could afford to ignore the expansion of Fidelismo. López Mateos' immediate response was positive but repressive. He dealt firmly with a rash of strikes, branding them illegal and jailing the labor leaders who had defied the government. He also imprisoned without trial leading radicals, including the painter David Siqueiros. The President made clear that he would not tolerate dissident activity that threatened the course of economic development. But he also ostentatiously embraced the cause of reform with a public announcement that his administration would move to the "extreme left within the Constitution." Overriding protests from the business community, the Congress pushed through legislation guaranteeing profit-sharing for the nation's workers. The government improved social security benefits and reemphasized its commitment to education by providing free books and breakfasts for students. The Constitution was amended to give an appearance of political democracy by the granting of increased congressional representation to minority parties. Despite the alarums raised by businessmen at the revived radicalism of the revolutionary government, however, López Mateos had no intention of downgrading economic development. By the end of his term of office in 1964 the nation had recovered, and the GNP annual increase surpassed six percent.

The popularity of López Mateos and his apparent success in pulling his country out of its brief recession pointed up both the strengths and weaknesses of the President's office. He was the most powerful man in the country, the leader of a government that brooked no real political opposition. He was the cynosure of public attention—always in the newsreels, on the television and radio, in the newspapers and periodicals. A village wanting a new water supply, a local politician aspiring to the governorship of his state, addressed petitions to Mexico City and to the President of the Republic. Respect for his person and his office ruled out public criticism, whatever his shortcomings. But he was also, in a sense, a prisoner of the system that chose him, and that he headed as Chief Executive. Because both extremes of the party exercised veto rights, the official candidate had to be a moderate. More, he could not risk offending influential politicians as he rose through the party ranks. A man did not become chief executive by bucking the system. No Mexican with the charismatic qualities of a Fidel Castro could achieve the presidency. And once he attained the highest office, the President lacked maneuverability. He had great power, but he could not use that power to offend or outrage important groups in the party or in public life.

López Mateos' successor, Gustavo Díaz Ordaz, fell into the same predicament—it was impossible to be bold and innovative. Had he so chosen, there was little that Díaz Ordaz could do to alter significantly the course set by his predecessors.

Gustavo Díaz Ordaz, from the state of Puebla, had served in López Mateos' cabinet as an efficient and, at times, ruthless Secretary of Gobernación. It was Díaz Ordaz who had silenced the government's most vociferous critics by jailing "Communists" and other "enemies" of the regime for "social dissolution." Leftists had predicted that his strong-arm tactics would damage him irreparably and that he could never be elected president, but he gained an easy victory in 1964 against slight opposition from PAN's ineffectual candidate, José González Torres. Lombardo Toledano's Partido Popular Socialista endorsed the official candidate and, as a reward, received ten seats in the Chamber of Deputies. PAN's twenty seats continued to give some semblance of opposition in the nation's congress. Díaz Ordaz inherited from López Mateos a going business concern. Though in his campaigning and in his early speeches as president he stressed the need for "integral" agrarian reform and a vast expansion of Mexico's secondary school system, he, like his predecessor, devoted most of his six-year term to industrial expansion. The annual GNP increase averaged more than six percent, and in some years surpassed seven percent.

Statistics and personal observations easily demonstrated the great strides taken by Mexico since the 1940s. The economy had been diversified to an extent unprecedented in a Latin American or, for that matter, any developing country. The 1960s saw the continued growth of basic industries—steel and cement for construction, and a new natural gas industry that produced enough fuel for Mexican needs and even allowed some exportation to the United States. At the same time, consumer-goods production mounted, and factories were established away from Mexico City to promote economic decentralization. Cuernavaca, Toluca, and Puebla became new industrial centers. Completion of the Malpaso hydroelectric plant and the Nezahualcóyotl Dam (fifth largest in the world) on the Grijalva River promised to speed up this decentralization. Agricultural production for export (cotton, coffee, tomatoes, citrus fruits, sugar) and for domestic markets (wheat, vegetables) climbed at an annual rate of four percent, largely because of irrigation, increased use of fertilizers, and better seeds. Mexico, once an importer of grains, became self-sufficient for most basic foodstuffs. (Maize shortages developed in the late 1960s, however, after a series of prolonged droughts interspersed with severe floods, and the crop failures necessitated a little-publicized importation program over several years.) Mexican agronomists worked with the 1970 Nobel Prize winner, Norman Borlaug and the Rockefeller Foundation to develop superior strains of dwarf wheat that could be grown not only at home but in countries such as Pakistan. The peso remained sound after the 1954 devaluation and by the 1960s served international banking agencies as a lending currency. Mexico, by the dint of hard work, had earned an excellent international credit rating. Through its agency, Nacional Financiera, the government took the leading role in directing this economic development—borrowing money abroad, encouraging domestic investments, and channeling funds to those industries that would most benefit the nation.

The rise in the standard of living was apparent everywhere, as Mexicans were better dressed, ate better food, lived in more modern houses, and bought radios, television sets, and even automobiles in ever greater numbers. The government supplemented working-class incomes with social security benefits (hospitalization and mobile food stores), subsidized entertainment in movie theaters (most tickets cost four pesos or 32 American cents), and free entertainment and instruction in the public parks. Though critics of the government decried the "bread and circuses," pointing to the problem of endemic poverty, there can be no doubt that most Mexicans lived better and longer than ever before.

Yet the vexing problems (old and new) showed no signs of disappearing. Though the level of support for social services continued to be high, too much of the federal budget went to debt servicing. Factors beyond the control of the Mexicans limited export trade—the reluctance of the United States to give Mexico's manufactured goods preferential treatment and the nationalistic jealousies and economic balkanization of Latin America, which prevented the formation of an effective Free Trade area. Internally there remained an obvious disparity of income, a yawning gap between the rich and the poor. Not that the rich got richer and the poor poorer, but the gap never narrowed appreciably. Compared with workers in the more advanced countries, Mexican labor was unproductive. Too many people performed useless or unneeded tasks—in a gasoline station, a bank, or a factory several men did the work of one. As a result, labor costs were high, despite low wages. Union leaders, many of them unmilitant hacks, showed little interest in improving the lot of the workers. The high prices of manufactured goods, coupled with the lack of buying power among the economically deprived classes, prevented the expansion of a mass market. Unless the rural and urban working classes could afford to buy an ever-increasing amount of consumer goods, production would be limited and prices would remain high.

Each chief executive taking office in the 1950s and 1960s publicly recognized the main problem facing his administration to be the agrarian sector. In 1965 Gustavo Díaz Ordaz declared that agrarian reform was either "complete or no reform at all." The situation had scarcely improved as he prepared to turn over the presidency to Luis Echeverría five years later. Even after fifty years of modernization and the Revolution's continued concern for the Indian population, perhaps a fifth of the Mexicans in the countryside remained marginal, taking little part in the economic or political affairs of the nation. The agrarian reform program, pushed by Cárdenas and his successors, could not be considered a success. Except for a few showcase ejidos, the cooperative farms fell short of the Revolution's goals, in part because they became entangled in politics, but also because of the campesinos' reluctance to modernize and cooperate. Many peasants distrusted the success of others, and all too frequently an enterprising man, a successful farmer or a bracero who had worked in the United States and had accumulated money, found himself compelled to waste it by paying for fiestas. Often campesinos saw the ejido as an opportunity to grow corn for their own consumption, rather than a more lucrative crop for sale. The largest part of Mexico's agricultural production came from private farms that made up less than ten percent of the rural landholdings. Despite continued and vigorous government action to increase agricultural production, the majority of the farmers resisted changes, preferring the familiar and age-old methods to the chemical fertilizers and modern technology. Nor did agrarian leaders fight effectively for the campesinos. Like the urban union leaders, many were politicians, lawyers, or intellectuals, who were more interested in agrarianism as a job than as a cause. The lack of opportunity in the countryside and the chronic poverty of the peasants drove more and more rural inhabitants to the cities, especially the nation's capital.

Improvements in sanitation and medical care reduced the death rate and permitted a constant population increase through the two decades after World War II. By the 1960s the annual increase had surpassed 3½%—one of the highest in the world. The demographic growth was most pronounced in the urban areas, already overcrowded through internal migration. Housing difficulties and other slum problems multiplied. Satellite cities grew and surrounded the older metropolis—Nezahualcóyotl adjoining Mexico City expanded in a decade from a few claim-jumpers to a population of more than a half million. The Federal District lacked financial means to provide schools, streets, sewers, police protection, and even water to these new areas. Yet the national government seemed to take scant notice of the ominous population growth. Alarmists, inside and especially outside Mexico, pointed to the dangers of the unchecked demographic explosion. Private birth control clinics worked with limited success. But Mexico's conservative Catholic heritage militated against effective contraceptive methods, and some influential politicians and businessmen saw the need for an ever larger population to give Mexico international power and to provide for an internal mass market. Meanwhile, the social and economic problems continued. In some rural areas landless peasants attempted to seize private properties only to be driven off by police and federal troops. A few took up arms, like the Zapatistas a half-century earlier, to redress their grievances. But the government and the Party of Revolutionary Institutions maintained a firm grip through Díaz Ordaz' six-year term of office. Criticism, if vocal, was ineffectual. The opposition parties proved incapable of giving the country a viable alternative to PRI rule.

The Party of National Action remained Catholic and conservative in its outlook. It drew its financial support from businessmen (especially in Monterrey) and perhaps from a government subsidy. But PAN fought an uphill battle against insuperable odds, for it won electoral victories only in Yucatán and the northwest, the two most disaffected areas in the country. The government nullified an apparent PAN victory in Mexicali in 1968 on the grounds that the mayoral candidate was not a Mexican citizen. Though PAN's candidates were often superior to the time-serving politicians imposed by PRI, the opposition party suffered the grave defect of its conservative origin and its religious coloration. The image of the Revolution, if tarnished by the 1960s, was too strong to be overcome by a party of the right. While the ground rules of politics in Mexico encouraged limited opposition, they did not permit attacks on the president or on the Revolution itself. Minority parties might criticize men or corruption but not institutions or principles. Neither the Catholic Church nor the National Action Party could mount an effective campaign against Mexico's social ills, for to decry widespread poverty and illiteracy was to imply that the Revolution had failed—an admission unacceptable to the government and the official party. In the end, the conservatives had no real campaign issue; if new reforms came, they would be in response to pressures from the left, not the right.

The Church in Mexico had long since acceded to the modus vivendi worked out by Cárdenas' government in the 1930s. The Catholic Social Action movement continued, but without the enthusiasm of the pre-1926 days. It promoted cooperative banks and Christian family groups —"busy work" but little else. As a trenchant critic of the Church in Mexico put it, Social Action was the "club which well-meaning, new middle-class families" could join to "agitate for their social privileges and their right for special treatment in the Catholic upbringing of their children." The worldwide agitation for change within the Catholic Church brought little clerical response in Mexico. Perhaps the most radical acts by churchmen in the 1960s were Bishop Sergio Méndez Arceo's removal of the statuary and other articles that had long cluttered his cathedral in Cuernavaca and the introduction of a mariachi mass. Pressures from the conservative Mexican hierarchy helped to bring about the Vatican's condemnation of Monsignor Ivan Illich's progressive center in Cuernavaca which trained missionaries from the United States to work in Latin America.

The public view of Mexican Catholicism in the daily press or weekly magazines (though distorted somewhat) was of aristocratic marriages, baptisms of wealthy babies, the first communions of little boys in outlandish uniforms and girls in white lace, and the fifteen-year birthday celebrations of adolescent girls dressed as brides. Like the Revolution, the Church's Social Action had become institutionalized. The old flames of protest burst out again only when the government compelled the Catholic schools to use textbooks that taught Martín Luis Guzmán's liberal view of Mexico's history, but these subsided when the contending parties reached a settlement. In May 1969 members of the hierarchy praised "separation of Church and State," insisting that the constitutional arrangement was in the "best interests" of Mexican Catholics.

The parties of the left, if more vociferous, were even less effective than the Party of National Action. The splintering of radical forces is a phenomenon not confined to Mexico, for the more cerebral the approach to politics, the less compromising and less tolerant of deviation are the partisans likely to be. The Popular Socialist Party of Lombardo Toledano steered a zigzag and lonely course between Marxism and the dominant official party. Lombardo Toledano breathed the fires of Marxism-Leninism and visited Communist China, but he was in reality a tame dragon who gave the government little trouble. His death in late 1968 led to a party schism, as the new leaders expelled Jacinto López, who had organized a dissident group of peasants, for disloyalty. Thereupon, López announced the formation of a new Labor-Agrarian Party. The more orthodox Communists split three ways, with different factions supporting the Soviet Union, China, and Castro's Cuba. Periodically, the parties of the left attempted to form coalitions, and during times of national indignation (the Dominican invasion in 1965, for example) they could unite in their common anti-Americanism. In 1961 a group of radicals, including Carlos Fuentes and Cárdenas' son, Cuauhtémoc, formed a National Liberation Movement to demand social reform and "solidarity with Cuba." But no party of the left was willing to subordinate itself to a coalition, and the leaders either drifted away or were co-opted into the Revolution's "establishment."

For the best part of the decade of the 1960s the most strident notes of radicalism came from the periodicals *Siempre* and *Política*. *Siempre* tried to maintain a façade of impartiality, carrying articles by PAN leaders, but its editorial policies were consistently pro-Cuban and anti-American. The editors had the wisdom not to attack the government or the Revolution, however, and so stayed in business. *Política*, which published its first issue in April 1960, was another matter. With a format like *Time* magazine, it was printed on slick paper and carried advertisements solely for a socialist bookstore in Mexico City. The high cost of publication was borne, according to some, by the Cuban embassy, according to others, by a subvention from the Mexican government. In any event, *Política* became increasingly radical during the 1960s, and early collaborators, such as Fuentes, dropped by the wayside. Violently anti-American, its chief concern was the United States' "fascist" involvement in Vietnam, Cuba, and the Dominican Republic. The editors attacked American influences on the Mexican government and in Mexican society and culture. They decried the "American way of life" in Mexico's television programming and demanded the banning of the Luce publication, *Life en Español*. But consistent and violent attacks on the person of Díaz Ordaz led the government to jail a *Política* editor and to withhold subsidized newsprint from the periodical. Unable to reconcile the ideological differences that split the left, and to buy enough newsprint on the open market, the magazine published its last issue in December 1967—an angry but defiant swan song of militant communism in Mexico.

The failure of the left to rally popular support was due to an inherent shortcoming of the radical leadership and to decisive action on the part of the national government. The ideologue, convinced that he alone was right, could not bring himself to accommodate the views of others. Moreover, he was a revolutionary only in the realm of ideas. He could complacently own a luxurious house in the Lomas de Chapultepec or the Pedregal and exploit servants by paying them low wages, while demanding social justice for the far-distant working classes. With reason, the lower classes distrusted the radical intellectuals, preferring existing privations to future uncertainties. The official party and the government bought off some obstreperous radicals with well-paying jobs. Others who would not be corrupted were imprisoned. A few, such as Rubén Jaramillo, a peasant leader in Morelos, were killed.

Through Díaz Ordaz' term of office the government continued to deal rigorously with dissident activity. It permitted mildly radical publications. It allowed public demonstrations, as long as they were carefully controlled. A parade or a manifestation of protest required a permit. The government stipulated the route and the time, size, and location of a demonstration. The Zócalo, once a grassy garden in front of Mexico City's cathedral and National Palace, became an asphalt staging ground, carefully marked with painted lines to maintain order during demonstrations. Plainclothesmen infiltrated protest groups to keep watchful eyes on potential troublemakers and to avoid possible violence. A strong day-and-night guard on the Paseo de la Reforma prevented surprise protest marches to the American embassy. But the government did not hesitate, in 1968, to use military force in suppressing preparatory and university student protests that seemed to threaten the Olympic Games in the nation's capital.

Though Mexico's revolutionary government had long stressed the importance of education (more money for schools than for the army), the problems that beset universities and preparatory institutions intensified during the 1950s and 1960s. The universities, especially the National Autonomous University (UNAM) in Mexico City, could not cope with the mounting number of students seeking higher education. By 1968 the complex National University enrolled more than 90,000 students—in facilities built for 30,000. During the 1950s the University moved to new and more modern quarters south of the capital with every intention of improving instruction by hiring permanent, full-time professors. But the size of the student body meant that most classes had to be taught by part-time teachers who stopped off at the university on their way to or from other jobs. Because they had no time for preparation and because the library could not provide books or space for so many students (it had fewer than 100,000 books for the 90,000 enrolled), the quality of instruction was consistently low. Few professors seemed to care whether students studied—and most did not. A single textbook and class notes sufficed for many courses. Only a third of those who enrolled at UNAM ever received a degree, and there was a great deal of time for political activity, both at the university and in the city.

The autonomy of the university, intended to protect it from government interventions, and student participation in the running of university affairs eventually proved harmful to the quality of education. The faculty and administration could not raise standards or limit admissions without protests and heated opposition from the students. And the cherished autonomy, instead of shielding the university, had the opposite effect of bringing national politics into internal university affairs, for the students took advantage of their privileged status to mount protests against social conditions in the country. While few students were Communists, many took a Marxian view of class-conflict, and most, like the adult intellectuals, cherished dreams of a future Elysium in which the oft-proclaimed ideals of the Revolution would reign, with free elections and an end to corruption and political repression.

To the UNAM students the most convenient symbol for the failure of the Revolution was the inadequate bus system of Mexico City. Moving the university from the center of the capital to the southern outskirts created an insuperable transportation problem. In any case, the young would have been frustrated by the obvious failure of the government to deal effectively with poverty in the midst of plenty, but this resentment was sharpened by the perennial difficulties of commuting to and from the university. Overloaded buses passed up crowds waiting at street corners, and students could never get anywhere on time. If the rebellious young could not achieve instant revolution and force the government to bow to their demands, they could at least burn or smash a bus. Most Mexicans, even in the lower classes, condemned the destruction of private property (many buses belonged to the drivers), and the students' violence cost them support in the general community. Elsewhere in Mexico similar university problems prevailed, and young people played an increasingly active and violent role in local politics. In June 1966 students in Durango seized an iron mine and held it for nearly a month until the government promised to build a smelter and to industrialize the state. In February 1967 students rioted in Hermosillo, capital of Sonora, to protest the gubernatorial candidate imposed by PRI. But the culmination of student difficulties came during the summer of 1968 in Mexico City as the nation prepared for the Olympics scheduled to open October 12. A seemingly minor incident touched off the students' anger and led to a widespread university strike. Before the flames had been brought under control, many students and bystanders had lost their lives, troops occupied the leading educational institutions, and the nation's capital, at the height of the tourist season, was under a virtual state of siege.

The strike had its origin in late July in an attack on the National Preparatory School by riot police trying to break up a schoolboy "rumble." For two months the students maintained their strike, and federal troops occupied the National University to prevent disruption of preparations for the nearby Olympic games. Significantly, the demands of the strikers did not deal with the internal problem of poor university education or with the need for social reforms. The issue, as stated by the students, was between them and the police, not between an alienated youth and an entrenched establishment. Whatever their real grievances and the basic causes of the student unrest, this strike was not a call for social revolution. The students were fully aware that the government would never permit them to demonstrate openly against the regime's failures. On October 2, ten days before the Olympic games began, thousands of students massed in Tlatelolco's Plaza of the Three Cultures to prepare for a march on the Polytechnic Institute. Skittish troops opened fire on the crowd, ostensibly because of snipers' fire, indiscriminately spraying the plaza and the adjoining apartment buildings with rifle and machinegun bullets. Later estimates placed the number of dead at between 50 and 600. It is unlikely that an accurate count will ever be released.

The massacre at the Plaza of the Three Cultures marked the turning point in the student disorders. The government had demonstrated that it would go to any extreme to keep order during the Olympics. And the students, lacking either popular support or a dynamic leader such as Daniel Cohn-Bendit or Mark Rudd, and with no transcendent and unifying cause such as the Vietnam conflict, were not prepared to go to the barricades to start a civil war. Through October and November an uneasy truce prevailed, while the Olympics, an outstanding success, went on as scheduled. To be sure, small incidents flared up—additional buses were burned, the police arrested more students, and several hundred young prisoners stayed in jail. With no hope of victory, however, the students finally capitulated, and in early December, urged by the UNAM rector and their strike committee, they voted to resume their classes.

In 1969 and 1970 the government continued to maintain its hard line. The Federal District brought from France some two dozen special riot trucks with high-pressure water cannons and displayed them ostentatiously in the capital. The student demands were not met, and as Díaz Ordaz neared the end of his term, large numbers of political prisoners, including students, languished in jail. Novelist José Revueltas was imprisoned for social dissolution, and Octavio Paz was removed as Ambassador to India for criticizing the government's handling of the student crisis. The literary review, El Corno Emplumado, which supported the students' cause, lost its government subsidy and was forced to cease publication. At the same time, the government made small gestures of reconciliation to the student protesters. The chief of police in the capital resigned "for reasons of health." In November 1969 Congress agreed to lower the voting age to 18, and in the following month the proposal was ratified by the 24 state legislatures. In July 1970, Article 145 of the Penal Code, under which the government had jailed opponents without trial, was repealed, and a number of long-term political prisoners were freed. But the new decade began with the national government and the official party firmly in control of the country. PRI announced as its candidate for the presidency Díaz Ordaz' Secretary of Gobernación, Luis Echeverría, who, with the governor of the Federal District, had been most closely identified with the repressive policies toward the students.

Yet the winds of change were blowing, and the defeated students did not stand alone in their rejection of old ways. In the arts, in literature, and in music a new generation turned its back on the parochialism and old-fashioned slogans of the Revolution and discovered the outside world. Young writers such as José Agustín and Fernando del Paso looked more to Burrough's Naked Lunch and Norman Mailer than to Octavio Paz and Agustín Yáñez. Carlos Fuentes no longer wrote of ancient Mexican revolutionaries; his Change of Skin (1967) described a crisis in the life of a middle-aged "beatnik," a "rebel without a cause," and his Cumpleaños (1970) was a short, bleak tale based on the modern European reincarnation of a thirteenth-century victim of the Inquisition. In music even Carlos Chávez experimented with serial techniques, and his younger colleagues, José Luis González, Eduardo Mata, Hector Quintanar, and Manuel Enríquez, began to explore the outer reaches of electronic composition with the aid of a Moog synthesizer and other advanced equipment. New artists, beginning with José Luis Cuevas, rejected the blatant nationalism of Rivera, and while the leap to Campbell soup cans was too difficult to negotiate abruptly, the works of Juan Soriano, Pedro Coronel, Roberto Donís, and Efrén Ordóñez, if traditionally representational, could have been executed in any Western country during the 1960s. Gone were the days when young Mexican artists could divert themselves with oils or water colors of clowns, cockfights, the bull ring, and doe-eyed Indian maidens holding calla lillies. As the youth of Mexico identified itself with the students of Paris, with Pop and Op artists, with Woodstock music, and with the "Turned-on" generation of Americans, it was questionable whether the party in power could long afford to give obsolete answers to the continuing social and economic problems.

But who was to lead Mexico along new paths if not the Party of Revolutionary Institutions? This was Mexico's dilemma at the beginning of the new decade. With reason Echeverría exuded optimism as he campaigned in 1970 for the presidency, because his election was assured. He invited the alienated young to rally to the Revolution's cause and to remain loyal to the *patria*. Few countries had as much liberty as Mexico, he boasted. (While he spoke, student leaders, still in jail after more than a year, announced a hunger strike to publicize their plight. The guards broke the strike by allowing other prisoners, hardened criminals, to rough up the young men in the presence of their families.) If Echeverría had discovered new answers, he did not reveal them, and his campaign speeches, filled with revolutionary platitudes, proposed six more years of the traditional policies. In his inaugural address, December 1, 1970, the new President stressed internal peace and uninterrupted economic growth. He would work for social improvement, not by extending political democracy, but through the strong and determined action of a paternalistic government. Echeverría warned the Mexican people to guard against "revolutionary dreamers, anarchists, provocateurs, and agitators" who stirred up student and peasant unrest. Nor should the country heed the alarmists who decried the rapid demographic growth. Predicting that Mexico's population would reach 100 million by the end of the century, Echeverría, father of eight children, rejected compulsory birth-control measures and all other "false, defeatist solutions" to urban overcrowding. As he took over the presidency, he gave no indication that he had heard the dissident voices, and he clearly intended to be another López Mateos or Díaz Ordaz.

At the end of the 1960s social problems were scarcely unique to

Mexico, but for fifty years Mexico had been vainly seeking to find ultimate solutions. Most Mexicans, though disillusioned with the Revolution, would vote overwhelmingly for PRI's candidates in the 1970s, because they had no other choice. Could PAN's outmoded Christian Democracy provide an answer? Could the fragmented and discredited left? What party could do more than PRI had done to improve the condition of most Mexicans? One might reasonably doubt that any government in Mexico could force the peasants to modernize, could nationalize industry under the bureaucrats, or, hardest of all, could compel Mexicans to undergo a personal reformation—to become in an instant altruistic and generous. The plain fact was that nowhere in the world had national socialization brought freedom and social justice. Because the Mexican Revolution promised much, too much was expected of it. Change was inevitable, for repression was no permanent answer to the demands of the young. But it would come slowly—far too slowly for many Mexicans.

Yet if only through the inexorability of aging and death, the young critics of the Revolution would one day guide the destinies of the nation. Each year the percentage of the population under 25 climbed, and, with the increase, the intensity of youthful alienation. In the meantime, PRI politicians and businessmen would rule Mexico, and the dislocations would continue in an unsatisfactory modus vivendi. Perhaps in this imperfect world that is all any people can ever achieve. Clearly, by 1970, the Mexicans had come farther than most developing nations in achieving the economic and social goals of Western democracies, and, compared with other Latin American, African, and Asian countries, Revolutionary Mexico, however flawed, was a success. But to the idealistic youth, the university and secondary students, partial success was not enough. In their eyes the problems and shortcomings far outweighed the accomplishments. And the electoral victory of Marxist Salvador Allende in democratic Chile meant that Mexico no longer headed the vanguard of revoltuionary, but peaceful change in Latin America. As though in response, President Echeverría abruptly changed his tune. By the spring of 1971, after three months in office, he had surprised Mexican politicians with his bold attacks on corruption and the failures of the agrarian program. For good or for bad, the year 1970 was a bench mark in Mexican history, certainly as important as 1940 and perhaps even 1910. The new generation had broken with the past and looked to the Echeverría years ahead—a few with gaurded hope, many with cynicism, and some with anticipation of violent social upheaval.

Bibliographic Essay

Europeans and Americans have long been fascinated by Mexico and by the Mexican people. As a result of this continued interest, there is no shortage of books on Mexico in many languages and in several disciplines. Scholars and interested laymen could occupy themselves profitably and with great pleasure for more than a lifetime just reading the good books in the English language alone. Because I have written this book for non-specialists—undergraduate students and members of the general public—I have limited the bibliography to works in English. Those who might want to pursue research topics can compile more specialized bibliographies from the books listed here.

The most useful and readable general account of Mexican history is Henry B. Parkes' *History of Mexico* (rev. ed. Boston, 1969). The book represents Parkes' research in the 1930s, however, and subsequent editions have not really kept it up to date. Lesley B. Simpson's *Many Mexicos* (Berkeley, 1966) is a delightful and not unprejudiced essay by a distinguished Mexicanist, which demonstrates that good history writing, if a disappearing art, still has its practitioners today. But Simpson, like Parkes, crystallized his views of Mexico before 1940. He is at his best in describing the events of the colonial era and the nineteenth century, and that best is very good indeed. Charles C. Cumberland's *Mexico: The Struggle for Modernity* (New York, 1968) stresses economic and social developments, rather than chronology and political events. The book provides in convenient form data unobtainable in similar general works.

Donald D. Brand, in *Mexico. Land of Sunshine and Shadow* (Princeton, 1966), gives a geographer's view of the country and its history. Anyone planning to travel to Mexico should start off by reading Brand's short volume. Preston James' *Latin America* (4th ed., New York, 1969), though older, provides the standard geographic description of Mexico. Víctor Alba, a Spaniard, writes of his adopted country in *The Mexicans. Making of a Nation* (New York, 1967). William W. Johnson, a journalist, wrote the text for the *Life* World Library's photographic essay, *Mexico* (New York, 1961). The photographs and maps are up to the usual high standard of *Time-Life* publications. J. Patrick McHenry's *Short History of Mexico* (Garden City, 1962) is just that. Frank R. Brandenburg's *Making of Modern Mexico* (Englewood Cliffs, 1964) offers a provocative and, at times, controversial explanation of recent Mexican history.

At the end of the nineteenth century, Justo Sierra wrote a Positivist's account of his country's history in *The Political Evolution of the Mexican People*. Now Edmundo O'Gorman has edited an abridged version (Austin, 1969). No bibliography of works in English would be complete without Hubert H. Bancroft's *History of Mexico* (6 vols., San Francisco, 1883–88). Bancroft directed a team of researchers and writers, and the various chapters are uneven. But anyone who writes on Mexico before the Porfirian period must begin with Bancroft and his extensive bibliography.

Many books place Mexico in a wider perspective. Among these are Richard N. Adams, *et al.*, *Social Change in Latin America Today* (New York, 1960); John J. Johnson (ed.), *Continuity and Change in Latin America* (Stanford, 1964); Frank Tannenbaum, *Ten Keys to Latin America* (New York, 1962); and the still-unsurpassed undergraduate textbook by Hubert Herring, *A History of Latin America* (2nd rev. ed., New York, 1968).

Bibliographic research starts in the *Handbook of Latin American Studies* (Cambridge, 1936–51; Gainesville, 1951–   ). Other helpful guides are Charles C. Griffin (ed.), *Latin America, A Guide to Historical Literature* (Austin, 1971); R. A. Humphreys, *Latin American History: A Guide to the Literature in English* (London, 1958); Arthur E. Gropp, *A Bibliography of Latin American Bibliographies* (rev. ed., Metuchen, N.J., 1968); David F. Trask, *et al.*, *A Bibliography of United States—Latin American Relations Since 1910* (Lincoln, 1968); *Mexico: Ancient and Modern. As Represented by a Selection of Works in the Bancroft Library* (Berkeley, 1962); Dale L. Morgan and George P. Hammond (eds.), *A Guide to the Manuscript Collections of the Bancroft Library* (Berkeley, 1963); C. J. Bishko, "The Iberian Background of Latin American History: Recent Progress and Continuing Problems," *Hispanic American Historical Review* (hereafter *HAHR*), XXXVI (February 1956), 50–80; Howard F. Cline, "Mexican Community Studies," *HAHR*, XXXII (May 1952), 212–42; Robert A. Potash, "Historiography of Mexico Since 1821," *HAHR*, XL (August 1960), 383–424; and Stanley R. Ross, "Bibliography of Sources for Contemporary Mexican History," *HAHR*, XXXIX (May 1959), 234–38.

For the Iberian backgrounds to the conquest of Mexico, the best single volume is John H. Elliott's *Imperial Spain, 1469–1716* (New York, 1964). Elliott writes with grace and wit and sorts out in admirable style the tangled skeins of political, economic, and social history. William C. Atkinson's *History of Spain and Portugal* (Baltimore, 1960) covers Iberian history from the earliest days. Harold V. Livermore, in his *History of Spain* (New York, 1968), sticks close to political chronology and often overlooks the forest for the trees, but he does provide a useful checklist of events.

A number of books by outstanding Spanish writers are available in English: Rafael Altamira y Crevea's *History of Spain* (New York, 1949), a condensation of his earlier four-volume edition; Américo Castro's *Structure of Spanish History* (Princeton, 1954), a philosophical investigation of the meaning of his country's civilization through great literary works; Jaime Vicens Vives' *Approaches to the History of Spain* (Berkeley, 1967), in which the Catalán historian stresses economic and social developments; and Salvador de Madariaga's *Spain. A Modern History* (New York, 1958), which reveals more about the author than about actual events.

Among the studies devoted to more specialized topics or to shorter periods in Spanish history are the *New Cambridge Modern History*. Vol. 4: *The Decline of Spain and the Thirty Years War, 1609–1648/59* (New York, 1970); John Lynch, *Spain under the Hapsburgs* (2 vols., New York, 1964, 1969); Reginald T. Davies, *Spain in Decline, 1621–1700* (New York, 1957); John H. Elliott, *The Revolt of the Catalans* (Cambridge, England, 1963); Henry Kamen, *The War of Succession in Spain* (Bloomington, 1969); Richard Herr, *The Eighteenth-Century Revolution in Spain* (Princeton, 1958); Gabriel H. Lovett, *Napoleon and the Birth of Modern Spain* (2 vols., New York, 1965); Raymond Carr, *Spain 1808–1939* (London, 1966); Julius Klein, *The Mesta: A Study in Spanish Economy, 1273–1836* (Cambridge, 1920); Earl J. Hamilton, *American Treasure and the Price Revolution in Spain, 1501–1650* (Cambridge, 1934); Garrett Mattingly, *The Armada* (Boston, 1959); and John H. Parry, *The Spanish Seaborne Empire* (New York, 1966).

The continuing interest in preconquest Mexico accounts for the never-ceasing spate of archaeological studies and histories of Indian civilizations. The best one-volume account (and that rarity of rarities, an excellently written textbook) is Gordon R. Willey's *Introduction to American Archaeology*. Vol. I: *North and Middle America* (Englewood Cliffs, 1966). The art work, both photographs and line drawings, is outstanding. Michael D. Coe has two first-rate volumes: *Mexico* (New York, 1962), which covers the area south to Oaxaca, and *The Maya* (New York, 1966), on southern Mexico, Yucatán, and the Central American countries. Sylvanus G. Morley's *Ancient Maya* (Stanford, 1956), revised and edited by George W. Brainerd, remains the classic early study by a master archaeologist. J. Eric S. Thompson, of the same generation as Morley, has updated his earlier work on *The Rise and Fall of Maya Civilization* (2nd ed., Norman, 1966). See also his *Maya History and Religion* (Norman, 1969). George C. Vaillant pioneered in archaeological and preconquest history studies of the Valley of Mexico. His widow, Suzannah Vaillant, published a revised edition of *The Aztecs of Mexico* (New York, 1962), based on more recent research and interpretations. Not new, but giving a Mexican's view of his country's Indian past, is Ignacio Bernal's *Mexico before Cortez: Art, History, and Legend* (New York, 1963). Another older book, still worth reading, is Frederick Peterson's *Ancient Mexico* (New York, 1962), for it covers both the highlands and Maya areas. The most detailed and authoritative project on Mexico's Indian cultures can be found in Robert Wauchope (ed.), *Handbook of Middle American Indians* (8 vols., Austin, 1965–71).

Other specialized volumes on Middle America are Richard S. MacNeish, *et al.*, *The Prehistory of the Tehuacán Valley* (Austin, 1967–   ), a detailed investigation of the cultural changes from paleolithic times to the coming of the Spaniards; Robert McC. Adams, *The Evolution of Urban Society. Early Mesopotamia and Prehispanic Mexico* (Chicago, 1966), comparing Teotihuacán in the Classic Period with the ancient Middle East civilization; John Paddock (ed.), *Ancient Oaxaca: Discoveries in Mexican Archaeology and History* (Stanford, 1966), essays by Paddock and others on the Zapotecs and Mixtecs; Ronald Spores, *The Mixtec Kings and Their People* (Norman, 1967), focusing on the sixteenth century just before and during the Conquest period; Michael D. Coe, *America's First Civilization. Discovering the Olmec* (New York, 1968) concerning the Olmecs and their influence on subsequent peoples; Alfonso Caso, *The Aztecs, People of the Sun* (Norman, 1958), on Aztec religion; Jacques Soustelle, *The Daily Life of the Aztecs on the Eve of the Spanish Conquest* (New York, 1962), for social history; and Laurette Séjourné, *Burning Water: Thought and Religion in Ancient Mexico* (New York, 1956), and Miguel León-Portilla, *Aztec Thought and Culture: A Study of the Ancient Náhuatl Mind* (Norman, 1963), studies of preconquest poetry, religion, and philosophy, viewed in a larger historical perspective.

Frances Gillmor has written two fictionalized histories of the Aztecs, *Flute of the Smoking Mirror* (Tucson, 1968), and *The King Danced in the Market Place* (Tucson, 1964).

The impressive preconquest remains have been recorded in many fine publications on art and architecture. Among the best are Miguel Covarrubias, *Indian Art of Mexico and Central America* (New York, 1957); Hans Helfritz, *Mexican Cities of the Gods* (New York, 1970), a particularly attractive guide for tourists; Pál Kelemen, *Art of the Americas. Ancient and Hispanic* (New York, 1969), an excellent paperback at a reasonable price; George Kubler, *The Art and Architecture of Ancient America: The Mexican, Maya, and Andean Peoples* (Baltimore, 1962), by a leading art historian; Tatiana Proskouriakoff, *An Album of Maya Architecture* (Norman, 1963), reconstructions of unsurpassed beauty; Donald Robertson, *Pre-Columbian Architecture* (New York, 1963), a useful survey of Middle and South America; and Paul Westheim, *The Art of Ancient Mexico* (Garden City, 1965), a knowledgeable summary by a pioneer in the field.

Of the several postconquest accounts of preconquest events several have been translated into English, notably Bernardino de Sahagún's *General History of the Things of New Spain* (Salt Lake City and Santa Fe, 1950–63); Motolinía's *History of the Indians of New Spain* (Washington, 1951); Diego Durán's, *Aztecs: The History of the Indians of New Spain* (New York, 1964); Alonso de Zurita's *Life and Labor in Ancient Mexico* (New Brunswick, 1964); and a Spanish-inspired book in the Maya language, *Popul Vuh* (Norman, 1950).

Distinguished American investigators have written of the lives and ideas of archaeologists: Robert Wauchope, *Lost Tribes and Sunken Continents. Myth and Method in the Study of American Indians* (Chicago, 1962), a witty analysis of stories on the origin of the Indians; and J. Eric S. Thompson, *Maya Archaeologist* (Norman, 1963), reminiscences from his long career of excavations in southern Middle America.

For an account of the historic voyages of Christopher Columbus, Samuel

Eliot Morison's Pulitzer Prize-winning *Admiral of the Ocean Sea* (2 vols., Boston, 1942) has no peer in any language. The tang of the salt sea winds pervades Admiral Morison's nautical prose to bring to life for the land-lubber the vicissitudes and accomplishments of Columbus and his men. Morison also wrote a shorter version, *Christopher Columbus, Mariner* (Boston, 1955). In contrast, Carl O. Sauer, a geographer-historian, provides an unflattering view of Columbus in his *Early Spanish Main* (Berkeley, 1966). The larger aspects of the overseas expansion are well covered in John H. Parry's *Establishment of the European Hegemony, 1415–1715* (3rd rev. ed., New York, 1966), and J. B. Brebner's *Explorers of North America, 1492–1806* (London, 1933). More literary and philosophical than factual are Ramón Iglesia's fine essays, *Columbus, Cortés, and Other Essays* (Berkeley, 1969), and Edmundo O'Gorman's *Invention of America* (Blooming-ton, 1961).

William H. Prescott's *History of the Conquest of Mexico,* written more than a century ago, may be hampered by florid Romantic prose and an exaggerated Yankeeism, but it remains the standard classic and will probably never be surpassed, if equalled, by another historian. Many complete edi-tions are available, as well as an abridged version (New York, 1964). Fred-erick A. Kirkpatrick's *Spanish Conquistadores* (2nd ed., New York, 1967) gives the best and most complete survey of the conquest period in both North and South America. Fernando Benítez, a Mexican journalist-historian, takes the reader *In the Footsteps of Cortés* (New York, 1952), on an imagi-native reconstruction of the march from Veracruz to Tenochtitlán. Salvador de Madariaga's *Hernán Cortés, Conqueror of Mexico* (New York, 1941) is a fanciful biography, while Irwin R. Blacker's *Cortés and the Aztec Con-quest* (New York, 1965) is a popularization for younger readers, beautifully illustrated by *Horizon* magazine. Correspondence between the Conqueror and the Emperor Charles V has been published as Hernando Cortés, *Five Letters* (New York, 1962) and can be compared with a first-hand account by one of his soldiers, Bernal Díaz del Castillo, *The Conquest of New Spain* (Baltimore, 1963). For a biography of Bernal Díaz, see Herbert Cerwin, *Bernal Díaz. Historian of the Conquest* (Norman, 1963). Two modern scholars have questioned the authenticity of Bernal Díaz' history, Ramón Iglesia, "Two Articles on the Same Topic," in his *Columbus, Cortés, and Other Essays*; and Henry R. Wagner, "Three Studies on the Same Subject," *HAHR,* XXV (May 1945), 155–211. Francisco López de Gómara provided a flattering contemporary portrait in *Cortés: The Life of the Conqueror of Mexico by his Secretary* (Berkeley, 1964).

More specialized studies of the conquest and of lesser figures are C. Harvey Gardiner, *Naval Power in the Conquest of Mexico* (Austin, 1956), *Martín López. Conquistador Citizen of Mexico* (Lexington, 1958), and *The Constant Captain: Gonzalo de Sandoval* (Carbondale, 1961); John E. Kelly, *Pedro de Alvarado. Conquistador* (Princeton, 1932); Donald E. Chipman, *Nuño de Guzmán and the Province of Pánuco in New Spain, 1518–1533* (Glendale, 1966); Frans Blom, *The Conquest of Yucatán* (Bos-ton, 1936); and Robert S. Chamberlain, *The Conquest and Colonization of Yucatán, 1517–1550* (Washington, 1948).

Another version of the conflict between Spaniards and Indians comes from postconquest histories by native chroniclers: Patricia de Fuentes (ed.), *The Conquistadors: First Person Accounts of the Conquest of Mexico* (New York, 1963); Miguel León-Portilla (ed.), *Broken Spears: Aztec Account of the Conquest of Mexico* (Boston, 1962); and Fernando de Alva Ixlilxóchitl, *Ally of Cortés* (El Paso, 1969). Robert C. Padden in *The Hummingbird and the Hawk* (Columbus, 1967) explores the conflict of the two cultures during the conquest and colonization periods, while George M. Foster in *Culture and Conquest: America's Spanish Heritage* (Chicago, 1960), demonstrates that a "concentrated" version of Spanish culture mixed with aspects of Indian culture to give birth to completely new forms.

The problems involved in the Christianization of the natives are delineated in Charles S. Braden, *Religious Aspects of the Conquest of Mexico* (Durham, 1930); Robert Ricard, *The Spiritual Conquest of Mexico* (Berkeley, 1966); Ursula Lamb, "Religious Conflicts in the Conquest of Mexico," *Journal of the History of Ideas*, XVII (October 1956), 526–39; and Nicolau d'Olwer, "Comments on the Evangelization of the New World," *The Americas*, XIV (April 1958), 339–410.

The colonial era has attracted and held the attention of distinguished Mexican, American, and European scholars throughout the twentieth century. General views are given by Edward G. Bourne, *Spain in America 1450–1580* (New York, 1904); by Charles Gibson in an updating of Bourne's volume, also *Spain in America* (New York, 1966), and by the quixotic Salvador de Madariaga, *The Rise of the Spanish Empire* (New York, 1947) and *The Fall of the Spanish Empire* (New York, 1948). In the latter volume, Madariaga attributes Spain's decline to the Jews, Jesuits, and Masons. In a class by itself is Clarence H. Haring's magisterial study of institutions, *The Spanish Empire in America* (New York, 1947). Other institutional investigations touching on Mexico have been made by Lillian E. Fisher, *Viceregal Administration in the Spanish-American Colonies* (Berkeley, 1926) and *Intendant System in Spanish America* (Berkeley, 1929); Charles H. Cunningham, *The Audiencia in the Spanish Colonies* (Berkeley, 1919); John H. Parry, *The Audiencia of New Galicia in the Sixteenth Century* (Cambridge, England, 1948); and Lesley B. Simpson, *The Encomienda in New Spain* (rev. ed., Berkeley, 1966). Woodrow Borah and Charles Gibson have looked at the perseveration of Spanish ways in "Colonial Institutions and Contemporary Latin America: Political and Economic Life" and "Social and Cultural Life," *HAHR*, XLIII (August 1963), 371–89.

Among the historians dealing with economic matters are William L. Schurz, *Manila Galleon* (New York, 1959), a superb study of trade between the Philippines and Acapulco; Woodrow W. Borah, *Silk Raising in Colonial Mexico* (Berkeley, 1943), on the abortive attempt to introduce silk cultivation; Robert C. West, *The Mining Community in Northern New Spain* (Berkeley, 1949); and William M. Dusenberry, *The Mexican Mesta* (Urbana, 1963), an account of the first stockman's association in the New World. Charles Gibson has meticulously studied the indigenous social structure and the impact of Spanish institutions in his *Aztecs under Spanish Rule* (Stanford, 1964). Lyle N. McAlister has a thought-provoking article, "Social Structure and Social Change in New Spain," *HAHR*, XLIII (August 1963), 349–70, which opens new avenues for research in

Colonial Mexico. John F. Bannon has assembled a useful book of readings, *Indian Labor in the Spanish Indies* (Boston, 1966). The most authoritative study of relations between Crown and Church is W. Eugene Shiels' *King and Church: The Rise and Fall of the Patronato Real* (Chicago, 1961). France V. Scholes' *Church and State in New Mexico, 1610–1650* (Albuquerque, 1937) is restricted to the northern frontier, but gives insight into general religious problems in the Indies. Nancy M. Farriss' *Crown and Clergy in Colonial Mexico, 1759–1821* (London, 1968) shows how diligent scholarship can bring new interpretations to old events. Lillian Estelle Fisher, in her *Champion of Reform, Manuel Abad y Queipo* (New York, 1955), looks at a socially conscious prelate, the Bishop of Michoacán, in the era of Ferdinand VII. Fintan B. (J. Benedict) Warren has studied an earlier reformer in *Vasco de Quiroga and his Pueblo-Hospitals of Santa Fe* (Washington, 1963). The role of the Society of Jesus in schooling and missionary activity has been surveyed by Jerome V. Jacobsen, *Educational Foundation of the Jesuits in Sixteenth-Century New Spain* (Berkeley, 1938), and Peter M. Dunne, *Pioneer Jesuits in Northern Mexico* (Berkeley, 1944). Asunción Lavrin examined Church property holdings in "The Role of the Nunneries in the Economy of New Spain in the Eighteenth Century," *HAHR*, XLVI (November 1966), 371–93.

The cruelties of the Spanish Inquisition have long titillated British and American readers. The classic, and far from unprejudiced, account is Henry C. Lea's *Inquisition in the Spanish Dependencies* (New York, 1908). More recently Richard E. Greenleaf has used modern scholarship methods in *Zumárraga and the Mexican Inquisition* (Washington, 1961) and *The Mexican Inquisition of the Sixteenth Century* (Albuquerque, 1969). The fullest report on the Inquisition's victims is Seymour B. Liebman's *Cultural History of the Jews in New Spain* (Coral Gables, 1970).

Lewis Hanke sparked the new interest in the sixteenth-century controversy between Bartolomé de las Casas and Juan Ginés de Sepúlveda with the publication of *The Spanish Struggle for Justice in the Conquest of America* (Philadelphia, 1949). For the response (in English) to the modern controversy see Edmundo O'Gorman, "Lewis Hanke on the Spanish Struggle for Justice in the Conquest of America," *HAHR*, XXIX (November 1949), 563–71; Lewis Hanke, "Bartolomé de las Casas, an Essay in Hagiography and Historiography," *HAHR*, XXXIII (February 1953), 136–51; Robert E. Quirk, "Some Notes on a Controversial Controversy," *HAHR*, XXXIV (August 1954), 357–64; Lewis Hanke, *Aristotle and the American Indians* (Chicago, 1959); and "More Heat and Some Light on the Spanish Struggle for Justice in the Conquest of America," *HAHR*, XLIV (August 1964), 293–340; John H. Parry, *Spanish Theory of Empire in the Sixteenth Century* (Cambridge, England, 1940); and Silvio Zavala, *New Viewpoints on the Spanish Colonization of America* (London, 1943).

Books on early Mexican art and architecture have proliferated. Among the more beautifully printed and expertly written are Manuel Toussaint, *Colonial Art in Mexico* (Austin, 1968); Pál Kelemen, *Baroque and Rococo in Latin America* (New York, 1951); George Kubler and Martin Soria, *Art and Architecture in Spain and Portugal and Their American Dominions, 1500–1800* (Baltimore, 1959); T. E. Sanford, *The Story of Architecture in Mexico* (New York, 1947); John McAndrew, *The Open-Air Churches of Sixteenth-Century Mexico* (Cambridge, 1965); Joseph A. Baird, Jr. and Hugo Rudinger, *The Churches of Mexico, 1500–1810* (Berkeley, 1962); and George A. Kubler, *Mexican Architecture of the Sixteenth Century* (2 vols., New Haven, 1948). For a general survey of literature which includes Mexico see Mariano Picón-Salas, *Cultural History of Spanish America from Conquest to Independence* (Berkeley, 1962). Other specialized monographs include John T. Lanning, *Academic Culture in the Spanish Colonies* (New York, 1940); and Irving A. Leonard, *Don Carlos de Sigüenza y Góngora* (Berkeley, 1929) and *Books of the Brave* (Cambridge, 1949).

Some historians have written on individual Spanish officials in Mexico: Arthur S. Aiton, *Antonio de Mendoza, First Viceroy of New Spain* (Durham, 1927); Lawrence F. Hill, *José de Escandón and the Founding of Nuevo Santander* (Columbus, 1926); J. Lloyd Mecham, *Francisco de Ibarra and Nueva Vizcaya* (Durham, 1927); Herbert I. Priestley, *José de Gálvez, Visitor-General of New Spain* (Berkeley, 1916); Bernard E. Bobb, *The Viceregency of Antonio María Bucareli in New Spain, 1771–1778* (Austin, 1962); Alfred B. Thomas, *Teodoro de Croix and the Northern Frontier of New Spain, 1776–1783* (Norman, 1941); and James Manfredini, *The Political Role of the Count of Revillagigedo, Viceroy of New Spain: 1789–1794* (New Brunswick, 1949).

No professional historian has dealt with the larger time spans within the colonial period in Mexico, but Fernando Benítez' *Century After Cortés* (Chicago, 1965) is a well-written, if partisan, account of the period before 1600. Other studies on that era include Charles Gibson, *Tlaxcala in the Sixteenth Century* (New Haven, 1952); Carl O. Sauer, *Colima of New Spain in the Sixteenth Century* (Berkeley, 1948); Woodrow Borah and Sherburne Cook, *Indian Population of Central Mexico, 1531–1610* (Berkeley, 1960); Phillip W. Powell, *Soldiers, Indians, and Silver: The Northward Advance of New Spain, 1550–1600* (Berkeley, 1969); and Howard F. Cline, "Civil Congregations of the Indians in New Spain, 1598–1606," *HAHR*, XXIX (August 1949), 349–69. Francisco Cervantes de Salazar's *Life in the Imperial and Loyal City of Mexico* (Austin, 1953) is a contemporary description of New Spain's capital in 1550 written in Latin for his students.

A few important works in English on the seventeenth century have appeared since 1950. Besides Gibson's *Aztecs under Spanish Rule*, which looks chiefly at the Valley of Mexico, there are Woodrow Borah's *New Spain's Century of Depression* (Berkeley, 1951), a seminal investigation which points to the consequences of a catastrophic population decline; François Chevalier's *Land and Society in Colonial Mexico: The Great Hacienda* (Berkeley, 1963), on the growth of large estates, principally in the north; and Irving A. Leonard's *Baroque Times in Old Mexico* (Ann Arbor, 1959), strong on literary history, but unfortunately, despite the title, neglecting art and architecture. First-hand and somewhat prejudiced information comes from a seventeenth-century English priest, Thomas Gage. His *New Survey of the West Indies* has been published in a modern edition as *Travels in the New World* (rev. ed., Norman, 1969).

The century before Independence has attracted the attention of scholars interested in the Bourbon reforms: Walter Howe, *The Mining Guild of New*

Spain and Its Tribunal General, 1770–1821 (Cambridge, 1949); Lyle N. McAlister, *The "Fuero Militar" in New Spain, 1764–1800* (Gainesville, 1957); Clement G. Motten, *Mexican Silver and the Enlightenment* (Philadelphia, 1950); David A. Brading, *Miners and Merchants in Bourbon Mexico, 1763–1810* (Cambridge, England, 1971); Brian R. Hamnett, *Politics and Trade in Southern Mexico, 1750–1821* (Cambridge, England, 1971); and Troy S. Floyd, *The Bourbon Reforms and Spanish Civilization* (Boston, 1966), a book of readings. Donald B. Cooper looked at medical history in *Epidemic Diseases in Mexico City, 1761–1813* (Austin, 1965). The indefatigable researcher, Lillian Estelle Fisher, described the *Background of the Revolution for Mexican Independence* (Boston, 1934). Still essential today for a grasp of the conditions in Mexico on the eve of Independence is Alexander von Humboldt's *Political Essay on the Kingdom of New Spain* (4 vols., New York, 1811); see also a one-volume edition (Lexington, 1957).

Unfortunately, a good survey of the Mexican Wars of Independence does not exist in any language. Instead, the reader must make his own synthesis from a number of well-researched monographs: Hugh Hamill, *The Hidalgo Revolt: Prelude to Mexican Independence* (Gainesville, 1966); Wilbert H. Timmons, *Morelos, Priest, Soldier, Statesman of Mexico* (El Paso, 1970); William F. Sprague, *Vicente Guerrero* (Chicago, 1939); William S. Robertson, *Iturbide of Mexico* (Durham, 1952); John V. Lombardi, *The Political Ideology of Fray Servando Teresa de Mier* (Cuernavaca, 1968); and John Rydjord, *Foreign Interest in the Independence of New Spain* (Durham, 1935); and from an unpublished dissertation, Jack A. Haddock, "The Administration of Viceroy José de Iturrigaray" (University of Texas, 1954). Three collections of essays, edited by leading Latin Americanists, shed light on the movement in Mexico: R. A. Humphreys and John Lynch, *Origins of the Latin American Revolutions 1808–1826* (New York, 1965); Arthur P. Whitaker, *Latin America and the Enlightenment* (New York, 1961); and Nettie Lee Benson, *Mexico and the Spanish Cortes, 1810–1822* (Austin, 1966). For the role of the Church see the Farriss book and Karl M. Schmitt, "The Clergy and the Independence of New Spain," *HAHR*, XXXIV (August 1954), 289–312.

Southwest United States was Spanish longer than it has been American, and its study forms a natural part of Mexican history. Herbert E. Bolton made monumental contributions to the area's history writing, though only two are mentioned here as examples: *Coronado. Knight of Pueblos and Plains* (New York, 1947) and *Spanish Borderlands* (New Haven, 1921). Good and readable recent surveys are W. Eugene Hollon, *The Southwest: Old and New* (New York, 1961), and Odie B. Faulk, *Land of Many Frontiers. A History of the American Southwest* (New York, 1968). Seymour V. Connor has edited a series on Texas, including his own *Adventure in Glory*, and Ernest Wallace, *Texas in Turmoil* and David M. Vigness, *The Revolutionary Decades, 1810–1836* (all Austin, 1965). Older, but still standard are William C. Binkley, *The Texas Revolution* (Baton Rouge, 1952), and Carlos Castañeda (ed.), *The Mexican Side of the Texas Revolution* (Dallas, 1928). From earlier days the great adventure story is *The Journey of Alvar Núñez Cabeza de Vaca* (Chicago, 1964).

Wilfred H. Callcott's studies of the nineteenth century have been largely superseded by recent monographic work but not replaced by similar broad studies, and they remain, with Bancroft, the starting point for the serious researcher: *Church and State in Mexico: 1822–1857* (Durham, 1926), covering more than the title implies; *Liberalism in Mexico, 1857–1929* (Palo Alto, 1931); and *Santa Anna: The Story of an Enigma Who Was Once Mexico* (Norman, 1936). Charles Hale has examined the crucial years before the Reform in *Mexican Liberalism in the Age of Mora, 1821–1853* (New Haven, 1968) to give a new interpretation to the complicated ideology of liberalism. Other important monographs dealing with the middle years of the century include Thomas E. Cotner, *The Military and Political Career of José Joaquín Herrera, 1792–1854* (Austin, 1949); Oakah L. Jones, Jr., *Santa Anna* (New York, 1968); Ralph Roeder, *Juárez and His Mexico* (2 vols., New York, 1947); Walter V. Scholes, *Mexican Politics during the Juárez Regime* (Columbia, 1957); Richard A. Johnson, *The Mexican Revolution of Ayutla* (Rock Island, 1939); Frank A. Knapp, Jr., *The Life of Sebastián Lerdo de Tejada, 1823–1889* (Austin, 1951); and Nelson Reed, *The Caste War in Yucatán* (Stanford, 1964). On the Empire and the French intervention, see, Egon Caesar Corti, *Maximilian and Charlotte of Mexico* (2 vols., New York, 1928); Jack A. Dabbs, *The French Army in Mexico* (The Hague, 1963); and Frank G. Weber, "Bismark's Man in Mexico: Anton von Magnus and the End of Maximilian's Empire," *HAHR,* XLVI (February 1966), 53–65.

Travel accounts and reports by foreign visitors form an important part of nineteenth-century Mexican historiography: Joel R. Poinsett, *Notes on Mexico Made in the Autumn of 1822* (New York, 1969); Henry G. Ward, *Mexico* (2 vols., London, 1829); *Mexico, 1825–1828. The Journal and Correspondence of Edward Thornton Tayloe* (Chapel Hill, 1959); John L. Stephens, *Incidents of Travel in Yucatan* (New York, 1843); Mme. Calderón de la Barca, *Life in Mexico* (Garden City, 1966); Waddy Thompson, *Recollections of Mexico* (New York, 1846); Carl Sartorius, *Mexico: Landscapes and Popular Sketches* (London, 1858); and Brantz Mayer, *Mexico as It Was and as It Is* (Philadelphia, 1847).

The Porfiriato deserves a first-rate, one-volume history, but to date none has appeared. Carleton Beals' *Porfirio Díaz, Dictator of Mexico* (Philadelphia, 1932) was inadequate when it appeared and has not aged well. Nevertheless, it is all that we have on Díaz in English that passes for scholarship. For studies of limited aspects of the era see, Karl M. Schmitt, "The Díaz Conciliation Policy on State and Local Levels," *HAHR,* XL (November 1960), 513–32; Thomas G. Powell, "Mexican Intellectuals and the Indian Question, 1876–1911," *HAHR,* XLVIII (February 1968), 19–36; and William D. Raat, "Leopoldo Zea and Mexican Positivism: A Reappraisal," *HAHR,* XLVIII (February 1968), 1–18. Economic development is studied by David M. Pletcher in his prize-winning *Rails, Mines, and Progress: Seven American Promoters in Mexico, 1867–1911* (Ithaca, 1958) and "The Fall of Silver in Mexico, 1870–1910, and Its Effect on American Investments," *Journal of Economic History,* XVIII (March 1958), 33–55; and by Alfred Tischendorf, *Great Britain and Mexico in the Era of Porfirio Díaz* (Durham, 1961). James D. Cockcroft has written a provocative and controversial study of the Porfiriato's downfall, *Intellectual Precursors of the Mexican Revolu-*

tion, 1900–1913 (Austin, 1968), in which he deals with the anarchistic Mexican Liberal Party. William Hendricks has also investigated the "Liberals" in his dissertation, "The Flores Magón Brothers and the Mexican Revolution," (University of Southern California, 1964).

Books by foreigners include Charles M. Flandrau's delightful and incomparable *Viva Mexico!* (Urbana, 1964); Fanny Chambers Gooch's *Face to Face with the Mexicans* (Carbondale, 1966); Frederick Starr's *In Indian Mexico* (Chicago, 1908); John K. Turner's *Barbarous Mexico* (Austin, 1969); and Edward I. Bell's *Political Shame of Mexico* (New York, 1914).

The Revolution has merited much attention from Mexican and foreign scholars alike. Because they have been too close to the events, most Mexicans have written partisan accounts of their recent history, and the best studies of the Revolution have come from foreigners—principally American and British. But these deal with particular periods or aspects of the Revolution, and there is as yet no synthetic treatment of events since 1910. Aside from Brandenburg's *Making of Modern Mexico*, the most thorough covering is in Frank Tannenbaum's *Mexico, the Struggle for Peace and Bread* (New York, 1950). Tannenbaum participated actively in the events he describes and was an intimate of leading figures in the Revolution. See also his *Peace by Revolution: An Interpretation of Mexico* (New York, 1966). Another close observer of the Mexican scene was Anita Brenner who wrote from firsthand experience her *Wind That Swept Mexico. The History of the Mexican Revolution, 1910–1942* (New York, 1943). Though now dated, this pictorial view of the Revolution is still eminently worth reading today. A younger scholar, James W. Wilkie, has looked at the budgets of revolutionary governments in *The Mexican Revolution: Federal Expenditures and Social Change Since 1910* (Berkeley, 1967). For dissenting views from Thomas A. Skidmore and Peter H. Smith and a reply by Wilkie, see "Notes on Quantitative History: Federal Expenditures and Social Change in Mexico Since 1910," *Latin American Research Review*, V (Spring 1970), 71–91. Frederick C. Turner's *Dynamic of Mexican Nationalism* (Chapel Hill, 1968) emphasizes the importance of xenophobia in the years since 1910. Useful readings books come from four leading historians: Charles C. Cumberland, *The Meaning of the Mexican Revolution* (Boston, 1967), Stanley R. Ross, *Is the Mexican Revolution Dead?* (New York, 1966), and James W. Wilkie and Albert L. Michaels, *Revolution in Mexico: Years of Upheaval, 1910–1940* (New York, 1969). An outstanding Mexican historian, Moisés González Navarro, interprets his country's recent history in "The Lopsided Revolution," from Claudio Veliz (ed.), *Obstacles to Change in Latin America* (New York, 1965). The dean of Mexican historians, Daniel Cosío Villegas, has compared Mexico's experience with that of Castro's Cuba in a perceptive and challenging essay, *Change in Latin America: The Mexican and Cuban Revolutions* (Lincoln, 1961). An American political scientist, Cole Blaiser, adds another dimension in "Studies of Social Revolution: Origins in Mexico, Bolivia, and Cuba," *Latin American Research Review*, II (Summer 1967), 28–51.

Professional historians who have written of the 1910–40 years tend to focus on individual revolutionaries or on short periods within the Revolution. As a result, the broader field has been left to amateurs who have made syntheses with varying degrees of success. Among the better books of this type are Ronald Atkins's *Revolution: Mexico, 1910–20* (New York, 1970); William W. Johnson's *Heroic Mexico. The Violent Emergence of a Modern Nation* (Garden City, 1968); and John W. F. Dulles' *Yesterday in Mexico* (Austin, 1961). At the end of the period a number of Mexican and foreign essayists combined to produce a summation, "Mexico Today," in the *Annals of the American Academy of Political and Social Science,* 208 (March 1940), 1–186. Edwin Lieuwen explores an important side of the Revolution in *Mexican Militarism: The Political Rise and Fall of the Revolutionary Army, 1910–1940* (Albuquerque, 1968).

Two leading American Mexicanists have written about the first revolutionary president: Stanley R. Ross, *Francisco I. Madero, Apostle of Mexican Democracy* (New York, 1955); and Charles C. Cumberland, *Mexican Revolution. Genesis under Madero* (Austin, 1952). Lowell L. Blaisdell has looked at an abortive rebellion of the Floresmagonistas in *The Desert Revolution: Baja California, 1911* (Madison, 1962). A new if perhaps unconvincing view of Huerta comes from William S. Sherman and Richard E. Greenleaf, *Victoriano Huerta, a Reappraisal* (México, 1960). A northern revolutionary has been studied by Michael C. Meyer, *Mexican Rebel: Pascual Orozco and the Mexican Revolution, 1910–1915* (Lincoln, 1967). For an account of the downfall of Huerta and the conflict between Carranza and the Convention, see Robert E. Quirk, *The Mexican Revoltuion, 1914–1915* (Bloomington, 1960). John Womack's excellently written *Zapata and the Mexican Revolution* (New York, 1969) received and merited critical kudos from book reviewers in several countries. Martín Luis Guzmán, in the *Memoirs of Pancho Villa* (Austin, 1965), gives a fictionalized account of the northern caudillo's military career.

Contemporary reports by foreigners provide significant and colorful commentary on events in Mexico: the socialist John Reed, *Insurgent Mexico* (New York, 1969); Edith O'Shaughnessy (wife of the American chargé d'affaires), *A Diplomat's Wife in Mexico* (New York, 1916) and *Diplomatic Days: A Story of the Díaz and Madero Regimes* (New York, 1917); Rosa E. King, *Tempest Over Mexico* (Boston, 1935), on her troubles with the Zapatistas; the Spanish novelist Vicente Blasco Ibáñez, *Mexico in Revolution* (New York, 1920); and Carl W. Ackerman, *Mexico's Dilemma* (New York, 1918).

The 1920s and 1930s are a scholarly desert with few oases. The best sources are still Dulles' *Yesterday in Mexico* and Ernest Gruening's *Mexico and Its Heritage* (New York, 1928). See also three dissertations: Donald D. Johnson, "Álvaro Obregón and the Mexican Revolution" (University of Southern California, 1946); Albert L. Michaels, "Mexican Politics and Nationalism from Calles to Cárdenas" (University of Pennsylvania, 1966); and Paul Nathan, "Mexico under Cárdenas" (University of Chicago, 1953). Two foreign observers wrote in the early 1920s: Carleton Beals, *Mexico, an Interpretation* (New York, 1923), and Emile J. Dillon, *Mexico on the Verge* (London, 1922). For sympathetic accounts of Cárdenas and his administration see William C. Townsend, *Lázaro Cárdenas, Mexican Democrat* (Ann Arbor, 1952); Nathaniel Weyl and Sylvia Weyl. *The Recon-*

quest of Mexico: The Years of Lázaro Cárdenas (New York, 1939), a Marxist view; and Robert P. Millon, *Mexican Marxist: Vicente Lombardo Toledano* (Chapel Hill, 1966).

Reports by knowledgeable foreigners during or at the end of the Cárdenas years include Verna Carleton Millán, *Mexico Reborn* (Boston, 1939); J. H. Plenn, *Mexico Marches* (Indianapolis, 1939); R. H. K. Marrott, *An Eye-Witness of Mexico* (London, 1939); John B. Trend, *Mexico, a New Spain with Old Friends* (Cambridge, England, 1940); Virginia Prewett, *Reportage on Mexico* (New York, 1941); Betty Kirk, *Covering the Mexican Front* (Norman, 1942); and Hudson Strode, *Timeless Mexico* (New York, 1944).

No book dealing with the past thirty years can match Howard F. Cline's *Mexico: Revolution to Evolution, 1940–1960* (London, 1962), for the author, Director of the Hispanic Foundation of the Library of Congress, has been thoroughly conversant with the country's history and current affairs. Of less authority is the journalist Irene Nicolson's *X in Mexico: Growth within Tradition* (London, 1965). Two groups of essays are worth noting: A. Curtis Wilgus, *The Caribbean: Mexico Today* (Gainesville, 1964), and "Mexico Today: An Atlantic Supplement," *Atlantic Monthly*, 213 (March 1964), 89–154. A Mexican Marxist, Jesús Silva Herzog, criticizes recent developments in "Rise and Fall of Mexico's Revolution," *Nation*, 169 (October 22, 1949), 395–96. Two valuable foreign appraisals of Mexico since 1940 are Herbert Cerwin's *These are the Mexicans* (New York, 1947) and John A. Crow's *Mexico Today* (New York, 1957). But most information on recent history is provided by political scientists and economists.

Under the watchful eye of the Mexican government, political scientists tend to study institutions and to describe conditions, rather than to probe deeply with questionnaire and interview techniques. Nonetheless, there is no shortage of literature, published and unpublished, on Mexican politics. Far and away the best analysis is by Robert E. Scott, *Mexican Revolution in Transition* (rev. ed., Urbana, 1964). Scott brought his study up to date with "The Established Revolution," in Lucian W. Pye and Sydney Verba (eds.), *Political Culture and Political Development* (Princeton, 1965), 330–95. Unfortunately, as Scott modernizes his political science vocabulary, he is less understandable to the outsider. Two other general studies are worth reading: William P. Tucker, *The Mexican Government Today* (Minneapolis, 1957); and L. Vincent Padgett, *The Mexican Political System* (Boston, 1966). A political sociologist, Pablo González Casanova, has made the only significant study of politics from within the Mexican culture, *Democracy in Mexico* (New York, 1970). The vogue for comparative politics led to two investigations which included Mexico: Gabriel Almond and Sydney Verba, *The Civic Culture* (Princeton, 1963), and Joseph A. Kahl (ed.), *Comparative Perspectives on Stratification: Mexico, Great Britain, Japan* (Boston, 1968). The latter includes excellent articles by González Casanova, Claudio Stern, and Rodolfo Stavenhagen.

For studies of the formal constitutional structure see H. N. Branch, "The Mexican Constitution of 1917 Compared with the Constitution of 1857," in *Supplement to the Annals of the American Academy* (Philadelphia, 1917); E. Victor Niemeyer's masters' thesis, "The Mexican Constitutional Convention of 1916–1917: The Constitutionalizing of a Revolutionary Ideology" (University of Texas, 1951); and W. R. Duncan, "The Mexican Constitution of 1917—Its Political and Social Background," *Inter-American Law Review*, V (July–December 1963), 277–309.

Several scholars have written on limited aspects of the political system: Stephen S. Goodspeed, "Mexico: President and Constitution," *Mid-America*, XXXVI (April 1954), 96–115; Philip B. Taylor, Jr., "The Mexican Elections of 1958: Affirmation of Authoritarism?" *Western Political Quarterly*, XIII (September 1960), 722–44; Martin C. Needler, "The Political Development of Mexico," *American Political Science Review*, LV (June 1961), 308–12; David T. Garza, "Factionalism in the Mexican Left: The Frustration of the MLN," *Western Political Quarterly*, XVII (September 1964), 447–60; Kenneth F. Johnson, "Ideological Correlates of Right Wing Political Alienation in Mexico," *American Political Science Review*, LIX (September 1965), 656–64; Leonard Cárdenas, Jr., "Contemporary Problems of Local Government in Mexico," *Western Political Quarterly*, XVIII (December 1965), 858–65; Bo Anderson and James D. Cockcroft, "Control and Coöptation in Mexican Politics," *International Journal of Comparative Sociology*, VII (March 1966), 11–14; James D. Cochrane, "Mexico's 'New Científicos,' The Díaz Ordaz Cabinet." *Inter-American Economic Affairs*, XXI (Summer 1967), 61–72; and José Revueltas, "A Headless Proletariat in Mexico," in Luis E. Aguilar (ed.), *Marxism in Latin America* (New York, 1968), 240–44.

Book-length studies on special topics include Karl M. Schmitt, *Communism in Mexico: A Study in Political Frustration* (Austin, 1965); Ward M. Morton, *Woman Suffrage in Mexico* (Gainesville, 1962); Merle Kling, *A Mexican Interest Group in Action* (Englewood Cliffs, 1961); Lawrence S. Graham, *Politics in a Mexican Community* (Gainesville, 1968); and Antonio Ugalde, *Power and Conflict in a Mexican Community* (Albuquerque, 1970).

A sampling of the many doctoral dissertations on Mexican politics includes Eugene M. Braderman, "A Study of Political Parties and Politics since 1890" (University of Illinois, 1938); Stephen S. Goodspeed, "The Role of the Chief Executive in Mexico: Politics, Powers, and Administration" (University of California, Berkeley, 1947); Ralph Eisenberg, "The Mexican Presidential Election of 1952" (University of Illinois, 1953); Jack B. Gabbert, "The Evolution of the Mexican Presidency" (University of Texas, 1963); James F. Creagan, "Minority Parties in Mexico: Their Role in a One-Party Dominant System" (University of Virginia, 1965); Patricia M. Richmond, "Mexico: A Case Study of One-Party Politics" (University of California, Berkeley, 1965); Anna Macías, "The Genesis of Constitutional Government in Mexico, 1808–1920" (Columbia University, 1965); Evelyn P. Stevens, "Information and Decision-Making in Mexico" (University of California, Berkeley, 1965); Thomas A. Porter, "Subversion, Opposition, and Legitimacy in Mexican Politics" (Harvard University, 1966); Elliott Kalmer, "The Political Role of the Intellectual: The Experience of Mexico" (Columbia University, 1968); Thomas H. Brose, "The Party of the Revolution and the Politics of Reform in Mexico" (Simon Fraser University, 1968).

The economic growth of Mexico has been studied intensively both inside and outside the country. Mexico has produced first-rate practical and theoretical economists. Beginning with Edwin W. Kemmerer, several distinguished American scholars have written treatises on the financial sector, industrialization, trade, and various aspects of the domestic economy. For general coverage see: Edwin W. Kemmerer, *Inflation and Revolution: Mexico's Experience of 1912–1917* (Princeton, 1940); Sanford A. Mosk, *The Industrial Revolution in Mexico* (Berkeley, 1950); William P. Glade, Jr. and Charles W. Anderson, *The Political Economy of Mexico* (Madison, 1963); Raymond Vernon, *The Dilemma of Mexico's Development* (Cambridge, 1963) and (ed.), *Public Policy and Private Enterprise in Mexico* (Cambridge, 1964); Robert L. Bennett, *The Financial Sector and Economic Development. The Mexican Case* (Baltimore, 1965); Robert T. Aubey, *Nacional Financiera and Mexican Industry* (Los Angeles, 1966); Dwight S. Brothers and Leopoldo Solís M., *Mexican Financial Development* (Austin, 1966); Raymond W. Goldsmith, *The Financial Development of Mexico* (London, 1966); Robert J. Shafer, *Mexico: Mutual Adjustment Planning* (Syracuse, 1967); Tom E. Davis (ed.), *Mexico's Recent Economic Growth. A Mexican View* (Austin, 1967); William O. Freithaler, *Mexico's Foreign Trade and Economic Development* (New York, 1967); Joseph S. La Cascia, *Capital Formation and Economic Development in Mexico* (New York, 1969); John B. Ross, *The Economic System of Mexico* (Stanford, 1970); David Barkin and Timothy King, *Regional Economic Development* (Cambridge, England, 1970).

Joseph A. Kahl compares two Latin American countries in *The Measurement of Modernism: A Study of Values in Brazil and Mexico* (Austin, 1968). John Fayerweather writes engagingly of the frustrations of doing business in Mexico in *The Executive Overseas: Administrative Attitudes and Relationships in a Foreign Culture* (Syracuse, 1959). An early prophet of doom, William Vogt, points to ecological problems ahead for Mexico and other countries in *Road to Survival* (New York, 1948). The relationship of population growth and economic difficulties is examined in Harold L. Geisert, *Population Problems in Mexico and Central America* (Washington, 1959), and in Harley Browning's doctoral dissertation, "Urbanization in Mexico" (University of California, Berkeley, 1962). Books on individual industries include J. Richard Powell, *The Mexican Petroleum Industry, 1938–1950* (Berkeley, 1956); Antonio J Bermúdez, *The Mexican National Petroleum Industry: A Case Study in Nationalization* (Stanford, 1963); John H. McNeely, *The Railways of Mexico, a Study in Nationalization* (El Paso, 1964); Marvin Bernstein, *Mexican Mining Industry, 1890–1950* (New York, 1965); William E. Cole, *Steel and Economic Growth in Mexico* (Austin, 1966); and Fredda Jean Bullard, *Mexico's Natural Gas. The Beginning of an Industry* (Austin, 1968). The pioneer study of Mexican unionization is Marjorie R. Clark, *Organized Labor in Mexico* (Chapel Hill, 1934). For developments since the 1930s, see Joe C. Ashby, *Organized Labor and the Mexican Revolution under Lázaro Cárdenas* (Chapel Hill, 1967); and Frederick Meyers, *Party, Government, and the Labor Movement in Mexico: Two Case Studies.* UCLA Report No. 170 (Los Angeles, 1967).

Few research topics have been so passionately explored, defended, and attacked since the early days of the Revolution as land reform. In English, representative studies are: George M. McBride, *Land Systems of Mexico* (Austin, 1923); Frank Tannenbaum, *The Mexican Agrarian Revolution* (New York, 1929); Eyler N. Simpson, *The Ejido: Mexico's Way Out* (Chapel Hill, 1937); Tom Gill, *Land Hunger in Mexico* (Washington, 1951); J. G. Maddox, *Mexican Land Reform* (New York, 1957); Clarence Senior, *Land Reform and Democracy* (Gainesville, 1958); John H. Mc-Neely's doctoral dissertation, "The Politics and Development of the Mexican Land Program" (University of Texas, 1958); Charles Erasmus, "The Land Reform in Northwestern Mexico," in *Man Takes Control* (Minneapolis, 1961), 209–37; Richard W. Parks, "The Role of Agriculture in Mexican Economic Development," *Inter-American Economic Affairs*, XVIII (Summer 1964), 3–27; Rodolfo Stavenhagen, "Social Aspects of Agrarian Structure in Mexico," *Social Research*, XXXIII (Autumn 1966), 463–85; François Chevalier, "The Ejido and Political Stability in Mexico," in Claudio Veliz (ed.), *The Politics of Conformity in Latin America* (London, 1967), 158–91; Ángel Palerm *et al.*, *Agrarian Reform and the Socio-Economic Development of Mexico* (Mexico, 1968); and Eduardo L. Venezian and William K. Gamble, *The Agricultural Development of Mexico* (New York, 1969).

Because of the nature of their discipline, anthropologists studying Mexico have tended to focus on the countryside. As a result, the best books, including general reviews, concern Indians or rural villages. The best general guide to indigenous Mexico is Eric R. Wolf's *Sons of the Shaking Earth* (Chicago, 1959). Older but still valuable works are Carleton Beal's *Mexican Maze* (Philadelphia, 1931), impressions of Mexico in the midst of change; Nathan Whetten's *Rural Mexico* (Chicago, 1948), a fine sociological investigation; and Sol Tax (ed.), *Heritage of Conquest* (Glencoe, 1952), essays on cultural change. See also: Betty Bell (ed.), *Indian Mexico: Past and Present* (Los Angeles, 1967), a symposium of six American and Mexican anthropologists.

Significant short studies of Mexican society include Nathan L. Whetten, "The Rise of the Middle Class in Mexico," in Theo R. Crevenna (ed.), *Materiales para el estudio de la clase media en América Latina*, II (Washington, 1950), 1–29; Woodrow Borah, "Race and Class in Mexico," *Pacific Historical Review*, XXIII (November 1954), 331–42; Munro S. Edmundson, "A Triangulation on the Culture of Mexico," *Middle American Research Institution Publication No. 17* (New Orleans, 1957), 201–40; Charles Wagley and Marvin Harris, "The Indians of Mexico," in *Minorities of the New World* (New York, 1958), 48–86; Orrin E. Klapp, "Mexican Social Types," *American Journal of Sociology*, 69 (January 1964), 404–14; Noel F. McGinn, "Marriage and Family in Middle-Class Mexico," *Journal of Marriage and the Family*, XXVIII (August 1966), 305–13; and Michael Maccoby, "On Mexican National Character," *Annals of the American Academy of Political and Social Science*, 370 (March 1967), 63–73.

Anthropologists have made their most significant contribution in studies of individual villages, towns, or limited geographic areas. For the Mexican Maya regions see Robert Redfield, *The Folk Culture of Yucatán* (Chicago, 1941) and *A Village that Chose Progress. Chan Kom Revisited* (Chicago, 1950); Robert Redfield and Alfonso Villa Rojas, *Chan Kom. A Maya*

Village (Chicago, 1934); Calixta Guiteras-Holmes, Perils of the Soul: The World View of the Tzotzil Indians (New York, 1961); Ricardo Pozas Arciniegas, Juan the Chamula (Berkeley, 1962); Frank Cancian, Economics and Prestige in a Maya Community: The Religious Cargo System in Zinacantan (Stanford, 1965); Evon Z. Vogt, Zinacantan: A Maya Community in the Highlands of Chiapas (Cambridge, 1969); and June Nash, In the Eyes of the Ancestors: Belief and Behavior in a Mayan Community (New Haven, 1970).

For Oaxaca and the South see Elsie W. Parsons, Mitla, Town of Souls (Chicago, 1936); Helen Augur, Zapotec (Garden City, 1954); Helen M. Bailey, Santa Cruz of the Etla Hills (Gainesville, 1958); Charles M. Leslie, Now We Are Civilized. A Study of the World View of the Zapotec Indians of Mitla, Oaxaca (Detroit, 1960); and Antone and Kimball Romney, The Mixtecans of Juxtlahuaca (New York, 1966). Of special interest is Paul Record (pseud.), Tropical Frontier, (New York, 1969), an exciting and well-written account of frontier life and justice. For the opposite end of the Republic see Charles J. Erasmus, "Cultural Change in Northwest Mexico," in Julian W. Steward (ed.), Contemporary Change in Traditional Societies (Urbana, 1967), III, 1–114.

Central and Western Mexico is well represented by Ralph L. Beals, Cherán: A Sierra Tarascan Village (Washington, 1946); William Madsen, The Virgin's Children (Austin, 1960); May N. Díaz, Tonalá: Conservatism, Responsibility, and Authority in a Mexican Town (Berkeley, 1966); Michael H. Belshaw, A Village Economy. Land and People of Huecorio (New York, 1967); and George M. Foster, Tzintzuntzan. Mexican Peasants in a Changing World (Boston, 1967).

No community has played a more important role in Mexican anthropological investigations than Tepotzlán, in the mountains above Cuernavaca. Robert Redfield began with his Tepotzlán, A Mexican Village (Chicago, 1930); two decades later Oscar Lewis made a critical assessment of Redfield's trail-blazing research in Life in a Mexican Village, Tepoztlán Restudied (Urbana, 1951). Taking advantage of tape-recorded interviews, Lewis followed his Tepoztlecos to Mexico City. No other American anthropologist has achieved (or merited) such heights of popular acclaim as Lewis with Five Families (New York, 1959), The Children of Sánchez (New York, 1961), an instant classic, and Pedro Martínez (New York, 1964). To sample the critical fallout from Lewis' investigations, see John Paddock, "Oscar Lewis' Mexico," Anthropological Quarterly, XXXIV (July 1961), 129–49; Oscar Lewis, "Children of Sánchez, Pedro Martínez, and La Vida: With a Discussion," Current Anthropology, VIII (December 1967), 480–500; and Berry Burgum, "The Sociology of Oscar Lewis as a Critique of Imperialism," Science and Society, XXXI (Summer 1967), 323–37. Oscar Luis Sánchez, Los hijos de Jones (Austin, 1963), is the Mexican economist Víctor Urquidi's apparently friendly parody of Lewis' Children of Sánchez. But under the surface, bitterness runs deep, and the Mexican sensitivity to foreign criticism shows through.

Studies of urban Mexico are few. American sociology is essentially inward looking, and its devotees have been disinclined to turn their attention to foreign cultures and exotic climes. Moreover, the Mexican political atmosphere, since *The Children of Sánchez*, has not been hospitable to research in the problem-ridden cities. For examples of urban research see Norman S. Hayner, "Mexico City: Its Growth and Configuration," *American Journal of Sociology*, L (January 1945), 295–304, and *New Patterns in Old Mexico* (New Haven, 1966); Louis K. Harris' doctoral dissertation, "Government for the People of Mexico City" (UCLA, 1956); Andrew H. Whiteford, *Two Cities of Latin America* (Beloit, 1960); Jorge Harth Deneke's doctoral dissertation, "The Colonias Proletarias of Mexico City. Low Income Settlements on the Urban Fringes" (MIT, 1966); Jay Moor (ed.), *Guanajuato: An Analysis of Urban Form* (Seattle, 1968); and David J. Fox and D. J. Robinson, *Cities in a Changing Latin America. Two Studies of Urban Growth in the Development of Mexico and Venezuela* (London, 1969).

Students of American as well as Mexican history have concerned themselves with diplomatic relations between the two countries. For the best general account, see Howard F. Cline's *United States and Mexico* (New York, 1963). Daniel James' *Mexico and the Americans* (New York, 1963) is reasonably objective, though it was published with support from a government intelligence agency. Larger problems of US-Latin American relations also involve Mexico. See Dexter Perkins' definitive *History of the Monroe Doctrine* (rev. ed., Boston, 1955) and Bryce Wood's prize-winning *Making of the Good Neighbor Policy* (New York, 1961). Important border problems are examined in Robert D. Gregg, *The Influence of Border Troubles: Relations between the United States and Mexico, 1876–1910* (Baltimore, 1937); Sheldon B. Liss, *A Century of Disagreement: The Chamizal Conflict, 1864–1964* (Washington, 1967); and Norris Hundley, Jr., *Dividing the Waters. A Century of Controversy between the United States and Mexico* (Berkeley, 1966). Stuart A. MacCorkle's earlier study, *American Policy of Recognition towards Mexico* (Baltimore, 1933), is still valuable. For an official view of Mexico's foreign policy, see Jorge Castañeda, *Mexico and the United Nations* (New York, 1958).

For early diplomatic problems which culminated in the Mexican War, see: George L. Rives, *The United States and Mexico, 1821–1848* (2 vols., New York, 1913); J. Fred Rippy, *Joel R. Poinsett, Versatile American* (Durham, 1935); Albert K. Weinberg, *Manifest Destiny* (Baltimore, 1935); Otis A. Singletary, *The Mexican War* (Chicago, 1960); Justin H. Smith, *The War with Mexico* (2 vols., New York, 1919); and Ramón Eduardo Ruiz (ed.), *The Mexican War: Was It Manifest Destiny?* (New York, 1963), a readings book. For a Mexican view of relations at the end of the nineteenth century, see Daniel Cosío Villegas, *The United States Versus Porfirio Díaz* (Lincoln, 1963).

The decade 1910–20 has been most assiduously studied by diplomatic historians. See Peter Calvert, *The Mexican Revolution, 1910–1914. The Diplomacy of Anglo-American Conflict* (Cambridge, England, 1968), based principally on British sources; Kenneth J. Grieb, *The United States and Huerta* (Lincoln, 1969), for a new view of the Mexican general; Arthur S. Link, *Woodrow Wilson and the Progressive Era* (New York, 1954), which gives new insight into Wilson's Mexican policies; Philip H. Lowry's doctoral dissertation, "The Mexican Policy of Woodrow Wilson" (Yale University, 1949), unfortunately never published; Harley Notter, *The Origins of the*

Foreign Policy of Woodrow Wilson (New York, 1937), now somewhat out of date; Robert E. Quirk, *An Affair of Honor: Woodrow Wilson and the Occupation of Veracruz* (New York, 1968); Henry Lane Wilson, *Diplomatic Episodes in Mexico, Belgium, and Chile* (Garden City, 1927), for the American ambassador's own story; Clarence C. Clendenen, *The United States and Pancho Villa* (Ithaca, 1961), a knowledgeable study by a retired army officer; and Herbert M. Mason, Jr., *The Great Pursuit* (New York, 1970).

In contrast with the diplomatic research on the years between 1910 and 1920, the period after 1920 is a scholarly wasteland. Oil and church problems dominated American interests. See Stanley R. Ross, "Dwight Morrow and the Mexican Revolution," *HAHR*, XXXVIII (November 1958), 506–28; Elizabeth Ann Rice, *The Diplomatic Relations between the United States and Mexico, as Affected by the Struggle for Religious Liberty in Mexico, 1925–1929* (Washington, 1959); and E. David Cronon, *Josephus Daniels in Mexico* (Madison, 1960).

Racial and cultural stereotypes have interested both Mexican and American scholars and social observers. As examples of early twentieth-century American prejudices based on pseudo-science see, Wallace Thompson, *The Mexican Mind. A Study in National Psychology* (Boston, 1922); Edward A. Ross, *The Social Revolution in Mexico* (New York, 1923); and C. A. Thompson, "Mexicans, an Interpretation," in *Proceedings of the National Conference of Social Work* (1928), 499–503. James D. Bell's doctoral dissertation explores the subject for a subsequent decade: "Attitudes of Selected Groups in the United States toward Mexico, 1930–1940" (University of Chicago, 1941). See also Norman D. Humphrey, "Ethnic Images and Stereotypes of Mexicans and Americans," *American Journal of Economic Sociology*, XIV (April 1955), 305–13; and Ralph H. Turner and Samuel J. Surace, "Zoot-suiters and Mexicans: Symbols in Crowd Behavior," *American Journal of Sociology*, LXII (July 1956), 14–20. The most complete and authoritative study is Cecil Robinson's *With the Ears of Strangers: The Mexicans in American Literature* (Tucson, 1963).

For Mexican views of the northern neighbor see: Luis Quintanilla, *A Latin American Speaks* (New York, 1943), by an outspoken diplomat; Norman D. Humphrey's "The Mexican Image of Americans," *Annals of the American Academy of Political and Social Science*, 295 (September 1954), 116–25; Julius Rivera's doctoral dissertation, "An Attitudinal Study of Mexican Contacts with the United States" (Michigan State University, 1956); Manuel Gamio (comp.), *The Mexican Immigrant: His Life Story* (Berkeley, 1961); John C. Merrill, *Gringo: The Americans as seen by Mexican Journalists* (Gainesville, 1963); and Vito Perrone's doctoral dissertation, "An Image of America Conceived in Mexican and Argentine Social Studies Textbooks" (Michigan State University, 1964).

The large number of books by Mexicans on relations between Church and State reflects the intensity of feelings concerning the conflict. Writings in English are less partisan and more objective. For a somewhat out-of-date general account, see J. Lloyd Mecham, *Church and State in Latin America* (rev. ed., Chapel Hill, 1966). Anthropologist William Madsen, examines evidences of preconquest religious influences on present-day Catholicism in

Christo-Paganism. A Study of Mexican Religious Syncretism (New Orleans, 1960). On the nineteenth century see Callcott's two volumes; Michael P. Costeloe, *Church Wealth in Mexico.* A Study of the *"Juzgado de Cape-llanías"* in the *Archbishopric of Mexico, 1800–1856* (London, 1967) and "The Mexican Church and the Rebellion of the Polkos," *HAHR,* XLVI (May 1966), 170–78; Jan Bazant, *Alienation of Church Wealth in Mexico* (Cambridge, England, 1971); and Robert J. Knowlton, "Some Practical Effects of Clerical Opposition to the Mexican Reform, 1856–1860," *HAHR,* XLV (May 1965), 246–56. For the Church under the Porfiriato see: Karl M. Schmitt's dissertation, "Evolution of Mexican Thought on Church-State Relations, 1876–1911" (University of Pennsylvania, 1954).

The Revolution's relations with the Church are explored by Robert E. Quirk, "Religion and the Mexican Social Revolution," in William V. D'Antonio and Fredrick B. Pike (eds.), *Religion, Revolution, and Reform: New Forms for Change in Latin America* (New York, 1964) and in Quirk's doctoral dissertation, "The Mexican Revolution and the Catholic Church. An Ideological Study, 1910–1929" (Harvard University, 1951). See also Robert F. Quigley's dissertation, "American Catholic Opinion of Mexican Anti-Clericalism, 1910–1936" (University of Pennsylvania, 1965); E. V. Niemeyer, "Anticlericalism in the Mexican Constitutional Convention of 1916–1917," *The Americas,* XI (July 1954), 31–45; Joseph Cirieco's dissertation, "The United States and the Mexican Church-State Conflict, 1926–1929" (Georgetown University, 1961); L. Ethan Ellis, "Dwight Morrow and the Church-State Controversy in Mexico," *HAHR,* XXXVIII (November 1958), 482–505; Lyle C. Brown, "Mexican Church-State Relations, 1933–1940," *A Journal of Church and State,* VI (Spring 1964), 202–22; and Earl K. James, "Church and State in Mexico," *Annals of the American Academy,* 208 (March 1940), 112–20. Two British novelists expressed their shock at events in the 1930s: Graham Greene, *Another Mexico* (New York, 1939); and Evelyn Waugh, *Mexico: An Object Lesson* (Boston, 1938).

Earlier American studies of Mexico's progress in education were most laudatory and optimistic. Those written in the 1960s tend to be more critical of obvious shortcomings. See Katherine M. Cook, *The House of the People: An Account of Mexico's New Schools of Action* (Washington, 1932); George I. Sánchez, *Mexico: A Revolution by Education* (New York, 1936), and *Development of Higher Education in Mexico* (New York, 1944); George F. Kneller, *The Education of the Mexican Nation* (New York, 1951); Marjorie C. Johnston, *Education in Mexico* (Washington, 1956); Ramón Eduardo Ruiz, *Mexico; the Challenge of Poverty and Illiteracy* (San Marino, 1963); and Charles N. Myers, *Education and National Development in Mexico* (Princeton, 1965).

Two special studies are worthy of attention: Blanca M. de Petricoli and Clark W. Reynolds, "The Teaching of Economics in Mexico," in *Education and World Affairs* (New York, 1967); and William S. Tuohy and Barry Ames, *Mexican University Students in Politics: Rebels Without Allies?* University of Denver Monograph Series in World Affairs, vol. 7 (Denver, 1969–70). See also the following dissertations: Walter R. Duncan, "Education and Ideology; an Approach to Mexican Political Development" (Fletcher School of Law and Diplomacy, 1964); Harry J. Carlson, "The

Impact of the Cárdenas Administration on Mexican Education" (University of Arizona, 1964); and Robert A. Monson, "Right-Wing Politics in Mexican Education: The Textbook Conflict" (Georgetown University, 1966).

Translations of Mexican literature and books in English about recent Mexican literature, philosophy, and art abound. A good general introduction to the thinkers of Mexico is W. Rex Crawford, A Century of Latin American Thought (Cambridge, 1961), which provides useful summaries of the works of writers such as José Vasconcelos and Samuel Ramos. Perceptive studies of leading fiction writers are provided by John Brushwood, Mexico in its Novel (Austin, 1966); and Joseph Sommers, After the Storm, Landmarks of the Modern Mexican Novel (Albuquerque, 1968). For conversations with writers and essays about literature see: Hubert C. Herring and Katherine Terrill (eds.), The Genius of Mexico (New York, 1931); Hubert C. Herring and Herbert Weinstock (eds.), Renascent Mexico (New York, 1935); Erico Verissimo, Mexico (New York, 1960); Luis Harss and Barbara Dohmann, Into the Mainstream: Conversations with Latin-American Writers (New York, 1967); and the Texas Quarterly, II (Spring 1959).

Works of Mexican fiction in English include Mariano Azuela, The Underdogs (New York, 1929) and Two Novels of Mexico. The Flies. The Bosses. (Berkeley, 1956); Martín Luis Guzmán, The Eagle and the Serpent (New York, 1930); Gregorio López y Fuentes, El Indio (New York, 1961); Agustín Yáñez, Edge of the Storm (Austin, 1963); Juan Rulfo, Pedro Páramo (New York, 1959); Carlos Fuentes, The Death of Artemio Cruz (New York, 1964) and A Change of Skin (New York, 1968); and Gertrude Diamont, The Days of Ofelia (Boston, 1942), and Josephina Niggli, Mexican Village (Chapel Hill, 1945), collections of short stories.

For the ferment in philosophy and the search for a national identity see, Patrick Romanell, Making of the Mexican Mind (Notre Dame, 1967); A. Robert Caponigri (trans.), Major Trends in Mexican Philosophy (Notre Dame, 1966); Martin Stabb, In Quest of Identity (Chapel Hill, 1967); Elizabeth Flower, "The Mexican Revolt against Positivism," Journal of the History of Ideas, X (January 1949), 115–29; Gordon W. Hewes, "Mexicans in Search of the 'Mexican': Note on Mexican National Character Studies," American Journal of Economic Sociology, XIII (January 1954), 209–23; John L. Phelan, "México y lo Mexicano," HAHR, XXXVI (August 1956), 309–18; and doctoral dissertations: A. P. Hogg, "The Search for Identity in Post-Revolutionary Mexican Writing" (University of London, 1967); Charles H. Haight, "The Contemporary Mexican Revolution as Viewed by Mexican Intellectuals" (Stanford University, 1956); George G. Wing, "Octavio Paz: Poetry, Politics, and the Myth of the Mexican" (University of California, Berkeley, 1961); and Edward H. Worthen, "The Reconquest of Mexico: a Panoramic View of Mexican Literary Nationalism" (University of Michigan, 1965).

The two most significant landmarks in twentieth-century philosophizing are Samuel Ramos' Profile of Man and Culture in Mexico (Austin, 1963); and Octavio Paz' Labyrinth of Solitude (New York, 1962). For a sampling and an assessment of José Vasconcelos' writings, see A Mexican Ulysses, An Autobiography (Bloomington, 1963); and John H. Haddox, Vasconcelos of Mexico: Philosopher and Prophet (Austin, 1967). Examples from Mexico's fine essayists and critical historians can be found in Daniel Cosío Villegas, *American Extremes* (Austin, 1964); Alfonso Reyes, *Mexico in a Nutshell* (Berkeley, 1964); José Luis Martínez, *The Modern Mexican Essay* (Toronto, 1965); and Merrill Rippy, "The Theory of History: Twelve Mexicans," *The Americas*, XVII (January 1961), 223–39.

The leading Mexican art historian, Justino Fernández, has written several works on various periods. His definitive study is available in English: *A Guide to Mexican Art: From Its Beginnings to the Present* (Chicago, 1969). See also Jean Charlot, *The Mexican Mural Renaissance, 1920–1925* (New Haven, 1963); José Clemente Orozco, *An Autobiography* (Austin, 1962); Mackinley Helm, *Man of Fire: J. C. Orozco, an Interpretive Memoir* (New York, 1953); Seldon Rodman, *Conversations with Artists* (New York, 1961); and José Luis Cuevas, "The Cactus Curtain: An Open Letter on Conformity in Mexican Art," *Evergreen Review*, II (Winter 1959), 111–20, and (in Spanish and English) *Cuevas por Cuevas* (México, 1965).

On the other aspects of Mexican culture see, Hans Beacham, *The Architecture of Mexico, Yesterday and Today* (New York, 1969); Frances Toor, *A Treasury of Mexican Folkways* (New York, 1947); Robert M. Stevenson, *Music in Mexico* (New York, 1952); and Merle E. Simmons, *The Mexican Corrido as a Source for Interpretative Study of Modern Mexico, 1870–1950* (Bloomington, 1957).

Index

148